D1737163

M.A. Jinnah
VIEWS AND REVIEWS

M.A. Jinnah

VIEWS AND REVIEWS

EDITED BY

M.R. KAZIMI

OXFORD
UNIVERSITY PRESS

OXFORD
UNIVERSITY PRESS

Great Clarendon Street, Oxford OX2 6DP

Oxford University Press is a department of the University of Oxford.
It furthers the University's objective of excellence in research, scholarship,
and education by publishing worldwide in

Oxford New York

Auckland Cape Town Dar es Salaam Hong Kong Karachi
Kuala Lumpur Madrid Melbourne Mexico City Nairobi
New Delhi Shanghai Taipei Toronto

with offices in

Argentina Austria Brazil Chile Czech Republic France Greece
Guatemala Hungary Italy Japan South Korea Poland Portugal
Singapore Switzerland Thailand Turkey Ukraine Vietnam

Oxford is a registered trade mark of Oxford University Press
in the UK and in certain other countries

ISBN-13: 978-0-19-597979-4
ISBN-10: 0-19-597979-6

Typeset in Adobe Garamond Pro
Printed in Pakistan by
New Sketch Graphics, Karachi.
Published by
Ameena Saiyid, Oxford University Press
Plot No. 38, Sector 15, Korangi Industrial Area, PO Box 8214
Karachi-74900, Pakistan.

Contents

Acknowledgements

I thank the following authors and editors/publishers for giving us the rights and permission to include the following articles: Dr David Page, Dr Stanley Wolpert and the late Mr B.N. Pandey (ed) *Leadership in South Asia*, New Delhi, Vikas, 1977. Mr Andrew Roberts and the editors of the *Sunday Times*, London, 18 August 1996. Dr Ian A. Talbot and Ms Juliet Gardiner, editor, *History Today*, London, 1984. Dr Francis Robinson, Dr R.J. Moore and the editor of *Modern Asian Studies*, Cambridge, 1983. Professor Alan Whaites and the editors of *Contemporary South Asia*, London, 1998. Dr Ayesha Jalal and Dr Syed Jaffar Ahmed and the editor of *Dawn*, Karachi, 23 March 2005 and 27 December 2003. Dr Betty Miller Unterberger and the editor of *Diplomatic History*, New York, 1981. I thank Professor Sharif Al Mujahid for favouring this publication with his paper. Dr Ansar Zahid Khan, editor *Historycus*, Karachi 2000, for permitting me to draw on an earlier version of my paper.

Special thanks are due to Dr Roger Long, who not only wrote his paper at our request, but who also sent us the text of a number of articles not available in Pakistan.

To Ms Ameena Saiyid, Managing Director, for her active encouragement, and Mr Ramik Akhund, Manager, Rights and Acquisitions, Oxford University Press, Pakistan for negotiating the rights and making this publication possible.

Introduction

We present in this volume studies of Mohammed Ali Jinnah by the most distinguished scholars of South Asian history. These scholars gained prominence after the 1976 Jinnah Birth Centennial. Debate on the aim and purpose of the Quaid-i-Azam reached a new level during the mid-1980s and since then has dominated the discourse on the role of Mohammed Ali Jinnah in securing the partition of India. Most of these essays had been neglected for the most part, and had not been available in Pakistan. The two authors whose full length studies have a wide circulation in Pakistan are also represented in this volume. Stanley Wolpert, with a paper which preceded his celebrated biography, and Ayesha Jalal, with an article which treats her treatise retrospectively.

Then, of course, there are distinguished authorities who have had occasion to write on the Founder of Pakistan. They do so in the backdrop of extensive and acclaimed studies of the history and politics of South Asia. We begin with a paper by David Page that dwells on the career of Mohammed Ali Jinnah as conditioned by the system of British Imperialist control—this study is conducive for an evolutionary vision of Jinnah's career. The earlier phase of Jinnah's politics, though perceived as having undergone a dramatic change in later life, was actually the formative phase and in no analysis of Jinnah's life and work can this period be overlooked.

David Page argues that by empowering only the provinces the British created a power vacuum at the centre which made partition attainable. This argument carries weight and provides a very credible background to Jinnah's personal endeavours. In dealing with Jinnah's superficial hold over provincial Muslim politicians—a recurring theme of this volume—David Page has unerringly identified the forces at work by distinguishing between the interests of the Agra and Oudh landlords in the first instance, and pointing to communalism being adopted as a conscious means of settling rivalry among the Hindu leadership in the second. However, David Page's interpretation of the final outcome in terms of Jinnah's personal ambition is less gradual than his preceding interpretation and leaves us with the feeling that had David Page not excluded consideration of the Cabinet Mission's visit, he could have explored impersonal forces with greater advantage. Even now, though written thirty years ago and well grounded in his *Prelude to Partition*, his paper gives us a deep insight into the intricacies of higher politics.

Andrew Roberts approached Jinnah through his study of Lord Mountbatten in his *Eminent Churchillians*. He follows the lead of Leonard Mosley from Mosley's *Last Days of the British Raj* in holding that had Lord Mountbatten not advanced the date of the transfer of power, the extent of the riots and bloodshed could have been contained. Roberts focused on Jinnah as the main victim of Mountbatten's impetuosity and noting the Viceroy's concern with his image, produced a short article on Jinnah's projection in the media. It is not Andrew Roberts' fault that the film *Jinnah* proved to be as disastrous to the understanding of the Quaid-i-Azam's mission as Sir Richard Attenborough's *Gandhi* has been. For all that, Roberts provides valuable lessons in the task of projecting Jinnah, all the more urgent in view of an ill-conceived attempt.

Stanley Wolpert, one of the main players of the ongoing debate, makes his appearance here with a 1977 paper on 'Congress Leadership in Transition'. Wolpert, who had previously written about Gopal Krishna Gokhale and Balgangadhar Tilak, now focused on a sharper and more momentous transition, that from Jinnah to Gandhi. Jinnah was a disciple of Gokhale and a compatriot of Tilak, and his role as a Congressman was crucial to understanding the political course he was to adopt since the transformation of the Congress and the Home Rule League on 4 October 1920. It was from this paper that grew not only *Jinnah of Pakistan* (1984) but also *Gandhi's Passion* (2001).

Stanley Wolpert depicts Gandhi's frustration during his 1918 loyalist phase and Jinnah's frustration in 1920 over Gandhi's expropriation of leadership which became the two biographical constructs of the unfolding course of Indian independence.

As against Wolpert who focuses on the 1920s, R.J. Moore focuses on the 1940s. Moore had previously published *Churchill, Cripps and India* (1979) and *Escape from Empire* (1979). In the 1940s, Jinnah enjoyed a more dominant role compared to the 1920s and was a stronger candidate for the Great Man role, however, it is precisely this premise that Moore questions. Despite the wealth of material Moore, observes:

> Yet the relation of Jinnah to rise of the League and its demand and movement for Pakistan is still obscure.

Moore stresses that in the crucial eighteen months preceding the Lahore Resolution 'Jinnah's role in the formation and expression of constitutional thought and strategy was certainly not that of an isolated, lonely and self-sufficient leader.'

Moore provides documentary evidence that Jinnah was less enthusiastic about partition than his followers. First he watered down the Sindh Muslim League resolution calling for two federations. Then Moore presents evidence to show that Jinnah read at Lahore in 1940 a speech heavily drawing upon draft supplied from Aligarh academics. This shows that Jinnah was led rather than followed, and that the theory that partition would not have been possible without Jinnah's leadership is considerably modified. Recounting Jinnah's adjustments to the different variants of the partition demand, Moore precludes the possibility that Jinnah was negotiating over the heads of his compatriots:

> Yet that outcome lends no support to the speculation that the Pakistan demand was Jinnah's bargaining counter in a united India, or that the Partition hoisted him with his own petard.

Ian Talbot's article 'Jinnah and the Making of Pakistan' is similar, in the sense that he does not attribute the 1945/1946 election victory of the Muslim League solely to Jinnah's leadership. Ian Talbot was later noted for his *Provincial Politics and the Pakistan Movement* (1988) and *Freedom's Cry* (1996) both of which contain findings that are at odds with his earlier assertation (1984) that:

Many of those who had voted for the Muslim League had done so more out of personal loyalty to its candidates than out of support for Pakistan.

There was no visible indicator of such a voting pattern, and no confirmation that Jinnah had misrepresented his mandate to play a 'confidence trick' on the British and the Congress. This position he was to modify radically on further inquiry. Talbot noted in *Freedom's Cry* that:

The growing groundswell of support for the League pressurized its Muslim landlord opponents to desert the Unionist Party (p. 9).

In his earlier *Provincial Politics*, Ian Talbot discovered that Jinnah's aloofness from provincial politics was not forced on him, but was by choice and he wielded more influence than was lately supposed. Is then Talbot's paper rendered redundant by his later full length studies? No, because, he was able to define Jinnah's role with great clarity. He holds that Jinnah 'manipulated' the popular appeal of Islam, the opportunities presented by the Second World War and the British urge to withdraw to 'temporarily' unite Muslims behind the Pakistan demand. He then attributed this outcome to the priority of a small Muslim elite. Ian Talbot, weighing Jinnah's role in the balance, ruled that:

His achievement in fact was far greater than such Pakistani propaganda can easily admit.

The quantum of influence wielded by Jinnah came to be tied in by later scholarship to the nature of his real strategy, therefore we inevitably come to consider the two most influential books on Jinnah yet written, *Jinnah of Pakistan* (1984) by Stanley Wolpert and *The Sole Spokesman* (1985) by Ayesha Jalal. Stanley Wolpert presented a biography which is rightly admired for being comprehensive and incisive and for its epigrammatic style. The opening sentence of the Preface is the most quoted assessment of Jinnah's life and work.

Quite unusually for any major work on a topic, Wolpert's biography of Jinnah was followed the very next year by a major study, Ayesha Jalal's *The Sole Spokesman*. This book received condemnation and rejection in the same measure as Wolpert's book had received praise and plaudits. Her view was known as the Revisionist Theory of Partition, most ably examined by Asim Roy.

Francis Robinson has reviewed both books together, noting at the outset their different scopes. He takes up Wolpert's book first, enumerating the paradoxes that Wolpert does not resolve. Wolpert's vision of Jinnah's political progress is 'strictly conventional', but further down, Francis Robinson concedes that Wolpert's analysis of Jinnah's motivation is 'less conventional' and makes a real contribution. In the course of comparison, Robinson shows that while Wolpert depicts Jinnah's motivation in psychological terms, Ayesha Jalal depicts them in strategic terms. Francis Robinson's tribute to Ayesha Jalal's treatise needs to be prominently highlighted:

> It is hard to believe that this is a first book. A novel thesis is brilliantly sustained from beginning to end. The understanding of politics is mature, the exposition sophisticated, the tone almost unnervingly confident.

The objections to Jalal's findings are sharp, they are widespread, some lie ahead in this collection itself and some objections are even valid, but the tribute paid by Francis Robinson is irreducible.

It is Alan Whaite who questions Jalal to the same effect that Francis Robinson questions Wolpert:

> 1971 did not entirely end the relevance or controversy surrounding the Pakistan ideal.

Alan Whaites challenges recent generalizations by asserting that far from catering to elitist interests, 'from 1937 onwards, the communal debate reached a point from where the elite leadership saw Pakistan in terms of loss of Muslim presence and leverage in

the minority areas' and of course, 'the communal violence in Bihar'
he argues, 'coloured attitudes'.

He forcefully argues that impending change in the centre
brought about a conceptual change in the Muslim majority areas
that the British had failed to anticipate. He applies the same
criticism to Ayesha Jalal, and it is on the basis of his analysis of the
changing Muslim majority attitude that he confronts the contention
of Ayesha Jalal:

> Yet Jalal's argument rests on an area only tangenitically explored in her
> work; that is the genuineness of Jinnah's conversion to the Pakistan
> idea after 1937.

What Whaites has achieved by pinpointing this aspect of her
treatise has been the ambition of every Pakistani apologist ever
since her revisionist theory made its appearance. Beyond noting
that her dissertation had been supervised by Anil Seale, Pakistani
polemicists have not been able to counter her arguments effectively.
Just where his findings lead the academic world to, is not quite
clear, but Whaites provides a corrective. How much academic space
his correction at present occupies, is also not quite apparent.

After featuring so much comment centred around the views of
Ayesha Jalal, it is only fair that we let her speak for herself. In a
very recent resume of her views, Ayesha Jalal does not deny that
she characterized the Pakistan demand as a bargaining counter. Her
main defence is that,

> In so far as politics is the art of possible, bargaining is an intrinsic part
> of that art. To suggest, as some have glibly done, that Mohammed Ali
> Jinnah used Pakistan as a mere ruse against the Congress is a gross
> distortion of not only my argument, but of the actual history.

Ayesha Jalal's restatement is not likely to close the gates of debate.
Nevertheless, her presence sheds lustre on, and adds depth to a
collection which is represented mainly by her antagonists, myself
not excluded. Revisionist or not, Ayesha Jalal's thesis does not
detract much substance from the Great Man theory. In her
dissertation, the role of the individual acquires added value, since

Jinnah, in her view, was able to play a vital role even if it was not his public role.

What was public and what was private in the stance of Mohammed Ali Jinnah can best be discovered by probing his relations with his lieutenant, Liaquat Ali Khan. In recent years, Roger Long and I have focused on Liaquat Ali Khan. Therefore, when I fixed on the necessity of including a paper describing Jinnah's relations with Liaquat, I also realized that Roger Long was best suited to this task. My confidence has been justified, and his paper is more comprehensive and insightful than my introduction to the *Jinnah-Liaquat Correspondence* (2003). It is also by far the better documented contribution and as such an added bonus for the reader.

The role of the individual in history is a theme implicit in every appraisal of the Quaid-i-Azam. It is appropriate that the task of making it explicit should have fallen to Sharif Al Mujahid, the doyen of Jinnah scholars in Pakistan. Coming from him, the observation that 'Jinnah was the most misunderstood man in Indian politics', is most startling. 'He begins by pointing to the difference in the estimate of contemporaries and historians regarding the personal contribution of Jinnah to the creation of Pakistan.

Sharif Al Mujahid does not skirt over the choice offered by the Cabinet Mission. This was a situation that tested the efficacy of the individual to the maximum because the Cabinet Mission formula stood out from the path historical forces had apparently chosen. Sharif Al Mujahid's example of Abul Kalam Azad is most pertinent to the debate on individual choice,

> What made Jinnah a Jinnah, and Azad an Azad at this juncture in Indo-Muslim history was the critical variable of their respective reaction to the influence from the historic realm and to the 1937–47 Muslim situation.

Another facet to judge the role of the individual, is not to address the historical forces with which he had to contend, but to examine the legacy an individual bequeaths. The pivotal role of the

Quaid-i-Azam would normally be the most influential in shaping the country of his creation, but as Syed Jaffar Ahmed shows in his 'The Lost Jinnah' this is not evident in the unfolding history of Pakistan,

> With religious intolerance and extremism looming large in the country, Jinnah seems to have become irrelevant today. But he is most relevant if Pakistan wishes to emerge from its present ashes of rage and hatred.

Pakistan's commitment to rise above intolerance and extremism has become a vital concern of the United States, Betty Miller Unterberger's article on 'American Views of M.A. Jinnah and the Pakistan Liberation Movement', becomes more than a bibliographical or historiographical study. She traces the appearance of Jinnah in the American press and his image in the diplomatic enclave of the United States. Noting that it was after cutting through much hostile propaganda that the US came to appreciate the justice of the Pakistan demand, she is able to point out, perhaps for the first time, that on independence day at Karachi, 'the United States was the first nation to extend diplomatic recognition, and the only foreign power to send an official delegate to the formal ceremonies.'

It is somewhat curious that her account passes over the efforts of M.A.H. Ispahani and Begum Jahan Ara Shahnawaz in publicizing the Pakistan demand in the United States. Since she originally wrote for *Diplomatic History*, Betty Miller Unterberger was precluded from assessing American academic dissertations on M.A. Jinnah and Pakistan, such as that of William S. Metz's *Political Career of M.A. Jinnah*, University of Pennsylvania, 1952, Walter Bennet's *Genesis of the Pakistan Idea*, University of South California, 1957. My own contribution, 'Indian Writers on Jinnah' is a humble tribute to the trail of country-wise historiographical accounts that Unterberger has blazed.

Muhammad Reza Kazimi
2005

1

Mohammed Ali Jinnah and the System of Imperial Control in India 1909–1930: A Case Study in Political Leadership and Constitutional Innovation
David Page

For students of the Partition of India, one of the most interesting questions about Mohammed Ali Jinnah is: How did the ambassador of Hindu-Muslim unity become the Father of a separate homeland for the Indian Muslims? Few historians of modern India and Pakistan have neglected to give an opinion on this issue, and such is the weight given to Jinnah's role in the creation of Pakistan that almost all of them have assumed that his political transformation is an essential part of Partition itself. Among Pakistani historians there have been two main approaches. Either they have concentrated on Jinnah's political career after his return to India in 1934 in an attempt to decide precisely when Partition became inevitable, or else they have given their interpretation in the context of a broad study of Muslim politics in the subcontinent, viewed generally from the standpoint of 1947. Neither of these approaches has proved particularly productive. The first has generally reduced itself to a study of the minutiae of political negotiations which has ignored the more general forces affecting Muslim India, and the second, which has involved an ideological interpretation of Jinnah's career, has generally failed to do justice to the political realities with which he had to work. Among Indian scholars, most of whom have deplored the Partition of India as much as Pakistani historians have praised it, emphasis has generally been placed either on Jinnah's personal ambition, or on the divisive tactics of the Raj, whose collaborator, it is argued, he was. These approaches too have very often indicated more about the intellectual climate of post-Partition India than about the political situation with which Jinnah had to deal. It is self-evident, therefore, that a new approach is necessary, and this article attempts to provide one. It begins with Jinnah as he was—a man with the highest respect for legal procedure and the norms of constitutional politics—and it examines his career as he pursued it for most of his political life—within the formal structure of politics setup by the Government. Few politicians of twentieth century India tried harder to deal with the Raj on its own terms than he did and it was only when it became superabundantly clear that the Raj could not be beaten on those terms that Jinnah finally donned the *sherwani* and *churidars* and became a mass politician. The advantage of this approach is twofold. First, it does not begin with assumptions about the desirability or inevitability of Partition. It attempts rather to study Jinnah's political evolution within the context of the political system he tried to work. And secondly, by providing a case study of the effect of constitutional innovation on Indian political activity, it provides a more systematic account of the Raj's own contribution to the making of Indian and Pakistani nationalism than the general run of 'Divide and Rule' history.

Born in Karachi in 1876, the son of a merchant of moderate means, Jinnah was a Khoja by religion, and though he did not practise his faith, his membership of this particular 'caste' undoubtedly affected his political perspective. Within Bombay Presidency at the time of Jinnah's youth, the Muslims formed only 20 per cent of the population, but as a Khoja, Jinnah was a member of a minority within a minority. The Khojas accounted for scarcely one per cent of the total Muslim community; and the Khojas were Shias whereas the vast majority of Muslims in the Presidency were Sunnis.

Though a minority, however, the Khojas, like the Bohras and the Memons, 'held a high position for wealth and enterprise and consequently for respectability'.[1] From their bases in Surat, Broach,

Ahmedabad, Karachi and Bombay, they controlled a considerable part of the Presidency's internal trade, not to mention the lucrative trade with East Africa and Mauritius, and within Bombay city, where the more prosperous ones congregated, the areas where they lived could boast large numbers of six-roomed Muslim houses and several very hospitable mosques.[2] In terms of English-medium education, they were not particularly advanced. Indeed, like the bulk of the Muslim population of the Presidency, only small numbers of them attended colleges and universities, and their share of the higher posts of the administration was very meagre indeed.[3] Where the Khojas were concerned, however, it would be incorrect to characterise this as backwardness, for in their own language— Gujarati—they were nearly as well educated as the most advanced Hindu castes, and if they were not educated in English, it was chiefly because they had little need to learn it. As a predominantly trading community, they could manage admirably with Gujarati, and the possession of a Government post was not for them, as it was for many others, the ultimate criterion of success.

This Khoja preoccupation with trade and industry affected their political outlook. At a time when competition for Government service was becoming a major source of communal antagonism, the Khojas, as a relatively self-contained and prosperous community, were much less affected by the communal virus than the majority of their co-religionists. They had less need of Government patronage and they were for this reason less inclined to quarrel with the more 'advanced' Hindus. On the positive side, moreover, as members of the commercial elite of Bombay not only did they share the rather easy-going cosmopolitan ethos of that city, but they also had commercial reasons for combining with members of other communities in order to secure relaxations of trading and financial restrictions.

Jinnah was an exception among the Khojas, however, in that his nationalism sprang not from commercial prosperity but from a thriving legal practice. Whilst still an adolescent, he decided not to go into business, but to travel to England to study for the Bar. Quite who supported him is uncertain. According to one legend, his studies were financed by wealthy patrons. According to another, his family fortunes collapsed while he was away and he was obliged to make ends meet as best he could. According to his nephew, it was at this time that he used to walk each day from Russell Road in West Kensington, where he had his lodgings, to the chambers in the City where he worked—to save the fare.[4] Whatever the truth of this—and if it is true, it does add a certain grandeur to Jinnah's later rise to fame—it seems very likely that his stay in London, which extended over four years, from when he was 16 to when he was 20, was a very formative period. Not only did he acquire the skills which were later to raise him to the heights of Malabar Hill, he also adopted English parliamentary and legal practices as his ideals and became alienated from his Karachi origins. Married before his departure, at his mother's instigation, he never returned to his wife, but chose instead, after a brief period in Karachi, to settle in Bombay. There, opportunities for success as a barrister were greater, and there too his taste for western dress and a western style of life were more appreciated.

After Jinnah returned to India, he devoted himself to the law. In Bombay, where he settled in 1897, he initially found the way ahead difficult. So much so, in fact, that he was obliged to take work as a Presidency magistrate in order to keep the wolf from the door. Gradually, however, his talents as a lawyer became known, and particularly after he had successfully represented Pherozeshah Mehta in an electoral petition against the Government, he left financial difficulties behind, and was able to turn his attention to politics.[5]

Jinnah's political views were typical of the arriviste lawyer of his day. He did not come from a class or community which had traditionally been recruited to Government service, and as a man who had educated himself successfully, he was anxious that merit should be rewarded. As a man who had been educated in England, he resented the differences of standards displayed by the British at home and abroad, and like many of those who had been through Oxbridge and the Inns of Court, he became committed on his return to 'the eradication of insolence on the one hand and of a feeling of inferiority and mortification on the other'.[6] Though zealous for Reform, however, his zeal was for constitutional reform, and for this his successful legal practice was responsible. He was typical of a class of men who had made themselves influential by their attachment to the principles of English justice and who used these principles to argue with their Imperial overlords.

Jinnah's early training as a lawyer undoubtedly affected his attitude to relations between the Muslim community and the Government. As a man who had pushed forward himself in the face of great difficulties, he believed that others should adopt the same recipe for success and he rigidly opposed any kind of special treatment for those who had fallen behind in the race for educational advancement. Asked by Lord Islington when he appeared before the Public Services Commission whether he was not concerned that under a system of simultaneous examinations the backward communities would be at a disadvantage, Jinnah was dogmatic in his support for a single competitive test; he said,

> I would have no objection if the result happens to be, of which I am now doubtful, that a particular community has the preponderance, provided I get competent men.

Another member of the Commission, Lord Ronaldshay, then carried the question still further, saying:

> It has been represented to me that difficulties might arise if you put a Hindu in charge of a Mohammedan population. Do you think that a Hindu who got a few more marks than an educated and influential Mohammedan would make a better and more efficient administrator when he was in charge of a population which was largely Mohammedan?
> I say (replied Jinnah) that in that case you will be doing the greatest injustice to the Hindu ... I do not see why a Hindu should not be in charge of a district where the majority happens to be Mohammedan.[7]

In Jinnah's early years, it was these kinds of views which made him a member of the Indian National Congress and not of the Muslim League.

The formal political arena in which Jinnah chose to ventilate these views was not local or provincial but national. Though he found Bombay a city full of congenial and like-minded men, and a convenient place for meetings with other politicians, so far as one can tell, Jinnah never had much interest in provincial politics. In the years before 1937, only in the mid-1920s did he involve himself in party-building at this level, and then for very obvious national reasons.[8] The reasons which made him focus his ambitions at the national or all-India level provide an interesting comment on the political structure of the time, for quite apart from his obvious ambition, there were very good reasons why he would not have succeeded at a lower level. Broadly speaking, the lower down the political structure a politician operates, the more local factors come into play and the less likely it is that an unrepresentative individual will become politically successful. The obvious course for the unrepresentative individual, therefore, is to work at as high a level of politics as his qualifications will allow, and in Jinnah's case this was the national level. As politics ceased to be consultative and became increasingly democratic, however, the inherent ambiguity of this position became more and more obvious, for with the spread of politicisation and the progressive integration of the local, provincial and national levels of politics, the all-India politician could only survive if his own following extended downwards to the roots of electoral power. This, indeed, was to be Jinnah's dilemma.

In 1909, in the first elections to take place under the Morley-Minto Reforms, Jinnah was returned to the Imperial Legislative Council by the Bombay Muslim constituency. Though returned by a separate electorate, however, Jinnah did not suffer from the pressures which affected many of the North Indian Muslims elected by the same method. In Bombay, those Muslims who were wealthy enough to qualify for a vote, were not interested in banging the communal drum, and throughout his long association with the constituency, which lasted with few interruptions until Partition itself, Jinnah was re-elected not only by Muslim votes but also with the assistance of many Parsi and Hindu friends.[9] Within the Viceroy's Council, Jinnah found himself sitting alongside some of

India's most eminent men. Like himself, many of them were Congressmen—Bhupendra Nath Basu, Dinshaw Wacha, Srinivas Sastri, Mazhar ul Haq, Tej Bahadur Sapru and Madan Mohan Malaviya. But others were Muslims outside Congress, with whom he was later to develop closer contact, notably the Raja of Mahmudabad and Sir Ali Imam. How far all these men were affected by their common membership of the Council is uncertain because the debates are too demure in tone and too limited in character to give the historian the sort of evidence he requires. But it cannot be sheer coincidence that these men, as members both of the Congress and the League, were later to be the leading advocates of Hindu-Muslim unity as a means to secure political reform. It would seem reasonable to argue that political organisation sprang from constitutional experience and that political activity was directed towards the Reform of existing institutions.[10]

During the initial period of his membership of the Viceroy's Council, Jinnah's political views remained unchanged. He showed no sign of adopting a more compromising attitude towards Muslim demands for special treatment. Indeed, at the Congress session of 1910, he and Mazhar ul Haq sponsored a resolution against the extension of separate electorates to local bodies. After a three year period in the Viceroy's Council, however, Jinnah was thoroughly dissatisfied with the progress which had been made. Members of Government had listened politely to any number of eloquent speeches, but they had shown few signs of doing anything more. Nor were they obliged to, for the Council had no real power. Non-official members were in a minority and they only had the right to speak to the Budget debate, to ask questions, and to introduce private members' bills subject to Government approval. Jinnah decided, therefore, not to stand for re-election, and though he was nominated by the Viceroy for the 1913 session to pilot through the Muslim Waqf Validating Act, he did not sit as an elected member again until 1915. His disenchantment with the reforms, however, did not stop there. He began, in fact, to work for their revision outside the Council, not only on the platform of the Congress, but also—and this was a new departure—within the Muslim League. In December 1912, at Bankipore, he attended his first Muslim League Council meeting, and from that time forward used his influence within both organisations to push them along the road to political union.[11] It seems to have become clear to him by this stage that the Government's use of Hindu-Muslim divisions as an argument against political devolution could only be countered effectively if the two organisations were brought together.

Where the Muslim League was concerned, Jinnah was very materially helped in the pursuit of this policy by the emergence at Lucknow, the headquarters of the League, of a group of like-minded men. These centred around the Raja of Mahmudabad, with whom Jinnah had worked in the Viceroy's Council, and they included Wazir Hassan, the League Secretary, Syed Nabiullah, later the Chairman of the Lucknow Municipal Board, and Samiullah Beg, an advocate at the Lucknow Bar. With the exception of the Raja, all these men were lawyers—and successful lawyers at that. Nabiullah, the oldest, had been called to the Bar in England, and the two others were among the leaders of their profession. Consequently, they shared Jinnah's political views, and though chiefly interested in reform at the provincial level, they were well aware that provincial demands would only be successful if put forward under a national umbrella. In the policy of union with the Congress, therefore, they were as forthright as Jinnah himself. It was Wazir Hassan, the League Secretary, who in 1912 reshaped the League's creed, and it was the same man, supported by the Raja, who in the years that followed steered a difficult course with skill to keep the League in the orbit of nationalist politics.[12]

Jinnah's efforts to achieve this end, however, were fraught by tensions within the Muslim community and by pressures from below encouraged by the working of the constitution in the localities. Indeed in the United Provinces itself, the Lucknow leadership was by no means universally respected, and its policy of cooperation with the Congress, far from being generally applauded, appeared to many as suicidal. One of the reasons for this difference of opinion is to be found in the different levels of development in different parts of the province. The province of Oudh, of which Lucknow was the capital, was in two ways an exception; firstly, in that the landed leadership of the community was in a fairly thriving condition; and secondly, in that Lucknow, both as a traditional Muslim centre and as a service centre for the colonial regime, was naturally a focus for the more educated and intelligent Muslims. In the province of Agra, on the other hand, both in the more populous western divisions of Meerut and Rohilkhund, and in the Agra and Allahabad divisions the landed position of the community was under severe attack, and educational advancement, particularly in the highly urbanised Rohilkhund division was extremely limited.[13] It is, of course, difficult to claim overwhelming reliability for generalisations of this kind. The evidence for degrees of educational advancement in different parts of the UP is by no means exhaustive. Nor is it true to say that all Muslims were losing land in the province of Agra. The Sheikhs appear to have been gaining in many districts—demonstrating in all probability that those Muslims who were increasing their holdings were also changing their titles to register their claims to higher social status. But insofar as these generalisations go, they do seem to have affected political attitudes. It is not a coincidence that loyalist Muslim leadership throughout the British period comes from the province of Agra, nor that Jinnah's allies in this period came from Lucknow.

But whatever the potential significance of varying levels of economic and educational development, such factors do not acquire political significance until they are activated, and such was not the case to any significant degree until the Morley-Minto constitution came into operation. Having come into operation, however, that constitution made two major changes in the context of politics. In the first place, by extending the franchise and by increasing the number of elected members, it brought a far larger number of local grievances to a far sharper political focus than had ever been the case before. The Raj itself had provided an important platform for the expression of grievances at the provincial level. It had recognised the representative character of those elected to it; and though it was not obliged to take notice of what they said, it had given them a position which was capable of exploitation. Consequently after 1909, those with grievances which needed to be settled at the provincial level were given a new incentive for involvement in the political system, and the educated and professional elite which was intent on modifying the existing system of control to improve its own position—in education, the services, and the judicial system—began to take to politics in a more systematic fashion. The second change wrought by the reforms, however, was less to the advantage of the 'nationalist' politician, for by making election to the provincial council dependent in a majority of cases on the votes of members of municipal and district boards, it greatly increased competition for position in those bodies and imported into local government elections a degree of factionalism and communalism which, despite the existence of general electorates, had previously been relatively uncommon.

If the United Provinces are taken as an example—and it was there that All-India Muslim politics had their focus at this time—the evidence suggests that in the municipalities and district boards prior to 1909 communal friction was the exception rather than the rule. The municipalities of the Rohilkhund division may have been an exception to this, particularly after the turn of the century, but except in that one division, Muslims did not suffer any very severe losses as a result of the working of the general electorate. Indeed in several of the larger towns, just before the 1909 Act was introduced, they made a number of gains. After 1909, however, Muslim losses increased, particularly in the eight most important towns with the right to elect a member to the Council.[14] Quite why this happened is uncertain. Whether it was, as a report from Mirzapur suggests, that the more established members of municipal boards were enrolling persons of their own religion to offset the challenge of the *vakils*, or whether it was the *vakils* themselves who were indulging in communal appeals to cut across the electoral alliances of the more traditional urban elites, is a question which can probably be answered in a different way in each locality. What is certain, however, is that the Muslims as a minority community could not help but suffer, and this undoubtedly explains why the demand for an extension of separate electorates increases in volume after 1909.

In attempting to marshal the forces for Reform within the Muslim community, therefore, Jinnah soon found himself entangled in a complex of conflicting interests. As an all-India politician, he personally was primarily interested in securing some devolution of power at the Centre. But in the face of Government recalcitrance, he was obliged to seek out provincial allies of a like mind, and in his involvement with them, he was also drawn into their more local rivalries and conflicts. During the period between 1912 and 1918, while Jinnah and the Lucknow politicians pursued their policy of cooperation with the Congress, these local conflicts form a sombre backcloth to their activities. In UP they showed themselves at the Agra League of 1913. On that occasion, Jinnah and Mazhar ul Haq attempted to persuade the League not to pass its regular resolution in favour of separate electorates in local self-government as an earnest of its intentions to work with the Congress. But they were voted down by the politicians of the UP Municipalities, and particularly those from the province of Agra.[15] At Bombay, in 1915, the first time that both organisations had held their sessions in the same city, local rivalries almost wrecked the possibility of a joint approach to the question of reform. Jinnah and his colleagues only carried the day against Cassim Mitha and his *goondas* by locking themselves up in the Taj Mahal hotel and holding their session in private.[16] But these local conflicts emerged onto the provincial and national stage most threateningly of all in UP in 1915 and 1916, when the UP Municipal Bill was introduced. This Bill, which proposed a large-scale devolution of power to the municipalities, sharpened communal demands in the localities at the very time that provincial and national leaders were anxious to keep out of sight. It brought the issue of 'separate versus joint electorates' to a head, and it obliged those politicians who were most anxious for a communal alliance at the provincial level to surrender local advantage for provincial profit.[17] At Lucknow itself, moreover, in December 1916, the bad feeling created by the Bill broke out again and threatened to wreck the chances of a national agreement. Jinnah himself was not involved in the settlement of the communal wrangles in the UP though he was very much involved in the national settlement at Lucknow in 1916. But it is a measure of the effect of these developments on his own capacity for manoeuvre that his views on separate electorates change dramatically by the time the Lucknow Pact is signed. In 1913, he had still been a passionate public advocate of joint electorates. By 1916, he is telling the Congress leaders that no settlement is possible unless the Muslim demand for separate electorates is granted.[18]

But the scope of the argument goes somewhat beyond the assertion that the working of the reform imposed important constraints on the activities of the 'nationalist' politicians. It would also suggest that the nature of the Reforms influenced the capacity of such politicians to overcome these constraints, to compose communal divisions, and to produce a united front against the Government. Where the controversy surrounding the UP Municipal Bill was concerned, it was the fact that there had been no real devolution of power at the provincial level which enabled provincial leaders of both communities to come together and to surrender local advantage for provincial gain. And when the same controversy re-emerged during the negotiations prior to the Lucknow Pact, it was because of the operation of very similar factors at the all-India level—because certain all-India leaders and other provincial leaders were in no mood to be baulked in their own ambitions—that the recalcitrance of Malaviya and Chintamani and the UP communal Hindu party was not allowed to stand in the way of national agreement.

In all this, there has been no mention of the Raj; merely of the formal structure of politics. Yet to talk of one without the other is plainly nonsense. For the formal structure of politics was ultimately the responsibility of the Imperial power, and the introduction of new constitutions was the Raj's response to political developments as it saw them. It is, of course, a different matter to find evidence to prove that the political results of the introduction of these constitutions were foreseen and intended by the Raj. The link between constitutional innovation and ensuing political events is obviously seen more clearly with hindsight. But even if the results were not foreseen by the Raj, these reforms, and the way in which they were introduced, do reflect very clearly the Raj's own estimate of where its real interest lay and where its real allies were to be found.

Generally speaking, the desire of the Raj was to give the maximum degree of influence possible to the more conservative elements in society. This was not an altogether reactionary motivation, because an Imperial power like Britain could only rule a country like India if it recognised the social economic realities which it found in existence in the different localities of the Empire. This indeed had been the criterion on which the Raj had acted in recruiting personnel to its services in the days before the electoral system was introduced, and from the 1880s onwards it had sought to reproduce the same system within the framework of electoral politics. Under the Morley-Minto Reforms, the working of this policy is to be seen in the granting of special electorates to the landlords, in the granting of separate electorates to the Muslims— to bolster the conservative landed class against the challenge of the new elite—and in the arrangement which made members of municipal and district boards the electorate for provincial constituencies. Moreover though the Congress and the League presented a joint demand for reform to the Secretary, Montagu, the Government persisted in the same policy. It may have been obliged, under pressure from Montagu, to put more power into Indian hands that it would have liked. But it endeavoured to do so in such a way as to strengthen its existing system of Imperial control.

What did this mean for Jinnah? In the first place—personal disappointment. If one looks at the policy of Hindu-Muslim cooperation enshrined in the Lucknow Pact from Jinnah's point of view, its whole purpose was to strengthen his bargaining position at the all-India level. In other words, in order to strengthen the chances of reform at the all-India level, Jinnah was prepared to ally himself with aspirants for political power at the provincial level in pursuit of a policy of reform at both levels. But what was the Government's response? To stand firm at the all-India level and only to make concessions at the provincial level. Having helped to keep the Congress and the League together right up to the point when Montagu visited India, therefore, Jinnah received no political pay-off. His own genuine distress and frustration at this are very

clear. Take, for example, his speech to the Imperial Legislative
Council in September 1918, when he said:

> Now my Lord, may I know why the Government of India is to remain
> so sacred and not to be touched? Is there no department in the
> Government of India which could not be brought under the control
> of the legislature? ... Why, I ask should there not be simultaneous
> advance?[19]

It was a good question. But the Raj had a good answer to it. Why
should it make concessions at the all-India level, when it could
disarm opposition by making concessions in the provinces?

In looking at this particular decision, however, one can discover
in it a more serious implication than the personal implication for
Jinnah himself. By standing pat at the Centre and devolving power
to the provinces, the Raj was attempting to offset the challenge to
its authority at the all-India level. In the process, however, it created
vested interests in the provinces, and introduced a centrifugal
tendency into all-India politics. Immediately after the introduction
of the new Reforms, this centrifugal tendency was more apparent
than real. The Raj was still firmly in control, and through the
Governments set up under the reforms in the different provinces,
it was able to maintain a relatively stable Imperium. The non-
cooperation movement was disarmed, and the lure of office
attracted even Congressmen back into the Councils. By the time
the Statutory Commission was appointed, however, these
Congressmen had been forced to accept that it was futile to work
the reforms on the Government's terms, and in 1930, another non-
cooperation movement began. This put the Government in a
serious political dilemma. Its powers of manoeuvre were being
reduced. It was becoming the victim of its own constitutional
innovation. Pressures created by the working of the existing system
made it necessary to grant a greater degree of devolution to the
provinces. But reluctance to give way at the Centre was increased
by the nature of the Congress challenge. So the Raj found itself
introducing provincial autonomy unhampered by the control of a
responsible central legislature. This meant, in effect, that the

eventual withdrawal of the Imperial power was to leave a vacuum at the Centre. At that stage centrifugalism found its fullest expression, and it is in these terms that the emergence of two separate states in 1947 is best understood.[20]

But while the Government's decision to stand pat at the Centre may explain the development of a centrifugal trend in all-India politics, it does not explain the nature of the challenge which the Raj faced to its authority, nor why centrifugalism and Muslim separatism became part and parcel of the same phenomenon. In order to explain these things, one has got to look at the manner in which power was devolved to the provinces. In the years before 1920, the men who demanded Reform were men like Jinnah—the educated lawyers, doctors and school teachers. But even in the provinces where certain departments of Government were transferred to the control of the legislature, it was not these men who benefited. The movement for reform had been essentially an urban movement, and the demand for reform had been intended to benefit the urban areas. But if one looks at the outcome of the reforms in the UP for example, one finds that out of seventy non-Muslim and Muslim elected seats, only ten were allocated to these areas. So who did benefit from the political devolution which took place? The answer is that the constitution was so devised that it bolstered the landed interest—the traditional allies of the Raj— either by giving weightage to the rural areas, or by extending the franchise beyond the canvassing powers of the politicians, or by both.

This manipulative device had important implications for the future. For it meant that those politicians who had been most vociferous in demanding reform had either got to retire from the formal arena of politics (take, for example, Wazir Hassan, the League Secretary, who concentrates increasingly after 1920 on his judicial career), or (and this is, of course, what happened to many Congressmen) to reject the Reforms in their entirety and to begin to agitate in the streets and fields for their revision. If one looks at Congress politics in the years between 1918 and 1935, and if one sees on the one hand the non-cooperation movement and the civil disobedience movement, and on the other, the frustrating experience of those Congress leaders who did try to work within the formal structure of politics, one can see how this kind of device was an indirect incentive to social disruption. For by bolstering the landed interest to counteract the aspirations of the political classes, the Raj was in effect challenging those classes to prove their representative standing, and hence encouraging them, however indirectly, to challenge the landed interest on its own home ground. The no-rent campaigns of the early 1930s may be seen within this context.

In a similar manner, the growth of Muslim separatism may be linked to the distribution of power within individual councils between the two main communities. By the terms of the Montagu-Chelmsford Reforms, the Government attempted to ensure that no community was in a position to benefit from the patronage of the transferred departments without Government cooperation (the support of nominated officials), and that no community could reject the Reforms without the cooperation of some members of the other community. The whole arrangement was devised to maximise the Government's own powers of leverage, and in the Muslim minority provinces—particularly UP and Bihar—it enabled the Government to maintain its old system of control with the support of a combination of Muslims and landlords. In the Muslim majority provinces, however, the situation was rather different, for by distributing power at least in some measure according to population the Reforms had the effect of bringing the Punjab and Bengal into the Muslim limelight. In those provinces, simply because the Muslims had larger numbers of seats in the councils than their coreligionists elsewhere, they stood a better chance of utilising the reforms for their own advantage. This was particularly the case in the Punjab, where the Muslims were given a virtual majority of the elected seats, and where their traditional ties with Government—notably in the military field—ensured them a good reception from the official benches. There, from 1920 onwards, Fazl-i-Hussain's Unionist party began to use the reforms for its own advantage, and a Muslim vested interest in the continuation and extension of the reforms of such power and influence was created that no all-India politician could safely leave it out of his calculations.

These methods of distributing power within individual councils undoubtedly contributed to the enormous increase in communal tension which characterised the period after the reforms were introduced. If one looks first at the Muslim majority provinces, such an explanation for the Punjab would go as follows. The Muslims were favoured by the reforms. They used the reforms to improve their position in local self-government, agriculture, health and education, and this improvement in their lot was at the expense of the economically and educationally more advanced urban Hindu community. Hence antagonism, particularly in the urban areas. Hence also the use of communal appeals by those hardest hit in order to broaden their support and defend their interests. Hence also rioting. In the minority provinces—in the UP for example—an explanation in terms of the structure of politics comes less easily. There the reforms were worked not by one community but by a combination of both, and so far as one can tell, the Muslims did not suffer undue discrimination. In the UP, the source of communal tension appears to have been not the domination of a minority by a majority, but rivalry within the majority community over the best tactics to be employed under the reformed constitution to achieve their objectives. The two leaders of these rival groups were Malaviya and Motilal Nehru, the two men who had clashed over the UP Municipal Bill compromise. In the 1920s, however, what was in dispute was not local but provincial advantage. Nehru had gained the upper hand by joining Gandhi's non-cooperation campaign, and subsequently emerged as the leader of the Swaraj party, favouring non-cooperation within the legislatures and maintaining, like Gandhi, that Hindu-Muslim cooperation was the best means of making this policy successful. Malaviya, on the other hand, who had important educational interests to consolidate, saw the advantage of working the reforms and securing control of the transferred departments. In order to do this, however, he had first to break Nehru's political ascendancy—and to put it bluntly, the communal appeal was the best means to hand. It served to divide Nehru from his Muslim colleagues, and to bind together the disparate elements of the Hindu community under his more orthodox leadership. But the main sufferers, of course, were the Muslims, for once the fire had been started it quickly spread and proved difficult to put out.[21]

In the period before 1920, when communal antagonism infected the localities, it was possible to localise it simply because politicians of both communities at the provincial and all-India level were playing for higher stakes. Once the communal virus affected the provinces, however, the chances of localising the infection were very slim indeed. When the Punjab, UP, Bihar and Bengal were affected, how could the all-India politician fail to take notice? The problem was compounded, moreover, when the Statutory Commission obliged provincial Muslim politicians to face the possibility of a national Government at the Centre. At that point, centrifugalism, which had been exhibited earlier chiefly by the Punjabis, joined hands with separatism in most provinces. How then could the all-India Muslim politician demand a unitary Government at the Centre?

Jinnah's career as an all-India politician under the Montagu-Chelmsford Reforms illustrates the working of these constraints. After he returned to the Central Assembly in 1923, he found the position much the same as when he had left it. There had been no introduction of ministerial responsibility and though the Chamber had been enlarged, the lines of confrontation were much the same as before. The Government put forward its arguments against a further devolution of power. The 'nationalists' continued to try to prove these arguments false on the Government's own terms. Where the forging of Hindu-Muslim political unity outside the Council was concerned, however, the Reforms had wrought changes which necessitated a change of tactics. Jinnah could no longer look to Lucknow for support. All that Lucknow had to recommend it by this time was a warm welcome from his old friend, the Raja of Mahmudabad. Instead, he was obliged to look to Lahore. Why was this? The reason is that in order to secure support for a devolution of power at the Centre, he needed provincial allies who were equally interested in Reform at their own level. And after 1920, the only Muslim interest group in India to fulfil this requirement was the Punjabis. It was not fortuitous, therefore, that when Jinnah decided to revive the League in 1924, he chose to do so at Lahore.

But the Lahore session of the League illustrated yet another constraint of the new system. Jinnah had hoped to secure Punjabi support for his plans for devolution at the Centre—had hoped, if reports are correct, to produce another Lucknow Pact. But the Punjabis were only interested in devolution at the Centre on their own terms, and when the resolution on reform emerged from the Subjects Committee, it was an almost entirely Punjabi affair. It looked forward to a Federal Government at the Centre, whose functions were to be confined to such matters as were of general or common concern; it demanded that no measure of territorial distribution should disturb Muslim majorities in Punjab, Bengal and the Frontier; and it paid scant attention to the position of the Muslim minorities. As a result of UP Muslim's objections, this resolution was subsequently amended to allow for 'adequate and effective' representation of Muslim minorities in every province. But this only added to Jinnah's problems. For far from securing the outright approval of the Punjabis for his own ambitions at the Centre, he in fact emerged from the Lahore League with a brief to secure from the Congress; as the price of cooperation, terms which exceeded those granted at Lucknow.[22]

Jinnah's efforts to fill this brief show clearly that the polarisation of communal relations in the provinces had made an all-India settlement virtually impossible by 1925. To bring the Muslims of the provinces into any form of political union at the all-India level, Jinnah had to put forward terms which had no chance of being accepted. For unlike in the period before 1920, when the absence of devolution at the provincial level acted as a spur to inter-communal political union, by 1925, communal division at the provincial level, brought about by the working of the reforms, had already poisoned relations at the national level. It was significant, for example, that those Hindus who took the lead in rejecting the Lahore League terms at the all-parties conference in 1925 were Lajpat Rai and Malaviya, the two chief provincial opponents of Jinnah's Punjabi and UP clients.

After the failure of his reform initiative in 1925, Jinnah did not attempt to play peacemaker again until the eve of the announcement of the Statutory Commission. At that stage; chiefly because of his hopes to secure at last what he had always been hoping for—namely responsibility at the Centre—he attempted to produce a new agreement, this time on the basis of joint electorates. This reversion to his earlier preference may well have been the result of his understanding that devolution at the Centre was less of an attraction to the provincial Muslims than it was to the Congress. But even so, agreement proved impossible, again chiefly because of communal Hindu opposition. Moreover, as the point of devolution came closer and Muslim demands increased, the terms on which Jinnah could continue as a viable Muslim leader at the all-India level also increased. From his four points of 1927, he graduates to 14 points in 1929, and except on the electorate question, there is by this stage virtually no difference between his position and that of the provincial Muslims. His own ambitions undoubtedly remain distinct. But he can only pursue them by compromising with provincial Muslim interests. The final compromise comes at the round table conference in 1930, when with extreme reluctance he agrees to the all-India Federation scheme. This scheme in effect makes impossible the strong central government with real powers which Jinnah had been working for since before the First World War, and it is not surprising that he loses interest in Indian politics and settles in England at this time.

As early as 1925, as an author of the Muddiman Committee minority report, Jinnah had demonstrated his awareness of the centrifugal trend introduced into all-India politics by the Montagu-Chelmsford constitution:

> ... with provincial governments fully responsible to their legislatures (ran the report) and the Central Government irresponsible in the last report, the Control of various kinds which is desired to be continued in the Central Government will be more difficult to enforce and the centrifugal tendency observed in many Federal states and especially marked in the history of India will manifest itself more and more making stable government unworkable.[23]

It was a prophetic insight, but not one which the Raj heeded. And so, between the pulls of provincialism and the recalcitrance of the Government, Jinnah ultimately lost his chance of high office in British India. But what he could not lose, despite his disillusionment, was his unique knowledge of all-India politics and its constraints, and he was later to put this knowledge to very effective use as the leader of the new Muslim League. In that role, however, the focus of his ambitions soon showed a marked change. He was no longer ambitious for power at the centre of the Indian political system. He was intent on creating a centre of his own.

NOTES

1. *Census of India, 1881, Bombay Presidency including Sind*, vol. i, pp. 135-136.
2. *Census of India, 1901, vol. xi, Bombay (Town and Island), part v*, Report by S.M. Edwardes, ICS, pp. 20, 77-82, and 105.
3. See *Progress of Education in India, Sixth Quinquennial Report, Cmd 7485 (1914)*, Table 16, p. 203, and Tables 217-218, p. 286. Also *Report of the Public Services Commission*, vol. i, Calcutta, 1917, p. 191.
4. Interview with Mr Akbar Peerbhoy, Bombay, Sept. 1970.
5. Interview with Jinnah's solicitor, Mohammed Ali Chaiwala, Bombay, Sept. 1970.
6. Speech by Sir Ali Imam at the All India Muslim League Annual Session, Amritsar, 1908. Quoted in S.S. Pirzada (ed.), *Foundations of Pakistan: All India Moslem League Documents 1906-47*, vol. i, Karachi, 1969, p. 53.
7. *Royal Commission on the Public Services in India, Appendix to the Report of the Commissioners*, vol. vi, (Cmd 7579), pp. 333 and 341-342.
8. See Purushotamdas Thakurdas papers (Nehru Memorial Museum, New Delhi), File 40: Jinnah to Thakurdas, circular letter, 22 May 1925; M.R. Jayakar, *The Story of My Life*, vol. ii, Bombay, 1959, pp. 558-560.
9. See Kanji Dwarkadas, *India's Fight for Freedom 1913-37*, Bombay, 1966, pp. 323-324.
10. One indication of this is the fact that the terms of the Lucknow Pact were first put to the Viceroy in Aug. 1916 as a memorandum from 19 members of his Council.
11. See Pirzada, *op. cit.*, vol. i, pp. 258-259.
12. See Ali Imam papers (Karachi University Library): Raja of Mahmudabad to Sir Ali Imam, 25 July 1917.

13. The evidence for these generalisations has been taken from UP district gazeteers published between 1903 and 1911, and from the censuses.

14. The most detailed examination of Muslim politics in the UP municipalities is to be found in F.C.R. Robinson's 'Municipal Government and Moslem Separatism' in Gallagher, Johnson and Seal (eds.), *Locality Province and Nation*, Cambridge, 1973, pp. 69-121. But I have differed from him in his assessment of the effect of the working of the general electorate on the Muslim community before 1909. Dr Robinson contends that the Muslims were losing seats in the Meerut, Agra, Rohilkhand and Allahabad divisions from 1883 onwards. But he does not appear to have taken into account the Municipal Reform Act of 1900, which reduced the membership of many municipal boards in order to provoke keener competition for membership. See annual *Reports on Municipal Taxation and Expenditure in the North Western Provinces and Oudh*, 1891/2-1898/9; *Reports on Municipal Administration and Finances*, 1900/01-1908/09.

15. See Pirzada, (ed.), *op. cit.*, vol. i, pp. 315-317.

16. *Ibid.*, pp. 324-361.

17. For an account of the Municipal Bill controversy, see Dr Robinson's article in Gallagher, Johnson and Seal (eds.), *op. cit.*, pp. 106-115.

18. See Government of India Home Political Department, Nov. 1916, B 452-453: Weekly report of the Director of Criminal Intelligence, 14 Nov. 1916.

19. *Indian Legislative Council Debates* 1918-1919, 7 Sept. 1918, p. 133.

20. For a fuller exposition of this theory, see my '*Prelude to Partition*: Karachi, Oxford University Press, 1987.

21. For a more detailed account of the development of communal antagonism in the UP and Punjab in the 1920s, see *ibid.*, pp. 48-72.

22. See Pirzada, *op. cit.*, vol. i, pp. 575-582.

23. *Reforms Enquiry Committee, Report*, London, 1925, *Cmd 2360*, p. 179.

2

Jinnah, Star of the East Reborn
Andrew Roberts

The news that Jeremy Irons might be playing Mohammed Ali Jinnah, the founder of Pakistan, in a movie has sparked a debate about whether it is politically correct for white actors to take non-white roles. Although actors may be called upon to impersonate people of a different age, class, religion or even sex, the race-relations industry now wants to restrict the pigmentations they can represent. It is a doctrine that would have deprived the British theatre of Ralph Richardson's 1938 Old Vic portrayal of Othello and Laurence Olivier's even more highly acclaimed interpretation of the same role in 1964.

Absurdities aside, the important, even glorious, news is that an epic film is to be made of the life of one of the century's greatest men. Jinnah's epicentral role in the partition of India and the formation of Pakistan has been consistently misrepresented and even traduced by journalists, politicians and some Indian historians over the past half century. This film, released to coincide with Pakistan's 50th anniversary this time next year, will try to set the record straight. The brainchild of the respected Islamic scholar Professor Akbar Ahmed, the film's script is a historically accurate representation of the extraordinary life of Pakistan's Quaid-i-Azam ('Great Leader').

Insofar as western filmgoers know anything about Jinnah at all, it is as the glowering, sulking villain in Sir Richard Attenborough's *Gandhi*. The film reduced Jinnah's arguments for a separate Muslim state to a simple jealousy of the Mahatma and of Pandit Nehru. It was as insulting to Pakistanis as it was historically inaccurate.

Worse still is the fanatical Indian Hindu BJP portrayal of Jinnah as an extreme Muslim communalist. In fact, far from practising the racial intolerance they themselves preach, Jinnah had a Parsi wife, Hindu doctor and British military secretary. He even recalled a British official from retirement to help run post-independence Pakistan. Equally dangerous libels come from the extreme Islamic attacks on his legacy. The Muslim fundamentalist Hisb-ut-Tahrir organisation, whose campaigning is making worrying headway on many British university campuses, believes that Ayatollah Khomeini, not Jinnah, should be their hero. Similarly, the late Dr Kalim Siddiqui, head of the so-called Muslim parliament, denounced the Jinnah film project, characterising its subject as a tool of western imperialism.

This would have surprised Lord Mountbatten, who as viceroy used every argument and threat to try to force Jinnah off his insistence upon a sovereign Muslim homeland. Mountbatten contributed to the slander against Jinnah, calling him vain, megalomaniacal, an evil genius, a lunatic, a psychotic case and a bastard, while publicly claiming he was entirely impartial between Jinnah's Pakistan and Nehru's India. Jinnah rose magisterially above Mountbatten's blatant bias, not even attacking the former viceroy when, as governor-general of India after partition, Mountbatten tacitly condoned India's shameful invasion of Kashmir in October 1947.

'We've decided that the fate of Kashmir is ultimately to be determined by the people,' said Nehru of the land of his ancestors. 'This pledge we have given not only to the people of Kashmir but to the world. We will not and cannot back out of it.' But Mountbatten allowed Nehru to do just that, and to this day the referendum Nehru promised Kashmir has not been held. Instead, Delhi has installed a series of puppet governments and the issue has developed into one of the world's longest running sores.

When the Queen visits the Indian subcontinent for the half-century celebrations next year, it is crucial that her programme is organised not overly to favour India over Pakistan, as did Mountbatten's arrangements for the transfer of power in 1947.

It is understandable that many Muslims feel that if even a great, tolerant, pro-western, moderate leader like Jinnah is ignored and underrated here, there is an argument for a Gadaffi or Khomeini figure who will force the West to take notice of Islam. Certainly, Pakistani moderates feel that a proper appreciation of the role of Jinnah in the West would in itself be a huge propaganda victory for those of them who are struggling against the neanderthal fundamentalism which threatens to engulf their country.

Without Jinnah there might never have been a Pakistan. The subcontinent would have been subjected to the horrific consequences of 90 million Muslims being forced into a unitary state dominated by 255 million Hindus. However unfortunate some parts of Pakistan's history have been—with three leaders shot, hanged and blown up—it cannot have been anything like as bad as the civil war which would undoubtedly have resulted had not Jinnah won partition.

Never more than today do Pakistanis need to be reminded of the tolerant, tough-minded, secularist pluralist who created their nation. India and Pakistan have fought three wars since independence, and are probably now both nuclear powers. Mutual trust can be built only through both sides appreciating each other's historical perceptions. In the subcontinent all border and political arguments between the countries inevitably return to 1947. A proper understanding of Jinnah's role is a crucial piece of the jigsaw puzzle. Only by placing him in his proper context, as an actor equally as great as Gandhi and Nehru in the 1947 drama, can Indians and Pakistanis gain a proper perspective.

Nevertheless, many Indian opinion-formers are consistently hostile to Jinnah's memory and castigate him, in the words of the title of a typical recent article, as *The Man Who Broke the Unity of India*. Because Jinnah is Pakistan's equivalent of Churchill, de Gaulle or George Washington, such unfair and often deliberately vicious criticism is bound to infuriate Pakistanis.

Hopefully this film will allow us to see the truth behind half a century of propaganda 'History,' said Jinnah in 1947, 'will be the ultimate judge of Pakistan.' In the meantime, we must rely on the silver screen.

3

Congress Leadership in Transition: Jinnah to Gandhi, 1914–1920
Stanley A. Wolpert

On the eve of the First World War Mohammed Ali Jinnah was in London at the head of a most prestigious National Congress deputation, which had been sent to lobby Secretary of State Crewe and other members of Parliament to open the Council of India to at least three (one-third its total composition) non-official Indians elected by members of British India's Imperial and Provincial Legislative Councils. It was the first major Council reform proposed since the inauguration of the Indian Councils Act of 1909, and the importance of Jinnah's role as leader of the deputation can hardly be overestimated. Though this young Bombay Muslim was only thirty-seven he had served his political apprenticeship as private Secretary to India's 'Grand Old Man', Dadabhai Naoroji, from 1906-10, was elected in 1910 to represent Bombay's Muslims on the Imperial Legislative Council where he became a close colleague of Gopal Krishna Gokhale, had accompanied Gokhale to Europe in 1913, and may thus be said to have ventured to London in 1914, not simply at the helm of another political deputation, but as potential heir to the Dadabhai-Pherozeshah-Gokhale mantle of Western-Indian National Congress leadership. At any rate Jinnah was certainly Western India's most brilliant young barrister and shrewdest parliamentarian-diplomat, 'the best talker of the pack',[1] as Lord Crewe so crudely put it in reporting to Viceroy Hardinge on his first meeting with the Congress deputation.

Mohandas Karamchand Gandhi at this time was forty-five, had just completed his South African *satyagraha* with what was to prove a short-lived and at best partial 'victory' over Smuts, and but for Gokhale's patronage, had no leadership status in the National Congress. He had, however, developed a uniquely potent method of agitation and mass resistance, which could so effectively tap the hitherto unused ocean of political energy stored within India's peasant population that his potential power at once impressed and so obviously frightened his ailing 'politic Guru' that Gokhale obliged Gandhi to vow abstention from politics for at least one year after he returned home. How exactly Gokhale planned to cope with his remarkable, all but unmanageable, disciple after that year ran out will never, of course, be known, since 'Baba Sahib' died at Poona before it was half over. We do, however, know that the Servants of India rejected Gandhi's subsequent candidacy membership in their Society, since Srinivasa Sastri, reflecting the feelings of most of his fellow members, found Gandhi's approach to political action fundamentally antipathetical to his own and dangerously disruptive.

The Congress leadership roles of Jinnah and Gandhi at the start of the First World War were, however, totally reversed, but two years after the war's end, Gandhi having captured all-power at Nagpur, where Jinnah 'carried no influence'.[2] This dramatic transition reflects at the least as much the complex and revolutionary impact of the war upon India's socio-political ideology and Nationalist aspirations as it does the leadership tactics or powers of either Jinnah or Gandhi, neither of whom basically changed his style of leadership in the course of the six year interlude under consideration. The climates of British and Indian opinion were, however, so radically and irreversibly, altered by the traumas of the war and its tragic aftermath that it was as though Jinnah and the moderate elitism he represented belonged thereafter to an era as irrevocably lost and remote as Edwardian England, while Gandhi and *satyagraha* seemed suddenly as timeless as eternity, offering India renewed hope of salvation, religious as well as political.

Only a month before the war started the Lords could still seriously debate and ultimately reject Crewe's singularly cautious council of India Bill as though its proposal to *select* two Indian members of Whitehall Council from a 'list of candidates' submitted by elected non-officials would 'destroy'[3] the Government of India. As Morley predicted in countering Ampthill's absurd argument that though 'sympathised with the aspirations of the people of India' it was not yet 'time to introduce this Bill' that 'time would never come'. Lord Ampthill was indeed 'like the rustic waiting on the edge of the stream until the waters flow by'.[4] Yet in just three years and one month's time Montagu would announce the Cabinet's readiness to advance much more swiftly toward 'responsible government' for India than any member of the Lords, including Morley or Crewe would have dreamed possible or considered desirable in 1914. And precisely three years after Montagu's August 1917 announcement, which had by then been translated into the most generous single measure of reform legislation ever enacted by the British for India, the Governor of Bombay would write morosely to his equally despondent chief in Whitehall that 'All the value and goodwill that one hoped from your reforms is being rapidly submerged on account of the actions of these two or three men (Gandhi and the Ali Brothers), and feeling has never been worse than at present since the Mutiny'.[5]

The almost equal yet opposite force that the First World War was to exert upon the political fortunes of Jinnah and Gandhi was not immediately apparent. Ironically enough, at the start of that holocaust, while Jinnah was still smarting from the dual rejection (by the India Office as well as the Lords) of his Congress deputation's demands, Gandhi urged resident Indians in England to 'think Imperially',[6] and was instrumental in organising a Field Ambulance Training Corps in London. As though compelled to relieve his African experience sequentially, however, Gandhi soon launched *satyagraha* against his Corps' Colonel, R.J. Baker, and quickly resigned from the service for which he'd so eagerly volunteered. Less than a month after returning to India, Gandhi attended a garden party reception given by the Gujar Sabha of Bombay, then Chaired by Jinnah, who presided. In 'thanking' Jinnah on this occasion Gandhi said he was 'glad to find a Mohammedan not only belonging to his own region's Sabha, but chairing it'.[7] The political effectiveness of so patronizing a remark was surely not lost on Jinnah, whose chances of achieving the dominant National leadership to which he aspired were undermined each time his minority religious status was so markedly noted in public. Perhaps the most ironic aspect of the Jinnah-Gandhi turnabout in Congress leadership during this interlude, and its enduring legacy to recent South Asian History, was the unrelenting religiously provincial character of Gandhi's 'secular' leadership, and the consistently secular national quality of Jinnah's communalism. Proper British Barrister that he was, Jinnah had groomed himself to be the perfect Indian Viceroy, and certainly proved, as Montagu noted in 1917, far sharper 'at dialectics'[8] than Hardinge's successor, Lord Chelmsford. Were it not for the war this 'Muslim Gokhale' might well have succeeded to national leadership over Congress as well as the League, drafting his meticulous briefs calling for more power, hurling his demands in high courts of Council across two continents, closing his contracts of political rapprochement (as at Lucknow in 1916) between Hindu and Muslim politicians ready to accept their promised share of seats and other such perquisites of power in the corporate enterprise of governing India.

By greatly accelerating the time-table of Indian political expectations (why else, after all, did Indian leaders universally express their loyalty to the Raj as soon as the war began?), while shortening the fuse of popular patience, the war offered Gandhi his historic opportunity to muster mass support for the programme of revolutionary action he had coincidentally developed at this opportune hour. As his brief and tortured London interlude in 1914 reveals, Gandhi was now determined to practise *satyagraha* wherever he went, but London hardly proved a congenial climate for such activity. Wartime India was a different matter. When it became all too obvious that Kitchener alone was correct in predicting a war of years rather than months, with the warship *Emden* wrecking havoc at Madras and in the Bay of Bengal, the prices of wheat and cotton goods skyrocketing, and cheap German manufactured items disappearing from bazaars across the subcontinent. Indians realised that for most of them war merely meant higher prices, more taxes, and less of everything else. For a minority of merchants and manufacturers, of course, it brought soaring profits, but when the British later tried to tap some of these they found that wealthy Marwaris like Bajaj and Muslim merchants like Chotani preferred to back revolutionary leaders like Gandhi and Shaukat Ali rather than surrendering their fortunes to foreigners. As Gandhi admitted in reflecting upon his Kheda *satyagraha* experience, 'the Bombay merchants sent us more money than necessary'.[9] For India's Muslim minority the war added even further cause of frustration and depressing ambivalence, but while Jinnah, in proper English style, remained aloof from any semblance of involvement in Pan-Islamic activity, Gandhi, prototypical Hindu that he was, not only dared to ride the tiger of Khilafat agitation, but used it as the staging ground for his rise to Congress leadership.

Making a virtue of the initial necessity his vow to Gokhale had imposed upon him, Gandhi assiduously avoided the trap of competing openly with the leadership of any established public organisation in India throughout the war. While courting Mahatma Munshiram (Swami Shraddananda) of the Arya Samaj, and keeping in touch with Congress and Home Rule League leaders, he disclaimed all interest in 'politics' as he travelled third-class across India, unobtrusively campaigning at every rural platform, building his own private band of followers, at Champaran, in Ahmadabad, Kheda, Madras, and Bombay. He soon correctly diagnosed India's wartime climate as 'a state of fear', and in February of 1916 did his best to help change that condition by speaking out fearlessly while Annie Besant and her Maharaja friends trembled at Benares. Whether or not 'some hidden violence in himself',[10] as Erikson suggests, helped Gandhi captivate that student audience while losing the support of their elders, from this time at least his popularity among India's silent majority grew in direct proportion to the anxiety and antipathy he generated among India's more conservative vocal leadership, including such 'moderates' as Annie Besant and Srinivasa Sastri.

Jinnah personally understood the phenomenon of Gandhi's meteoric rise to popular fame as well as his own destiny to be dubbed the dupe of alien rule so long as he retained faith in the ultimate responsiveness of a system that was losing its lifeblood on Flanders and Mesopotamian battlefields. He explained it to Meston in 1917 as clearly as Gokhale had once explained the same sort of political problem to Morley a decade earlier.

> The Extremist has a definite programme, impracticable perhaps, but appealing keenly to the pride of the people. The Moderate has no particular creed, except trust in Government. If he goes on the platform and asks his audience to trust Government they immediately challenge him to tell them what Government is going to do for them. He is unable to reply. Government has not confided its intentions to him; and he is shouted down. The Extremist on the other hand, is definite, plausible, and unless he breaks the law, there is nothing to show that Government disapproves of his propaganda.[11]

From within the Imperial Legislative Council Jinnah laboured in vain to convince Government of the urgency of announcing British post-war plans for Indian constitutional reform. The memorial, inspired by Gokhale's 'political testament', which was presented to the Viceroy in October 1916 by nineteen members of the Imperial Council, including Jinnah, became the basis of the Congress-League demands agreed upon jointly at Lucknow in December. Calling for substantial and effective constitutional reforms, the Memorial, as well as the Lucknow Pact with its detailed scheme of minority representation, reflected Jinnah's Nationalist leadership style at its best. Explaining the new demands to Bombay's Sixteenth Provincial Conference, over which he presided, Jinnah noted that 'India has ... turned a corner ... There is now a bright and a great future in front of her. We are now on a straight road, the Promised Land is within sight'.[12] Two months later at Lucknow he could 'rejoice to think that a final settlement has at last been reached which sets the seal on Hindu-Muslim cooperation and opens a new era in the history of our country'.[13] It was, however, all but the end of the brief interlude of Congress-League cooperation, and certainly the peak of Jinnah's personal rise to National leadership.

The debacle in Mesopotamia, resulting in Chamberlain's forced resignation and Montagu's August promise, only added fuel to fires of Indian impatience and frustration with the British and their war. Montagu came too late to bolster the tottering line of loyalist leaders, like Jinnah, who had fashioned themselves in Whitehall's image, and were made targets of popular ridicule or what in some ways was worse, mass ostracism. Craddock, O'Dwyer, and the old Guard had won their delaying action, and even after Montagu arrived on the Indian scene he could barely make sense of the turbulent reality that confronted him, misreading Gandhi as 'a pure visionary',[14] vainly 'racking my brains as to how I am going to get something which India will accept and the House of Commons will allow me to do without whittling it down'.[15] It was an impossible equation to balance, and Montagu destroyed himself seeking to solve it.

While Jinnah fretted about legislative reforms and communal rapprochement, Gandhi went to Champaran, where he found himself 'face to face with God',[16] in confronting Indigo peasants. From Bihar he returned home to popular victories at Ahmadabad and Kheda, the latter marking, as he called it, 'the beginning of true political education' for the peasants who joined him, or rather whose struggle for economic survival he joined as the Leader with a Method. Which is not to negate the inspirational power of Gandhi's leadership, but merely to note that without the eagerly predisposed, willing followers, marshalled by his 'subcontractor' Patels, and Prasads in Gujarat and Bihar, he could no more have achieved success with his *satyagraha* than he did in trying to recruit soldiers for Chelmsford after the Viceroy's War Conference in April 1918. As long as he tapped the well-springs of Hindu-Jain-Buddhist faith in Ahimsa and Mother India's soil, Gandhi was capable of magnetising millions, but once he abandoned his message of love and belief in India's capacity to 'conquer all by soul-force',[17] and sought instead to assist Western Europe defend its soil in a titanic battle of brute-forces he lost his audience.

The Summer months Gandhi laboured in 1918 as Chelmsford's recruiting sergeant in Gujarat are critical to any understanding of his leadership powers and its limits, for as though consciously to test his charisma the Mahatma returned to Kheda, to those very peasants who had been ready to sacrifice their lives at his command less than a year before. 'My optimism received a rude shock', Gandhi confessed. 'Whereas during the revenue campaign the people readily offered their carts free of charge, and two volunteers came forth when one was needed, it was difficult now to get a cart even on hire, to say nothing of volunteers'.[18] He walked himself weary, spoke himself hoarse, but accomplished virtually nothing, except to rouse the skepticism and wonder of his most devoted co-workers, many of whom thought he had gone mad to abandon Ahimsa for war. Actually, Gandhi was merely practical enough to realise that the war offered India a unique opportunity to train its own army, and though his Bania loyalties would not permit him to agree to help raise more money for the war, he did not scruple against urging peasants to take advantage of the martial training that was being offered to village volunteers. The mass rejection of his call proved so painful a defeat to Gandhi that he became 'deathly ill' (as he had been during his volunteer service days in London), suffering total mental and physical breakdown from which he did not begin to recover until he heard about the Armistice, and had 'no longer to worry myself'.[19] Still his recovery was slow, as 'all interest in living had ceased'[20] while he waited in 'agony' to emerge from that 'helpless state'. It was a bitter lesson; one he never forgot. Hereafter, the campaigns Gandhi led (until his assassination) were all popular, if not politically, successful. He might in future seek to withdraw from the whirlwind aftermath, or 'Himalayan blunders' of *satyagraha*, but would not soon launch another campaign that by its inherent nature was doomed to futile failure, among the mass of followers on whom he was constrained to focus his leadership talents.

Jinnah was, of course, equally constrained by the limits of followership in his efforts to lead British India toward the dawn of Dominion status. Though intellect, training, and predilection made him tailor his political image to the model of Gokhale, religious heritage and political opportunity gave him the seat on the Imperial Legislative Council which indelibly identified him as a communal minority member. If Gandhi could not wean the majority of Hindu India's peasant population from their faith in non-violence, a Muslim Jinnah could no more have hoped to win their allegiance for any cause, whatever its intrinsic popularity, than would a Jewish Montagu. What Jinnah hoped to accomplish, however, precisely as Montagu did, was through education, and other social, as well as economic and political reforms, sufficiently to transform the basic character of British India (we now call that process 'modernisation') so as to retain his leadership over it, despite his birth within a religious minority. Though it has become fashionable to speak of Jinnah, Gokhale, and other such 'Moderates' as practitioners of the 'politics of limitation', reflecting the limited demands as well as numerical size of the literate urban constituencies they represented, it seems equally important to remember that their goals were often hardly more 'limited' than those of the most 'extreme' or revolutionary of their contemporaries. Their tactics were, of course, quite different, as were their time-tables.

Perhaps the best indication of how radically nationalistic Jinnah's agitation on behalf of Home Rule had begun to sound to British ears by early 1918 is provided by Willingdon's 'including' him (and Malaviya) with Tilak and Mrs Besant among those 'extremists' who 'have no feeling of what is their duty to the Empire at this crisis'.[21] Chelmsford was equally frustrated by Jinnah's outspoken criticism in Council, and should have assured him a permanent place on India's Nationalist Role of Honour merely by naming Jinnah with Malaviya, Sarma, and Patel as four members of the Imperial Council in whom the Viceroy detected 'a root of bitterness ... which cannot be eradicated'.[22] Sir George Lloyd, Willingdon's successor as Governor of Bombay, was later to wax even more eloquent in warning Montagu against 'Jinnah and Mrs Naidu ... both fair of speech and black of heart—real irreconcilables'.[23]

Jinnah was second only to Sarma in resigning from the Viceroy's Council as his personal protest against passage of the Rowlatt Acts in April of 1919. He had been elected President of the Bombay Home Rule League after Annie Besant's internment in 1917, consistently called for constitutional reforms in accord with the Memorandum by the Council Nineteen and the Lucknow Pact, urged amnesty for political prisoners upon Montagu's appointment as Secretary of State, argued most eloquently for opening commissioned officer ranks in the services to Indians, for expanding educational opportunities for all, and for Hindu-Muslim unity. His diction was flawless, his appearance impeccable, yet his appeal was either ignored or answered in too little portion too late by Viceroys and Governors who failed to recognise his frank warnings as the honesty of friendship rather than the critical assault of an enemy, or feared his brilliance, distrusted his sage counsel, and finally drove him to the wilderness of resignation.

But for the war of course, and the rising tide of prices, popular discontent, official repression, and terrorism, the Rowlatt Acts would never have been proposed in the first place, or passed in the face of such widespread, articulate, and legitimate Indian opposition. By August of 1920, George Lloyd could single them out with the remarkably sound vision of hindsight as the first of a 'series of blunders'[24] committed by Simla. For Jinnah as well as Gandhi these Acts proved unique catalysts, critical determinants of their future leadership roles. Both men reacted with the same sort of Barrister-fired indignation: Gandhi's *satyagraha* pledge called the Bills 'unjust, subversive of the principles of liberty and justice, and destructive of the elementary rights of individuals on which the safety of the community, as a whole and the State itself is based'; Jinnah's letter of resignation to the Viceroy stated:

> ... by passing this Bill, Your Excellency's Government have ... ruthlessly trampled upon the principles for which Great Britain avowedly fought the war. The fundamental principles of justice have been uprooted and the Constitutional rights of the people have been violated at a time when there is no real danger to the State by an overfretful and incompetent bureaucracy which is neither responsible to the people nor in touch with real public opinion.[25]

Their remedies, however, were diametrically different, for Jinnah resigned his Council seat in Simla, not to rouse mass civil disobedience to the 'Black Acts' but to shift the venue of his Fabian-like politics in this era from the echoless chamber of the Viceroy's Council to what he believed would be the more responsive ambiance of London's Whitehall. He tendered his resignation, feeling

> that under the prevailing conditions I can be of no use to my people in the Council nor consistently with one's self-respect is cooperation possible with a Government that shows such utter disregard for the

opinion of the representatives of the people ... In my opinion, a
Government that passes or sanctions such a law in times of peace
forfeits its claim to be called a civilised Government and I still hope
that the Secretary of State for India, Mr Montagu, will advise His
Majesty to signify his disallowance to this Black Act.[26]

Gandhi, of course, turned to another audience, pledging his mass
of followers to 'refuse civilly to obey these laws', affirming 'that in
this struggle we will faithfully follow truth'.

In the anguished months that followed, Chelmsford closed ranks
behind the barbarism of Dyer and O'Dwyer, and Gandhi moved
from initiating the anti-Rowlatt *satyagraha* to his admission of a
'Himalayan miscalculation' dictating its temporary demise. Jinnah
went to London again that summer, this time at the head of a
Muslim League deputation to appeal to Montagu and present
testimony before Lord Selborne's select Committee on the Reforms.
His success was modest and undramatic, but he returned to
Bombay convinced that 'if India were to send her real representatives
(to London), say half-a-dozen, who will carry on propaganda work
there backed up by substantial financial help and public opinion,
a great deal can be done. But it must be a continual and
permanently established institution carried on by men not only
who go there for a few months, but permanently'.[27] Obviously,
Jinnah himself was prepared to serve as one of those permanent
emigree representatives, still 'confident that Mr Montagu will not
fail us', believing more could be accomplished on India's behalf in
London than anywhere under the iron heel of the Government of
India's Rowlatt Act rule. He had 'no hesitation in saying that Lord
Chelmsford's administration has been a failure and the sooner he
is recalled the better for all concerned'.[28] Jinnah's prescription
sounded much like that voiced several decades earlier by William
Wedderburn and Gokhale, and though it might well have proved
the swiftest, most rational, and surely least painful, path to
Dominion status for a united India, it evoked no resonant echo
from the political leadership of post-war Delhi, Amritsar, Calcutta,
Ahmadabad, Nagpur, or even Bombay.

The war had raised too many hopes, shattered too many illusions. Montagu's high-sounding words of 1917 had lost all their sterling ring with the inflation, devaluation, and increased taxation that by 1919 made even his noble Act of Reform seem but a bitter pill for the earthquakes of protest that rocked post-Rowlatt Delhi, Amritsar, and Lahore. The new plateau of political impatience and popular frustration called for new measures of opposition, new outlets of active protest. Though Montagu might label him a 'fanatic',[29] Craddock a 'Misguided Saint',[30] and Chelmsford 'a d ... d nuisance',[31] the only Indian capable of launching and sustaining such post-war protest was Gandhi. He had, as the Viceroy was by now sufficiently astute to detect, 'passive resistance on the brain',[32] and with the support of Marwari, Gujarati, and Memon money, and the millions of Muslims he gathered by joining forces with Shaukat and Mohammed Ali, making the Khilafat issue the first plank of his nationwide *satyagraha* of 1920, the Mahatma became a new rallying point of independence, and the symbol of unrelenting suffering, for India's down-trodden 'wretched of the earth', penurious middle-class, and furious nouveau riche.

Gandhi's Vishnu-like stride to the peak of Congress power from Amritsar, through Calcutta to Nagpur, has been so thoroughly analysed by Judith Brown[33] and Richard Gordon[34] as to require no elaboration here. The longer range significance for recent Indian history of the Mahatma's phenomenal rise to popular acclaim must, however, be viewed in the light not only of Gandhi's rise, but also of Jinnah's fall. Though the Rowlatt Acts and Chelmsford were anathema to Jinnah, he viewed non-cooperation as a fundamentally religious rather than political attack, and came to consider Gandhi a disruptive rather than unifying force in India's public life. Was it jealousy at having lost the mantle of Gokhale's leadership to this intruder from the South African bush? Or indignation at finding himself beaten in a battle of parliamentary tactics over the Home Rule League, whose name was changed to *Swarajya Sabha* by Gandhi as he seized control of it in October 1920 in Jinnah's own citadel of Bombay? Or frustration at finding this Hindu Bania presiding over the most popular political movement of Muslims ever started on Indian soil? Or mere personal exasperation at finding himself unable to speak without heckling interruption by thousands of illiterates, whose cheaply purchased votes had somehow become equated with his own at Nagpur? Perhaps it was just that at 43, Jinnah felt it was too late for him to start all over, redesigning his political style, changing the character and content of his public image and message to suit the radically altered times, yet knowing that if ever he hoped to regain the pinnacle of power he would have to do something like that. For Congress had fallen for a Mahatma, as did most of Muslim India.

'Your methods have already caused split and division in almost every institution that you have approached hitherto', Jinnah berated Gandhi after losing leadership of the Home Rule League, 'and in the public life of the country not only amongst Hindus and Muslims but between Hindus and Hindus and Muslims and Muslims and even between fathers and sons; people generally are desperate all over the country and your extreme programme has for the moment struck the imagination mostly of the inexperienced youth and the ignorant and the illiterate. All this means complete disorganisation and chaos. What the consequence of this may be, I shudder to contemplate ... I do not wish my countrymen to be dragged to the brink of a precipice in order to be shattered'.[35] It was a fearsome image to invoke, but we may wonder if that contemplative 'shudder' was Jinnah's moment of rude historic awakening to the harsh realisation that his dream of attaining National leadership over an Indian Dominion was irrevocably 'shattered'? Were that so, he would have no options other than to abandon public life entirely, or try to find—perhaps at 'the brink of a precipice'—another Nation to call his own.

NOTES

1. Lord Crewe to Lord Hardinge, 14 May 1914, Letter No. 21, p. 37, *Hardinge Papers*, Cambridge University Library.
2. Sir Frank G. Sly, Chief Commissioner, Central Provinces, 'Confidential' Report to Lord Chelmsford, 1 Jan. 1921, Nagpur, *Chelmsford Papers*, MSS Eur. E 264/26.

3. Lord Curzon speaking to the Council of India Bill, 30 June 1914, *The Parliamentary Debates*, (official Report) Fifth Series, XVI, *House of Lords*, Second Volume of Session 1914, 5 May to 16 July, p. 495, Column 1.

4. Lord Morley re. Lord Ampthill's earlier remark on the Council of India Bill, 7 July 1914, *ibid.*, p. 789, Column 1.

5. Sir George Lloyd to 'My dear Montagu', 13 Aug. 1920, Ganeshkhind, Bombay, *Montagu Papers*, MSS. Eur. D 523/25.

6. M.K. Gandhi at a reception in his honour at the Cecil Hotel, London at which M.A. Jinnah was present, *India*, London, 14 Aug. 1914, p. 71.

7. M.K. Gandhi at the Gurjar Sabha reception, Bombay, 14 Jan. 1915, *Collected Works of Mahatma Gandhi*, XIII, Publication Division, Ministry of Information Delhi, 1964, No. 8, p. 9. (Hereafter cited as *CWMG*).

8. Edwin S. Montagu, *An Indian Diary*, (ed.) Venetia Montagu, London, 1930, William Heinemann Ltd., 26 Nov. 1917, Delhi, pp. 57-58.

9. Mohandas K. Gandhi, *An Autobiography: The Story of My Experiments With Truth*, first Beacon Paperback edition, 1957, p. 436. (hereafter cited *GA*).

10. Erik H. Erikson, *Gandhi's Truth*: On the Origins of Militant Non-violence, N.Y., 1969, W.W. Norton and Company, p. 283.

11. Montagu to Chelmsford, 11 Jan. 1917, Vol. 18, No. 14, pp. 16-19, *Chelmsford Papers* MSS Eur. E 264/18.

12. M.H. Saiyid, *Mohammad Ali Jinnah*, Lahore, 1945, Shaikh Muhammad Ashraf, p. 127.

13. Jinnah's Presidential Address to the Muslim League, Lucknow, 1916, *ibid.*, Appendix III, pp. 873-877.

14. Montagu, *op. cit.*, 26 Nov. 1917, Delhi, p. 58.

15. *Ibid.*, 10 Nov. 1917, Bombay, p. 10.

16. *GA*, p. 412.

17. Gandhi's speech at the Gujarat Political Conference, Godhra, 3 Nov. 1917, *CWMG*, XIV, No. 13, p. 53.

18. *GA*, pp. 445-446.

19. *Ibid.*, p. 452.

20. *Ibid.*, pp. 452-453.

21. Lord Willingdon to Edwin Montagu, Bombay, 30 Apr. 1918, pp. 50-51 *Montagu Papers*, MSS Eur D 523/18.

22. Chelmsford to Montagu, Simla, 17 Sept. 1918, *Chelmsford Papers*, MSS Eur. E 264/4.

23. Lloyd to Montagu, 12 June 1919, *Montagu Papers*, MSS Eur. D 523/25.

24. Lloyd to Montagu, 13 Aug. 1920, Ganeshkhind, *Montagu Papers*, MSS Eur. D 523/25.

25. Jinnah to Chelmsford, 28 Mar. 1919, Bombay, reprinted in Saiyid, *op. cit.*, pp. 238-239.

26. *Ibid.*

27. Jinnah's 'exclusive interview' in the *Bombay Chronicle* of 17 Nov. 1919, *Chelmsford Papers*, MSS Eur. E 264/23.

28. *Ibid.*
29. Montagu to Chelmsford, 22 Apr. 1919, London, *Montagu Papers*, MSS Eur. D 523/3.
30. Quoted by Sir Michael O'Dwyer to Chelmsford, 21 Apr. 1919, Lahore, No. 236, *Chelmsford Papers*, MSS Eur. E 264/22.
31. Chelmsford to Montagu, 9 Apr. 1919, Dehra Dun, *Montagu Papers*, MSS Eur. D 523/8.
32. Chelmsford to Montagu, 20 Mar. 1919, Delhi, *Montagu Papers*, MSS Eur. D 523/8.
33. Judith M. Brown, *Gandhi's Rise to Power: Indian Politics, 1915-1922*, Cambridge, 1972, at the University Press.
34. Richard Gordon, 'Non-Cooperation and Council Entry, 1919 to 1920', *Modern Asian Studies*, 7, 3, 1973, pp. 443-473.
35. Saiyid, *op. cit.*, pp. 264-265.

4

Jinnah and the Pakistan Demand
R.J. Moore

In an age sceptical of the historic role of great men there is universal agreement that Mohammed Ali Jinnah was central to the Muslim League's emergence after 1937 as the voice of a Muslim nation; to its articulation in March 1940 of the Pakistan demand for separate statehood for the Muslim majority provinces of north-western and eastern India; and to its achievement in August 1947 of the separate but truncated state of Pakistan by the Partition of India. Subcontinental judgements of Jinnah are bound to be *parti pris* and to exaggerate his individual importance. While Pakistanis generally see him as the Quaid-i-Azam, Great Leader, or father of their nation, Indians often regard him as the Lucifer who tempted his people into the unforgivable sin against their nationalist faith. Among distinguished foreign scholars, unbiased by national commitment, his stature is similarly elevated. Sir Penderel Moon has written:

> There is, I believe, no historical parallel for a single individual effecting such a political revolution; and his achievement is a striking refutation of the theory that in the making of history the individual is of little or no significance. It was Mr Jinnah who created Pakistan and undoubtedly made history.[1]

Professor Lawrence Ziring believes that Jinnah's 'personality ... made Pakistan possible' and that 'it would not have emerged without him'.[2] Sir Cyril Philips has argued that without Jinnah's leadership regionalism would probably have competed seriously with Muslim nationalism as the aim of the Muslim majority provinces.[3] Professor Nicholas Mansergh looks to Jinnah for 'the classic exposition of the two-nation theory' in his March 1940 address prefiguring the Pakistan resolution and revises sharply upwards the determining influence of the concept upon the interplay of men and events that culminated in the Partition of India.[4]

Yet the relation of Jinnah to the rise of the League and its demand and movement for Pakistan is still obscure. Eminent contemporaries were puzzled by the sources of his apparent power. For example, as last Viceroy, Lord Mountbatten thought the idea of Pakistan 'sheer madness' and wrote of Jinnah in bewilderment: 'I regard Jinnah as a psychopathic case; in fact until I had met him I would not have thought it possible that a man with such a complete lack of administrative knowledge or sense of responsibility could achieve or hold down so powerful a position.'[5] Mountbatten saw Jinnah as a leader whose 'megalomania' was so 'chronic' that he pursued his own power to the material detriment of his misguided followers.[6] British statesmen and officials and Congress leaders alike attached immense significance to vanity and pride in Jinnah's quest for Pakistan and their views continue to influence the historiography of the Partition.[7]

In a perceptive analysis Professor Khalid Bin Sayeed seeks the key to the relationship between Jinnah's personality and the Pakistan movement in the 'congruence' between the ambition of Jinnah, a domineering man whom reverses in life had made desperate, and the needs and characteristics of his people, 'a community ... booking for a great saviour ... who was prepared to unite the community and bring earthly glory to Islam'.[8] Nevertheless, for Sayeed 'it continues to be an enigma how these people followed a leader who was so austere and so remote from them'.[9] The link, he speculates, was 'that this power-conscious man promised to them the political power which the Qur'an had promised to them and which their forbears had wielded in India'.

Historians have also emphasized the enigmatic nature of Jinnah's 'promise'—the vagueness of the Pakistan demand and the variety of constitutional reforms that Jinnah seemed willing to accept in satisfaction of it.'[10] Some have sought to resolve the paradox by construing the demand as a bargaining counter, whereby Jinnah sought to enhance the power of the League and himself within a united free India.[11] Others have argued that Jinnah was 'hoist with his own petard': he fell captive to his promise of separate statehood for six provinces and was left by the Partition with the truncated state that was alone consistent with the concept of a nation defined by the religious map of the subcontinent.[12]

The following analysis seeks to clarify the relation between Jinnah and the Pakistan movement during the decade preceding partition, in terms of both his charisma and his constitutional strategy, but not, it should be stressed, in terms of party organization and political mobilization, on which much more work remains to be done.[13]

I. Sources of Charisma

Jinnah was born on Christmas day 1876 in a tenement house in Karachi. He was to be the eldest of seven children of a hide merchant, whose means were modest but sufficient to despatch Jinnah at the age of sixteen direct from the Sind Madrasa to London for commercial experience. The precocious youth instead registered at Lincoln's Inn and as an exemplary pupil qualified for the Bar. During his short four-year absence his mother and his child-wife died and his father suffered financial ruin. He chose to make his way at the Bombay Bar. After three briefless and penurious years his powers of application, analysis, and advocacy brought him rapid success and wealth, the springboard to his political career. By the age of forty he had been prominent in the Indian National Congress, toured Europe with Gokhale, represented the Muslims of Bombay in the Imperial Legislative Council, and acted as principal negotiator of the Lucknow Pact for Congress-Muslim League unity. When Edwin Montagu visited India in 1917 he recorded meeting this 'young, perfectly mannered, impressive-looking ... very clever man', who, 'armed to the teeth with dialectics' tied the Viceroy up in verbal knots.[14]

By the standards of his gilded youth the next twenty years of Jinnah's life were leaden. Poised to scale political heights he fell and suffered disappointment. Gandhi's Congress-Khilafat non-cooperation movement, which was inimical to his constitutionalist style, was partly responsible for his eclipse, but perhaps as important was the shift that the dyarchical provincial councils effected in Muslim politics. Given the realities of office and patronage the Punjab Unionist Party became the powerhouse of Muslim policy.[15] Confronted with Congress initiatives to inherit the central government of India, the All-India Muslim Conference, led from the Punjab by Mian Fazl-i-Husain, espoused schemes for entrenching the Muslims in quasi-sovereign provinces, yielding to a federal centre only such powers as they chose and given effective safeguards for Muslim interests. Jinnah remained a leader of the League and a member of the Central Legislature but the action had moved elsewhere. In 1928 he was worsted by the forces of Hindu orthodoxy when he sought accommodation with Congress on an all-parties constitutional scheme. At the Round Table Conference he was suspected by the dominant Muslim delegates as an unreliable conciliator, and he seemed to speak for no one but himself. For three or four years he turned his back on India and tried to settle in London, living in Hampstead and pactising at the Privy Council Bar. When he returned to India in 1936 to set up the League's Parliamentary Board to contest the 1936 elections under the India Act of 1935's provisions for provincial autonomy, he was shunned by the Punjab Unionists. He remained hopeful of achieving an all-India Hindu-Muslim settlement under a Congress-League *rapprochement* until, after its electoral triumph, Congress made it apparent that its terms were the League's capitulation.[16]

Jinnah's personality and experience disposed him to feel bitterly the Congress denial of the Muslims' political identity. Lacking inherited status, from an early age his place in the world had rested wholly upon his own efforts. By observing a regimen of discipline and self-denial he had earned a place of dignity in Indian politics. The single-minded pursuit of professional and political success left him little opportunity to cultivate a private life that might mitigate the sense of public rejection. The exaggerated refinement of the English dress and personal style that he adopted seem more like carapaces than indulgences. The political reverses of middle-age were unrelieved by any of the usual pleasures of personal or domestic life. His marriage at the age of forty-two to the eighteen-year-old daughter of a Parsi friend had, after several unhappy years, finally collapsed in 1928. Her death soon afterwards left him bereaved and with a sense of guilt. For the rest of his life his sole companion was his loyal sister Fatima, who, from living with it daily, came to share his acute sense of persecution.[17]

Like Jinnah's personal standing the status that the Muslims had achieved by 1937 had been hard won. Late-comers to western education, official employment and party politics, they had, as collaborators of the British Raj, advanced rapidly in the twentieth century. In the United Provinces they had consolidated their tenure of land and won weightage well beyond their numbers in councils and government service.[18] Since the first elections to the Montford councils they had succeeded to decades of Congress ascendancy in Bengal and won office in Punjab. The All-India Muslim Conference had defended separate electorates in both majority provinces and applied a strategy of 'provincial balance' to secure the separation of Sind from Bombay and its elevation, together with that of the North West Frontier Province, to full provincial status. In 1936, the last year of his life, Fazl-i-Husain could reflect that the Muslim position was now 'adequately safeguarded'.[19] The sense of achieved security owed much to checks that the India Act of 1935 seemed to place on the power of the Congress, for in its contemplated all-India federation a third of the seats were reserved to the Muslims and a third to nominees of the Indian princes. The emergence of Congress dominance in 1937 changed all that.

In March 1937, when Nehru remarked that the Congress and the Raj were the only two parties in India, Jinnah replied to the rebuff by claiming the Muslim League as a third, a rightful 'equal partner' of the Congress.[20] It was the Muslims of the Congress provinces who first apprehended the dangers of Hindu ascendancy under a Congress Raj and reacted with a sense of persecution.[21] Muslim grandees in the United Provinces grew anxious when Congress denied them a share in government and threatened their culture, property and prospects of public employment.[22] In Muslim minority provinces it seemed that under responsible government the Congress could withhold their participation in office permanently. In Muslim majority provinces Congress sought power through alignments with Muslim factions. Rajendra Prasad commented:

> The attempt of our party in most [of these] provinces has constantly been to win over members of the government party and thus secure a majority for itself, so that it may form a ministry. In effect its action has been not so much to consider the criticised government measures on their merit and secure the adoption of its own programme by the government, but to try somehow or other to oust the party in power. The result ... has been to create much bitterness against the Congress...[23]

At the all-India level the Congress High Command pursued its advantage by pressing the princes to fill their federal seats by election instead of nomination, which would open the prospect of sufficient Congress victories to destroy the statutory check upon its power.[24] Jinnah became convinced that parliamentary government would mean Congress 'totalitarianism' in India.[25] The only safeguard of equal rights to India's Muslims lay in their achievement of equality of power through their solidarity within the All-India Muslim League. Under his organization the League's membership grew from a few thousand to several hundred thousand in 1937-8.

Jinnah harped on the theme of equality. At the League's annual session at Lucknow in October 1937 he insisted that 'an honourable settlement can only be achieved between equals'.[26] He demanded of Nehru that Congress must recognize the League 'on a footing of perfect equality'.[27] He internalized the Muslims' sense of 'suffering and sacrifice' from the 'fire of persecution'. He expressed himself with personal conviction: 'I have got as much right to share in the government of this country as any Hindu'; and 'I must have [an] equal real and effective share in the power'.[28] The appeal was underpinned by an assertion that Islamic society was based on the equality of man.

The essential link between Jinnah's leadership and the emergence of a Muslim national consciousness was that Jinnah personified the sense of persecution felt by Muslims—more precisely, Urdu-speaking Muslims—at the Congress denial of their achieved status. The widespread assumption that vanity, pride, ambition and megalomania were the dominant facets of his personality has masked it. In a similar way, the extension of impressions of his personality to generalizations about his political style has exaggerated the intellectual distance between the leader and his followers, obscuring the doctrinal cut and thrust from which emerged the constitutional strategy that would afford a refuge from persecution.

II. From Karachi to Lahore

Almost all who observed Jinnah described him as reserved, remote, aloof and, above all, lonely. His remoteness in later life was caused partly by his chronic bronchial infection, which had probably appeared in 1936,[30] and from July 1943 partly by the precautionary measures of up to three official bodyguards who were assigned to him after he was attacked by an assassin. But clearly he did not enjoy physical contact and kept the world at a distance. The famous monocle and frequent changes of clothing seem, like his aversion to shaking hands and travelling by train unless in a first class coupé, expressions of immaculacy. When Sir Stafford Cripps visited him in December 1939 he noted: 'Altogether he gave me the impression of an intensely lonely man in perpetual conflict with himself and with no-one in whom he could confide or who could give him reliable advice, but he put his case with great ability and clarity.'[31] In January 1942 Sir Reginald Coupland visited him at his new house on Malabar Hill and was struck by the 'great forensic ability ... admirable lucidity ... and clear conclusions' of this 'very able advocate'.[32] His notes suggest Jinnah's clinical detachment and self-sufficiency, living and working in a mansion with 'beautiful rooms, lavishly furnished, and a most attractive curving marble terrace, with lawn beneath it sloping to a belt of trees with a gap in it through which the sea'. Jinnah plied him with League literature, 'largely reprints of his own speeches'. A few weeks later Coupland

described Jinnah as 'virtually dictator' of the League,[33] a judgement
that A.V. Alexander echoed at the time of the Cabinet Mission:
'Mr Jinnah, the so-called Man of Destiny of the Muslim League
[is] a clever lawyer ... and I should think in his own way pretty
near to being a complete dictator'.[34] Mountbatten believed that 'the
only adviser that Jinnah listens to is Jinnah'.[35]

Yet in the crucial eighteen months preceding the proclamation
of the Pakistan demand at Lahore Jinnah's role in the formation
and expression of constitutional thought and strategy was certainly
not that of an isolated, lonely and self-sufficient leader.

In October 1938 Jinnah returned to a king's welcome in the city
of his birth, Karachi, for a conference of the Sind branch of the
All-India Muslim League.[36] He rode from the railway station in an
open limousine at the head of a procession three miles long. Some
20,000 delegates were assembled, among them the provincial
premiers Sir Sikandar Hayat Khan (Punjab) and Sir Fazlul Haq
(Bengal), the UP leaders Liaquat Ali Khan (Secretary of the
League), the Raja of Mahmudabad and Choudhry Khaliquzzaman,
the old Khilafat leader Shaukat Ali, and prominent Sindhis. The
main object of the Sindhis in organizing the conference was to
bring to bear upon the province's faction-ridden Muslim
establishment the unifying influence of the national body. The
benefits of the separation from Bombay of this majority province
had been squandered by the recourse of its Muslim premiers to
Hindus for their survival. In July 1937 M.H. Gazdar (a future
mayor of Karachi) had written to Jinnah in disgust at the state of
Sind politics and proposed the creation of an independent Muslim
state comprising the four north-western provinces.[37] The initiator
and reception committee chairman of the conference was Sir
Abdoola Haroon, a self-made merchant and industrialist prince of
Karachi, campaigner for the separation of Sind, member of the
Central Legislature (1926-42), founder of the Sind United Party
on the model of the Punjab Unionists, and member of the League's
Working Committee.[38] In his opening address he focused attention
upon the need for an all-India Hindu-Muslim settlement, failing
which Muslims may need 'to seek their salvation in their own way

in an independent federation of Muslim states', in the division of Hindu India and Muslim India 'under separate federations'.[39]

Haroon was moving further and faster towards a separatist objective than Jinnah, who emphasized the primary need to consolidate Muslims to resist Congress oppression. Fourteen months later Jinnah was still professing to be as much an Indian nationalist as Nehru, and in January 1940 he could still write of India as the 'common motherland' of Muslims and Hindus.[40] He was disquieted when Haroon incorporated the goal of an independent Muslim state in a resolution:

> The Sind Provincial Muslim League Conference considers it absolutely essential in the interests of an abiding peace of the vast Indian continent and in the interests of unhampered cultural development, the economic and social betterment and political self-determination of the two nations, known as Hindus and Muslims, that India may be divided into federations, namely, the federation of Muslim States and the federation of non-Muslim States. This conference therefore recommends to the All-India Muslim League to devise a scheme of constitution under which Muslim-majority-provinces Muslim Indian States and areas inhabited by a majority of Muslims may attain full independence in the form of a federation of their own...[41]

Jinnah is reported to have entered a caveat: 'The Government is still in the hands of the British. Let us not forget it. You must see ahead and work for the ideal that you think will arise 25 years hence.'[42] Next day, with his tacit consent, Haroon's draft was passed thus modified:

> This conference considers it absolutely essential, in the interests of an abiding peace of the vast Indian continent and in the interests of unhampered cultural development, the economic and social betterment and political self-determination of the two nations, known as Hindus and Muslims, to recommend to the All-India Muslim League to review and revise the entire conception of what should be the suitable constitution for India which will secure honourable and legitimate status to them.[43]

While the two nations theory now became the League's creed it was clearly not synonymous with separatism. Even the mover of Haroon's original resolution, Shaikh Abdul Majid, expected that the Hindu and Muslim federations would be linked by a common centre for foreign affairs, defence and the settlement of disputes.[44] Clearly, too, Jinnah was drawn this far by the initiative of the Sindhis and the need to accommodate policy to it in the interests of solidarity.

Jinnah was unwell during the following weeks and made no speeches until 26 December at the League's annual session at Patna, when he spoke impromptu. He then observed the awakening of a 'national consciousness among the Muslims' comparable to that of the Hindus, but warned that a 'national self and national individuality' had yet to be developed.[45] The session authorized him to explore suitable constitutional alternatives to the 1935 Act,[46] and the following March the Working Committee set up a committee to examine those that had already appeared and others that might emerge.[47] Jinnah was to head the committee and eight others, including Haroon, Liaquat, Sikandar, Nazimuddin (Bengal), and Aurangzeb Khan (NWFP) were empanelled. Next month Jinnah intimated that several schemes were before the committee, including one for dividing the country into Hindu and Muslim India. In fact the committee never met and the initiative remained in Haroon's hands.

During the interim between the Karachi and Patna conferences Haroon took a number of steps to advance the general cause of a separate federation of Muslim provinces and states. His resolve was strengthened by Congress activities in the states towards the end of the year.[48] He failed in an attempt to enlist the support of the Aga Khan.[49] However, the Council of the League now established a Foreign and Inland Deputations subcommittee, and Haroon became its chairman. It was to send deputations abroad, to explain the views of Muslim India and counter Congress allegations that the Muslims were reactionary and unpatriotic, and from the Muslim majority to the minority provinces, to consolidate links between their organizations.[50] The committee performed some of the functions appropriate to offices for foreign affairs and propaganda. Haroon also involved it in planning when he asked Dr Syed Abdul Latif to meet it in Lahore in January 1939 to discuss his ideas for the recognition of the two nations by the redistribution of India into cultural zones.[51] Though Latif's approach was to accommodate the two nations within a 'common motherland' under a single federal authority, rather than to pursue the separate federations that he himself favoured, Haroon advanced Rs 2000 for the publication and foreign distribution of Latif's scheme in expanded booklet form.[52] The circulation of Latif's views in 1938-9, in pamphlets, newspapers and the booklet, stimulated controversy over the constitutional future of Muslim India.

Much of the constitutional planning occurred in the Punjab, where there was already a significant legacy of separatist thought. As president of the League in 1930 the philosopher-poet of Lahore, Sir Muhammad Iqbal, had called for the amalgamation of the four northwestern provinces, less some non-Muslim districts, into 'a Muslim India within India'.[53] As the religious units of India had never been inclined to sacrifice their individualities in a larger whole 'the unity of an Indian nation must be sought, not in negation, but in mutual harmony and co-operation'. The 'effective principle of co-operation' in India was the recognition of 'homelands' in which the Muslim might enjoy 'full and free development on the lines of his own culture and tradition'. In 1933 the Cambridge student Rahmat Ali, the Punjabi coiner of the name 'Pakistan', proposed the separation from India of a Muslim state embracing the four provinces and Kashmir, and soon afterwards launched the Pakistan National Movement.[54] During the year preceding his death in April 1938 Iqbal's opposition to a single Indian federation had hardened and he had urged Jinnah to demand one or more separate Muslim states, though he was silent as to their relations with the rest of India.[55]

In March 1939 the fact that the League Working Committee had Latif's scheme before it provoked Ahmad Bashir, secretary of the youthful and intellectual Pakistan Majlis, Lahore, to petition Jinnah, Liaquat, Haroon, Fazlul Haq and Sikandar.[56] Latif's scheme would prejudice the political and economic integrity of Pakistan by casting the eastern tracts of the Punjab and Kashmir into a Hindu-Sikh zone:

> As the scheme is likely to influence the natural boundaries of Pakistan I feel the interest of Pakistan and the Movement started towards the creation of an independent state in the North-West of India comprising the whole of the Punjab, Kashmir, the North Western Frontier Province, Sind and Baluchistan would materially suffer if the Cultural Zones Scheme is extended towards the North West of India... The Pakistan mind is slowly believing in its physical whole and any attempt to disintegrate this natural geographical identity will certainly be detrimental to the cause of Muslim India.[57]

The references to the Pakistan Movement and the claim to the full four north-western provinces plus Kashmir reveal the influence of Rahmat Ali on the Pakistan Majlis but they also drew on Iqbal's ideas. The Majlis's full title, 'Majlis-i-Kabir Pakistan, Lahore', reflected its reverence for the saintly poet who was also the prophet of Indian unity. In the spirit of Iqbal, Ahmad Bashir wrote to Jinnah: 'Nobody questions India's unity but how that unity can be achieved is a matter that deserves special attention of all the parties concerned. It is a matter ... [that] must be given precedence to everything else.'[58] The recognition of 'separate homelands by dividing India into autonomous homogeneous states' was 'the one and the only way to India's unity'. Ahmad Bashir was to supply Jinnah with ringing passages for his inspiring Lahore presidential address.[59]

In summer 1939 the alternatives open to the League were clarified by Sikandar's formulation of a scheme for a loose all-India federation of zones including provinces and states,[60] and its rejection first by Ahmad Bashir[61] and then by scholars at Aligarh. The latter favoured the division of British India into 'three wholly independent and sovereign states'.[62] Two Aligarh authors, Professor Syed Zafarul Hasan and Dr M.A.H. Qadri, insisted that the Muslims of India, 'a nation by themselves', must not be 'enslaved into a single all-India federation with an overwhelming Hindu majority in the Centre'. The three sovereign states of British India would be North-West India or Pakistan, Bengal, and Hindustan.

The principalities within these states or exclusively on the frontier of one of them would be attached automatically, while those adjoining more than one state might choose their attachment. But Hyderabad must recover Berar and the Karnatic and become a fourth sovereign state, 'the southern wing of Muslim India'. Pakistan would include the four north-western provinces, Kashmir and other adjacent states. Bengal would embrace the existing province less the districts of Howrah, Midnapur and Darjeeling, but plus the districts of Purnea (in Bihar) and Sylhet (in Assam). Both Pakistan and Bengal would be Muslim states. Hindustan would comprise the rest of India but within it two new autonomous provinces—Delhi and Malabar—should be formed with strong Muslim minorities. The three states would have separate treaties of alliance with Britain and should join together in a defensive and offensive alliance. The Hasan-Qadri scheme was commended warmly by eight Aligarh scholars who, at the same time, deplored Latif's proposals.[63] The scholars claimed to have discussed 'the Aligarh scheme' with its authors in principle and detail and were convinced that it went as far as possible to meet the just claims of the 'two nations'.

By September 1939, when Britain shelved the paper federation of the 1935 Act, Muslim constitutional thought was certainly turning against the federal principle, even as expressed in the zonal schemes of Latif and Sikandar. A year after the adoption at Karachi of the two nations theory its practical application was a live issue. On 18 October, when Lord Linlithgow spoke of India's destiny in terms of unity,[64] Ahmad Bashir protested to Jinnah at his blunt rejection of 'the national demand of the Muslims regarding the recognition of their separate national status'.[65] Next month the Aligarh group was provoked when Gandhi attacked the theory of separate Muslim nationhood.[66] On 15 November Professor Hasan, together with Dr Zaki Uddin and Dr Burhan Ahmad (two of the eight who commended the Aligarh scheme), and Ubaid Ullah Durrani, petitioned Jinnah at length upon the matter. They concluded: 'Neither the fear of British bayonets nor the prospects of a bloody civil war can discourage [the Muslims] in their will to achieve free Muslim states in those parts of India where they are in majority.'[67] Soon afterwards the several Muslim authors of constitutional plans met for ten days 'to evolve a consolidated scheme', which they sent to Jinnah confidentially.[68] This 'fresh plan on the basis that Moslems are a separate Nation' so constituted Muslim zones in the north and the east as to include seventy-two per cent of the total Muslim population of India. A Delhi province was added to the northern zone and all of Assam to the eastern. A third of the land mass of India was claimed.

On 1 February 1940 Haroon presided at New Delhi over a joint meeting of his Foreign Committee and the authors of schemes. It resolved to recommend that the Working Committee 'state its mind in unequivocal language with regard to the future of the Indian Moslem Nation'.[69] India's Muslims were a separate nation entitled to self-determination. In order to make that right effective 'the Moslems shall have separate National Home in the shape of an autonomous state'. The meeting's resolutions were sent to Liaquat (as League Secretary) and to Jinnah on 2 February. Two days later the Working Committee adopted the nub of them[70] which was, of course, expressed in the Lahore resolution's call for independent Muslim states the north-western and eastern zones of India.[71]

The Lahore expression of the two nations theory as a demand for separate Muslim statehood was thus the culmination of eighteen months of controversy. The variety of its analogues goes far to explain the vagueness of the resolution over the delineation of the contiguous Muslim regions of north-western and eastern India and the contemplated relations between them. The notoriously obscure provision for 'territorial readjustments' was clearly a hold-all for additions to, as well as reductions of, existing provinces.[72] Doubts about the desirable relations between the regions are revealed by the authorization of the Working Committee to frame a scheme providing 'for the assumption finally, by the respective regions, of all powers' such as 'defence, external affairs, communications, customs and such other matters as may be necessary'. Again, 'finally' suggests an antithesis to an interim period of co-ordination by a common authority, such, perhaps, as the resolution's seconder, Khaliquzzaman, favoured.[73] However, it is clear that by its separatist emphasis the resolution marked the firm rejection of Sikandar's view that Muslim India's national destiny might be achieved within an all-India federation. He indeed acknowledged that his own preferred resolution was lost.[74] One possibility left open was that of an independent Bengal nation, the destiny most favoured by the resolution's proposer, Fazlul Haq.[75]

No more than the resolution itself was Jinnah's Lahore address the achievement of the Quaid unaided. The most remembered passages in his speech were drawn essentially unchanged from the representations of Ahmad Bashir and the Aligarh group. After roundly condemning the 1935 Act as unsuitable to India he followed Hasan and Qadri in quoting for criticism a London *Times* leader of 1 April 1937 that had consigned the difference between Hindus and Muslims to the realm of transient 'superstition', no real impediment to the emergence of a single nation. He then took his refutation of British views from Ahmad Bashir's condemnation of Linlithgow's statement of 18 October 1939:

Ahmad Bashir

His Excellency the Viceroy thinks that this unity can be achieved with the working of the constitution as envisaged in Government of India Act, 1935. He hopes that the passage of time will harmonise the inconsistent elements in India. May be he holds this view with sincerity, but it is in flagrant disregard to the past history of the sub-continent as well as to the Islamic conception of society. The nationalities which, notwithstanding thousand years of close contact, are as divergent as ever, can never be expected to transform into one nationality merely by being subject to the same constitution. What the *Unitary* Government in India has failed to bring about can not be achieved by the imposition of the *Federal* Government.

It is, however, satisfying to note that His Excellency the Viceroy and the Secretary of State along with the House of Lords are fully alive to the fundamental differences between the peoples of the Indian continent. Yet unfortunately, they are unwilling to recognise their separate national status. It is more than truism to say that the Hindus and Muslims represent two distinct nationalities. Therefore, any attempt to dissolve their present differences which disregards this vital fact is doomed to precipitate. Hindu-Muslim problem is not an intercommunal issue and will never be solved on intercommunal lines. It is manifestly an international problem and therefore it must be treated as such. It will submit itself to a permanent solution on that basis alone. Any constitution be it in the form of Dominion Status or even 'Complete

Independence', which disregards this basic truth, while destructive for the Muslims cannot but be harmful to the British and Hindus.

If the British Government is really serious and sincere in bringing about peace in the sub-continent, it should not only appreciate the difference but also allow the two nationalities separate homelands by dividing India into autonomous homogeneous states. These states shall not be antagonistic to each other, they on the other hand, will be friendly and sympathetic to one another; and by an international pact of mutual goodwill and assistance they can be just as united and harmonious as today are France and Great Britain. This is the one and the only way to India's Unity.

We are confident that it shall ensure eternal harmony, calm and friendliness between the Hindus and Muslims and materially accelerate the progress of the sub-continent.

If this method for the salavation of India's problems is not adopted the fate of the Muslims as a nation is sealed in India and no revolution of stars and no rotation of the earth would resuscitate them.

Jinnah

So according to the London Times the only difficulties are superstitions. These fundamental and deep-rooted differences, spiritual, economic, cultural, social and political have been euphemised as mere 'superstitions'. But surely, it is flagrant disregard of the past history of the subcontinent of India as well as the fundamental Islamic conception of society *vis-à-vis* that of Hinduism to characterise them as mere 'superstitions'. Notwithstanding thousand years of close contact, nationalities which are as divergent today as ever, cannot at any time be expected to transform themselves into one nation merely by means of subjecting them to a democratic constitution and holding them forcibly together by unnatural and artificial methods of British Parliamentary Statutes. What the unitary government of India for 150 years had failed to achieve, cannot be realised by the imposition of a central federal government. It is inconceivable that the fiat or the writ of a government so constituted can ever command a willing and loyal obedience throughout the subcontinent by various nationalities except by means of armed force behind it.

The problem in India is not of an intercommunal but manifestly of an international character and it must be treated as such. So long as this basic and fundamental truth is not realised, any constitution that may be built will result in disaster and will prove destructive and harmful not only to the Mussalmans, but also to the British and Hindus. If the British Government are really in earnest and sincere to secure peace and happiness of the people of this subcontinent, the only course open to us all is to allow the major nations separate homelands by dividing India into 'autonomous national states'. There is no reason why these States should be antagonistic to each other. On the other hand the rivalry and the natural desire and efforts on the part of the one to dominate the social order and establish political supremacy over the other in the government of the country, will disappear. It will lead more towards natural good-will by international pacts between them, and they can live in complete harmony with their neighbours. This will lead further to a friendly settlement all the more easily with regard to minorities by reciprocal arrangements and adjustments between the Muslim India and the Hindu India, which will far more adequately and effectively safeguard the rights and interests of Muslims and various other minorities.

The Ahmad Bashir text was thus the source of Jinnah's 'quiet assertion' of the international status of the Indian problem that Mansergh has held to be 'the essence of his case'.[76] Jinnah notably dropped the emphasis (following Iqbal) upon present division as 'the only way to India's Unity' in future.[77] He continued by drawing upon the Aligarh petition of 15 November 1939 to fill out the rhetoric of his 'classic exposition of the two-nation theory'. Again, where the scholars' target was specifically Gandhi, Jinnah's is more generally the Hindus:

Aligarh scholars
It is extremely difficult to explain Mr Gandhi failing to appreciate and understand the real nature of Islam and Hinduism. Islam as well as Hinduism are not only religions in stricter sense of the word, but are in reality different and distinct social orders governing practically every individual and social aspect of their adherents. It should be clear beyond doubt that Hindus and Muslims cannot evolve a common nationality. A few following arguments must convince Mr Gandhi on this issue.

1. That the Hindus and Muslims belong to two different cultures. They have totally different religious philosophies, social customs, laws and literature. They neither inter-marry nor inter-dine together and, indeed, belong to two different civilizations which are in many aspects based on conflicting ideas and conceptions...

2. That the Hindus and Muslims drive [*sic*] their inspiration from different sources of history. They have different epics, different heroes and different episodes. Very often a hero of one is a foe of the other and likewise, their victories and defeats overlap...

The above facts must convince every body that all those ties which hold people together as one social unit (Nation) are entirely wanting in the case of Hindus and Muslims of India. Nor there is any possibility of their ever being created here.

Mr Gandhi and other Congress leaders stress the significance of a common country and cite the examples of Egypt, Turkey and Persia. They only state a half truth in this argument. Egypt, Turkey and Persia are wholly Muslim countries and the Muslims there are naturally free to determine their own future.

A discontent is bound to occur wherever two different people are yoked under a single state one as minority and the other as majority. A number of instances like those of Great Britain and Ireland, Czechoslovakia and Poland an exemplify the above. Further it is also too well known that many Geographical tracts which otherwise should have been called as one country, much smaller than the Indian sub-continent have been divided into as many states as are the nations inhabiting them. The Balkan Peninsula comprises of as many as eight sovereign states. The Iberian Peninsula is also likewise divided between the Portuguese and the Spaniards.

Mr Gandhi stresses the historical unity of India even during the days of Muslim kings. We cannot accept his contention. No student of history can deny the fact that all along the last 12 hundred years India has always been divided into a Hindu India and a Muslim India. The extent of one or the other might have been varying from time to time, but the fact remains untarnished that Hindu and Muslim Indias have always been co-existing. The present unity of India dates back only to the British conquest....

We want to assure Mr Gandhi that the ideal of having free sovereign Muslim states in India which now inspires a very large number of Muslims is not actuated by a spirit of hatred or revenge. It is initiated by an earnest desire of solving Hindu Muslim problem on an equitable basis and epitomises the natural desire of Muslims of India to determine their future independently in the light of their own cultures and history.

Jianah

It is extremely difficult to appreciate why our Hindu friends fail to understand the real nature of Islam and Hinduism. They are not religions in the strict sense of the word, but are, in fact, different and distinct social orders and it is a dream that the Hindus and Muslims can ever evolve a common nationality, and this misconception of one Indian nation has gone far beyond the limits and is the cause of most of our troubles and will lead India to destruction if we fail to revise our notions in time. The Hindus and Muslims belong to two different religious philosophies, social customs, and literature. They neither intermarry, nor interdine together and indeed they belong to two different civilisations which are based mainly on conflicting ideas and conceptions. Their aspects on life and of life are different. It is quite clear that Hindus and Mussalmans drive [sic] their inspiration from different sources of history. They have different epics, their heroes are different, and they have different episodes. Very often the hero of one is a foe of the other and likewise their victories and defeats overlap. To yoke together two such nations under a single state, one as a numerical minority and the other as a majority, must lead to growing discontent and final destruction of any fabric that may be so built up for the government of such a state.

History has presented to us many examples such as the Union of Great Britain and Ireland, of Czechoslovakia and Poland. History has also shown to us many geographical tracts, much smaller than the subcontinent of India, which otherwise might have been called one country but which have been divided into as many states as there are nations inhabiting them. Balkan Peninsula comprises as many as 7 or 8 sovereign states. Likewise, the Portuguese and the Spanish stand divided in the Iberian Peninsula. Whereas under the plea of unity of India and one nation, which does not exist, it is sought to pursue here the line of one Central Government when, we know that the history of the last 12 hundred years, has failed to achieve unity and has witnessed during the ages, India always divided into Hindu India and Muslim India. The present artificial unity of India dates back only to the British conquest and is maintained by the British bayonet, but the termination of the British regime, which is implicit in the recent declaration of His Majesty's Government, will be the herald of the entire break-up with worse disaster than has ever taken place during the last one thousand years under the Muslims.

Jinnah was carried to Karachi on the shoulders of his fellow Sindhis and soared to Lahore on the wings of young intellectuals of the city and scholars of Aligarh. The Great Leader who personified Muslim apprehensions synthesized plans to assuage them in acceptable formulations of Muslim nationalism (the two nations theory) and separatism (the Pakistan demand).

III. *The Meaning of 'Two Nations'*

In October 1939, when Lord Linlithgow called Jinnah into discussions with the Congress leaders about participation in government during the war, he was certainly recognizing him as the Muslim leader *par excellence*.[78] But in large measure Jinnah had earned the status by the solidarity that the League had then achieved. In May 1939 Sikandar, the senior Muslim premier, had observed publicly that Jinnah had answered for Muslims the question: 'Are we content to lose our identity and to be relegated to the position of political pariahs?'[79] Jinnah's mobilization of the

League in reaction to Congress 'totalitarianism' under the 1935 Act had made it the voice of the putative nation. In December 1939 Liaquat estimated that it had over three million two anna members. In the early war-time negotiations Jinnah could, pursuant to the two nations theory, make acceptance of the League's status as sole Muslim spokesman the precondition of co-operation with government or Congress, thereby outflanking dissidents (be they even premiers) by appeals to the national will. It was another corollary of his theory that as one of the two nations Muslim India must be treated as the co-equal of Hindu or Congress India. In consequence, the League called for the right to consultation prior to any British statement about India's constitutional future and to veto any scheme. By November, Rajendra Prasad (now Congress President) shrewdly perceived that Jinnah's insistence upon the League's equality with Congress would mean not only 'equality in the matter of negotiations' but also 'division of power in equal shares between the Congress and the League or between Hindus and Muslims, irrespective of population or any other consideration'.[80]

The meaning of the two nations theory and its implications for Jinnah's leadership became manifest in League Working Committee resolutions in June 1940. In any war-time reconstruction of the central or provincial governments the League must receive half of the seats (more if the Congress was non-cooperating), Jinnah alone might negotiate with Viceroy or Congress, and without his consent no League member might serve on war committees.[81] The resolutions were a rebuff for Sikandar, who, appalled at the grave implications for India of the allies' defeats in Europe, was negotiating with Congress leaders for a constitutional settlement.[82] In August a British statement, effectively according the Muslims a veto on any constitutional scheme, seemed to remove the danger of a Hindu raj.[83] Here was a major victory for the two nations theory. Another was soon to follow.

Leading Muslim politicians, including the premiers, were now prepared to join war committees on a basis short of parity. By so doing they would, in effect, be compromising the cause of Muslim equality embodied in the two nations theory. In summer 1941

Jinnah brought the theory to bear in order to force their resignations from the Viceroy's Defence Council. That this was no mere exercise of personal power but rather the execution of essential League policy is revised by Liaquat's advice to Jinnah a month before the Working Committee met to consider the matter. Liaquat advised that Jinnah's condemnation of the collaborators had 'given expression to the feelings of a vast majority of Musalmans on the subject'.[84] The question now was 'whether the disciplinary action ... should be taken by you or by the Working Committee and the Council' (an elected body of 465 members). Liaquat strongly advised the latter course:

> Let us put up an imposing show and I think the people will appreciate [it] if the Council is given an opportunity of expressing its views on the conduct of those who have let down the League... Let it not be said that the decision is of only one individual or a few persons. Let the whole Council which is the most representative body of the League give its verdict and I have no doubt as to what the verdict will be....

On 24 August the Working Committee demanded the collaborators' resignations from the Defence Council and expelled from the League those who resisted the verdict. The Council did not meet to ratify the action for two months but its attitude was not in doubt. Jinnah was, of course, aware of allegations that he was a dictator.[85] The two nations theory enabled him plausibly to brand as 'traitors' Muslims who collaborated with the Raj on a basis short of parity. As national leader he saw it as his duty to identify their 'mistakes', leaving the Working Committee and the Council to determine their punishment.[86]

By applying the theory vigorously Jinnah engineered the nationalization of Muslim politics throughout the war. The theory's meaning was revealed most dramatically at Simla in June 1945, when Jinnah demanded not only Hindu-Muslim parity in the Viceroy's executive but also that all the Muslim members must be League nominees. The demand destroyed Lord Wavell's attempt to reconstruct his government on the basis of party representation.

IV. *Defining 'Pakistan'*

In February 1941 Jinnah explained the meaning of 'Pakistan', for the term had not been used at Lahore:

> Some confusion prevails in the minds of some individuals in regard to the use of the word 'Pakistan'. This word has become synonymous with the Lahore resolution owing to the fact that it is a convenient and compendious method of describing [it] ... For this reason the British and Indian newspapers generally have adopted the word 'Pakistan' to describe the Moslem demand as embodied in the Lahore resolution. I really see no objection to it...[87]

But the resolution was obscure on the demarcation of the Pakistan regions, their relation to each other, and any interim constitutional rearrangement prior to their 'finally' assuming such powers as defence, foreign affairs, communications and customs. While Jinnah demanded parity as the basis of participation in government, the vagueness of 'Pakistan' was such as to make impracticable its acceptance by the Raj a precondition of co-operation. He did, however, insist that no constitutional scheme that was inconsistent with its eventual achievement must be imposed. The 'Pakistan' demand meant that Muslim India's right to national self-determination must not be transgressed, not that separate statehood must be embodied in a constitutional settlement. Jinnah drew the distinction explicitly in his speeches.[88] The diversity of the schemes embodying 'Pakistan' that were extant in March 1940 helps to explain the obscurity of the Lahore resolution. Any precise scheme must surely divide the League. However, the resolution did provide for the Working Committee to prepare a particular scheme. Haroon's Foreign Committee seems to have continued to discharge the primary planning function.

In February 1941 a scheme recommended by the Haroon committee was leaked to the press.[89] Consistently with the direction pursued by the Aligarh scholars and the assemblage of authors during winter 1939-40, it delineated sovereign Muslim states: the four north-western provinces plus a Delhi province; and Bengal (save Bankura and Midnapur districts) plus Assam. The principalities adjoining them might federate with them, and Hyderabad would become a separate sovereign state. For a transitional period the four powers listed at Lahore for assumption finally by the regions would be exercised by a co-ordinating central agency. Jinnah denied that the Working Committee had adopted the scheme and on 22 February it merely reaffirmed the Lahore resolution. The main effect of the leakage was to draw from Sikandar a long, reasoned denunciation of 'Pakistan', if it meant separatism.[90]

In his presidential address to the League's session at Madras in April 1941 Jinnah emphasized the goal of 'completely Independent States in the North-Western and Eastern Zones of India, with full control of Defence, Foreign Affairs, Communications, Customs, Currency, Exchange etc.'[91] The League would 'never agree' to an all-India constitution 'with one Government at the Centre'. As if to suggest that the two nations theory did not restrict future development to the emergence of only two states he explained that in Hindu India there was a Dravidian nation, Dravidistan, to which the Muslims would stretch their 'hands of friendship'. In amplification of this trend in his thinking he told the Governor of Madras that he envisaged four regions—Dravidistan, Hindustan, Bengalistan, and the north-west Muslim provinces.[92] They would be separate self-governing dominions, each with its own governor-general controlling its foreign affairs and defence and responsible to the British parliament through the secretary of state. Here was a scheme for subordinate dominions, with the princely states joining them and remaining apart under a Crown Representative. It bore some resemblance to Haroon's leaked scheme.

In February 1942 Khaliquzzaman explained a similar proposal to Coupland:

The Moslem demand is that Britain, after the war, should by Act of Parliament, establish the zonal system, before considering further Swaraj. British control would be still required at the Centre—apparently for an indefinite period—since Defence and Foreign Policy (which is practically all the Centre would deal with) should still be in

British hands. The zones would have fiscal autonomy. If they couldn't agree on tariff policy, the British at the Centre would settle it. Pakistan, moreover, would require British aid and capital for its development before it would be able to stand alone.[93]

Khaliquzzaman seemed to be saying that in the event of a complete British withdrawal the Muslims would accept nothing short of sovereign Pakistan; but that they would welcome a protracted British presence—in effect, Indian unity under the Crown, with the sub-national zones standing as recognition of Muslim nationhood. Unlike Jinnah he was opposed to the cession of the non-Muslim districts of Punjab (Ambala division) and Bengal (Burdwan division).[94]

On the eve of Cripps's arrival in India Coupland analysed Jinnah's position on the Pakistan demand:

(i)   While claiming Dominion status for Pakistan, Jinnah has more than once intimated that it need not be full Dominion status and that he would like Foreign Affairs and Defence to remain, at least for the time being, in British hands; and

(ii) he has never asked that H.M.G. should accept Pakistan, but only that it should not be ruled out of discussion nor the chances of its adoption prejudiced by the form of an interim constitutional system. Nevertheless, *Pakistanism might triumph as a counsel of despair*.[95]

The Cripps declaration proposed Dominion status for a Union of India, but though it did not accept Pakistan it did accord provinces the right to secede from the Union and become separate dominions.[96] Jinnah and the League saw it as recognizing the principle of Pakistan.[97] From the notes of Coupland, Cripps and the Intelligence Department there can be no doubt that Jinnah and the League were disposed to accept the offer.[98]

On 28 March 1942 Jinnah 'stated [to Cripps] the League's acceptance of the Declaration'. On 7 April he intimated that 'he must hold back the League's acceptance till after the Congress has accepted'.[99] Coupland foresaw that if Congress rejected the offer the League would follow suit, 'so wording their rejection as to obtain some British and world support without losing face as Indian patriots'. On 9 April, when Congress seemed poised to accept, Jinnah was reported as saying 'that Pakistan could be shelved', given a satisfactory position in the Viceroy's executive and a suitable procedure for the secession of provinces.'[100] When Congress rejected the declaration the League did likewise, deprecating H.M.G.'s objective of Union, the provision for a single constituent assembly in the first instance, and the eligibility of non-Muslims to participate in the Muslim provinces' decisions on secession.[101]

In February 1944 Jinnah stated that Britain 'should now frame a new constitution dividing India into two sovereign nations', Pakistan and Hindustan, with 'a transitional period for settlement and adjustment' during which British authority over defence and foreign affairs would remain.[102] The length of the period would depend upon the speed with which the two peoples and Britain adjusted to the new constitution. Though the statement clearly contemplated continued subordination to Britain it is too vague to be read as a shift from the notion of zonal dominions.[103] In September 1944 the Gandhi-Jinnah talks concentrated attention on the precise meaning of the Pakistan demand. The Bengal Provincial League now wanted 'a sovereign state in N.E. India that will be independent of the rest of India', though it was divided over the cession of the Burdwan districts, with some members arguing that their retention would win Hindu approval.[104] The talks themselves did little to clarify Jinnah's conception of Pakistan but he reiterated that for the regions in which the Muslims predominated it was they alone who must determine their future. Jinnah also spoke now of Pakistan as a single state.[105]

Throughout the war Jinnah contemplated the post-war emergence of one or two Pakistan 'dominions', coexisting with one or two Hindustan 'dominions' and the princely states, and with Britain retaining power over defence and foreign affairs. The separateness and equality of the Pakistan and Hindustan 'dominions' would be a recognition of the validity of the two nations theory and of their right to eventual sovereign independence. The conception resembled that which some British Conservatives formed at the time of the Cripps Mission and espoused until the eve of the transfer of power.[106]

V. *Definition by Circumstance*

With Labour's assumption of office in July 1945 it was soon apparent that there was not to be a gradual demission of power by stages but an early and complete withdrawal.[107] Jinnah now became adamant that there must be a single state of Pakistan and the League fought the elections of 1945-6 on that platform.[108] The announcement in February 1946 of the imminent despatch of a Cabinet Mission to settle the basis for independence and Jinnah's first meeting with the Mission on 4 April confirmed that Labour was in a hurry. Fortified by the League's electoral triumph, on 7 April Jinnah led a convention of 470 League members of the central and provincial legislatures to an unequivocal resolution in favour of 'a sovereign independent state comprising Bengal and Assam in the North-East zone and the Punjab, North-West Frontier Province, Sind and Baluchistan in the North West zone'.[109] Acceptance of this precise demand for Pakistan and its implementation without delay; by the creation of a Pakistan Constituent Assembly, was made the *sine qua non* for the League's participation in an Interim Government. The opening of the imperial endgame had precipitated an immediate and full-blooded definition of the Pakistan demand.

By 10 April Cripps had prepared a draft proposal for discussion with the Indian leaders and a few days later the Mission confronted Jinnah with two alternative approaches that it advocated: either a truncated Pakistan, independent and fully sovereign but limited to the Muslim majority areas, and thus short of far more of the territories of Punjab, Bengal and Assam than the League had contemplated; or the grouping together of the whole of the six claimed provinces, beside a Hindustan group, within a Union exercising power over defence, foreign affairs and communications.[110] When Jinnah refused to choose either alternative Cripps prepared a draft that rejected a fully independent Pakistan. But it proposed a powerful subnational Pakistan, with its own flag, forces to maintain internal order, and enjoying parity with Hindustan in an all-India government. The League would draft its constitution and join with Congress on the basis of parity to draft the Union constitution.[111] The Mission was willing to concede its right to secede from the Union after fifteen years.[112] This remarkable scheme was the furthest that H.M.G. ever went towards accepting the full Pakistan demand.

It is scarcely surprising that Jinnah and the League were drawn into negotiations on the basis of this scheme, though some Leaguers speculated that Jinnah's departure from the Legislators' full-blooded resolution evidenced vacillation among 'weak-kneed' members of the Working Committee.[113] During the subsequent month of negotiations the Mission reduced the concessions to the demand in order to woo Congress, so that when its scheme was published on 16 May it was far less attractive to the League.[114] It split the six 'Pakistan' provinces into two groups, the formation of which was to depend upon the voluntary accession of each province to its assigned group. It abandoned parity in the making of the Union constitution, enlarged the Union's power to include finance, and failed to provide for the secession of groups or provinces from the Union. Though some Leaguers feared that the Union's powers would enable Congress to abort the emergence of Pakistan,[115] the counsels that prevailed were that the Cabinet Mission's scheme met 'the substance of the demand for Pakistan'[116] First, it provided that the provinces must enter constitution-making 'sections' that were conterminous with the groups. Secondly, the section constitution-making procedure was to precede Union constitution-making. Thirdly, the Working Committee assumed, on the basis of discussions that Jinnah had had with the Viceroy, that the League would enjoy parity with Congress in an Interim Government, which seemed a tacit admission of Pakistan's right to separate nationhood.

Jinnah received written letters of advice from Aurangzeb Khan and Jamil-ud-din Ahmad that emphasized the advantages of accepting the Mission's scheme.[117] Ahmad, then Convenor of the

League's Committee of Writers, expressed the 'prudent' strategy vigorously. The League should

> work the Plan up to the Group stage and then create a situation to force the hands of the Hindus and the British to concede Pakistan of our conception. ... [We should] make known in most emphatic terms our objections to the Plan specially with regard to the Centre and declare that we will ... not be bound to submit to a Union Centre which does not accord us a position of equality. We [should] give a chance to the Hindu majority to accommodate us at the Centre. ... After we have made the constitutions of Groups B and C according to our wishes our position will be stronger than what it is now if we use our opportunities properly. We will have some foothold. When we reassemble in the Union Constituent Assembly we can create deadlocks on really important issues.... If the worst comes to the worst and the Hindu majority shows no willingness to compromise we can withdraw from the Assembly in a body, and refuse to honour its decisions. Ours will be a solid bloc as there won't be more than two or three non-League Muslims in the Assembly... We will be on strong ground morally and politically because firstly we will have previously declared that we can never acquiesce in any Centre which reduces us to a subordinate position and secondly we will be in power in the Groups, and will be better able to resist the imposition of an unwanted Centre.

In the spirit of this advice the League resolved that:

> ... inasmuch as the basis and the foundation of Pakistan are inherent in the Mission's plan by virtue of the compulsory grouping of the six Muslim Provinces in Sections B and C, [it] is willing to co-operate with the constitution making machinery proposed in the scheme outlined by the Mission, in the hope that it would ultimately result in the establishment of complete sovereign Pakistan....[118]

Jinnah was authorized to negotiate for the entry of the League to the Interim Government. He wrote to Wavell to emphasize that his assurance of parity therein had been 'the turning point' in the League Council's acceptance.[119]

The League's strategy was destroyed by the Congress's refusal to contemplate parity in the Interim Government or the compulsory grouping of provinces for constitution-making, together with H.M.G.'s conviction that Congress goodwill was vital for a peaceful transfer of power.[120] In August 1946 Jinnah was driven to a course of 'direct action' by his mistrust of the Congress and H.M.G.'s infirmity.[121] Certainly, by December, when he and Nehru were called to London in a desperate attempt to secure agreement on sectional procedure, Jinnah had abandoned his mid-year hopes of realizing Pakistan through the Mission's scheme. He now reverted to the notion of a Pakistan dominion and rehearsed it not only with Attlee and the Cabinet Mission ministers[122] but also with British Opposition leaders.[123] Churchill, for whom a secret telegraphic address was established, assured him that the Pakistan areas could not be turned out of the Commonwealth as part of an Indian republic.[124] Indeed, in parliamentary debate Churchill affirmed that Muslim India and the princes should be accorded Commonwealth membership.[125] That winter Jinnah sought assurances that other Conservatives would support Pakistan's dominionhood. His inquiries converged with intrigues for separate princely dominions, to which he gave his blessing.[126]

Jinnah welcomed the prospects of a transfer of power on a provincial basis that Attlee's time-limit statement of 20 February 1947 foreshadowed.[127] In his first discussions with Mountbatten he sought a Pakistan dominion comprising the full six provinces,[128] but he did not oppose the option of separate sovereign provinces that the 'Dickie-bird' or Ismay plan ('Plan Balkan') offered. His objection to Plan Balkan was that it envisaged the severance from Punjab and Bengal of their non-Muslim areas. When he first saw the Plan he argued 'that power should be transferred to Provinces as they exist today. They can then group together or remain separate as they wish.[129] When Mountbatten asked his views on H.S. Suhrawardy's proposal for 'keeping Bengal united at the price of its remaining outside Pakistan' he replied: 'I should be delighted. What is the use of Bengal without Calcutta, they had much better remain united and independent; I am sure that they would be on friendly terms with us.'[130]

Whereas in 1946 Jinnah had been prepared to find the Pakistan demand realized, at least temporarily, by the grouping of the six provinces within the Union of India, in 1947 he was willing to see it satisfied by the separate dominionhood of provinces. Now again he was frustrated by Congress, which was no less opposed to the instant loss to India of non-Muslim areas of provinces than it had been to their distant loss by secession from the Union. The outcome of negotiations in 1947, a dual transfer of power to a single truncated Pakistan dominion and a single Indian dominion (to one of which the states were obliged to accede), flowed from Congress policy and H.M.G.'s acquiescence in it.[131] Given the reversals that he suffered in the three-sided discussions from April 1946 to May 1947 it is scarcely surprising that Jinnah eschewed the prolongation of triangularity implied in proposals for Mountbatten to become Governor-General of both dominions and the retention of a Joint Defence Council.[132] However, at the end of the Raj he still acknowledged Pakistan's need for British agency. The retention by Pakistan of British governors, chiefs of staff and civil and military officers was consistent with his expectation that the transfer of power would be a phased process.[133]

VI. *Man and Movement*

At the age of sixty Jinnah made the cause of Muslim India his life. An extraordinary match of man and movement followed. Ambition, pride and vanity were less important to it than his refined sense of Muslim injury under Congress rule and his capacity to express the hurt and specify the cure. Like Gandhi he evoked national consciousness in opposition to felt wrongs.[134] While Gandhi had experienced India's emasculation by British imperialism Jinnah felt the impotence of Muslim India under Congress totalitarianism. Jinnah articulated not the Qur'an's promise of political power nor memories of the Mughals but the Muslim's sense of persecution at the sudden threat to all that he had achieved in the twentieth century. When the Congress governments resigned in November 1959 he rallied Muslims to celebrate their 'deliverance from tyranny, oppression and injustice'.[135] Jinnah's constitutional remedies were not of his own making. The Pakistan demand was no pet scheme of which he dreamed alone but an ideal to which he was converted by others, colleagues of long-standing like Haroon, thinkers in the line of Iqbal, scholars of the Aligarh school. His very formulation of the two nations theory drew upon their thoughts and words. His amplification of the theory into a demand for parity was a brilliant tactical manoeuvre, but its effectiveness rested on the willing support of the League, most notably when Linlithgow set up his Defence Council and Wavell attempted to reconstruct his executive. The tactic consolidated the League as the microcosm of the Muslim nation and Jinnah as its leader.

It is a paradox that the demand for separate Muslim statehood based on the existing Muslim provinces with territorial adjustments should finally have found recognition in a Pakistan truncated to a degree never envisaged by Jinnah and the League. It is inconceivable that they did not realize that the truncation was a logical corollary of the distribution of the peoples of the two nations. The arguments that they adduced to resist it could scarcely be accepted with justice by a departing Raj, whether they emphasized the need for hostages or for matching minority populations for exchange in case of need, or for non-Muslim territories to make Pakistan viable economically. The incorporation of the full six provinces in Muslim zones could only have been secured by a British award, and it seems most likely that Jinnah envisaged such an award as a line of advance consistent with Britain's continuing presence in her own interests. In other words, he probably assumed a British withdrawal by stages, at the first of which the Pakistan zones would receive subordinate dominionhood, secured like the princely states by H.M.G.'s continuing control over defence and foreign affairs (as the 1935 Act had stipulated). His reference in October 1938 to a further twenty-five years of imperial rule, the Lahore resolution's emphasis upon all powers 'finally' passing to independent states, his war-time comments, his play for Pakistan dominionhood from December 1946, his reliance on British agency after August 1947, all support such a thesis. His acceptance of the Cabinet Mission's scheme

might be seen similarly as evidence of a readiness to postpone full
sovereign statehood, provided that the conditions of its eventual
emergence were safeguarded, that is Muslim zones and parity in
government. He was willing to associate the Muslim nation with
central government on the basis of parity but he doubted that such
a government could endure. He told Coupland as much:

> Assume a 50:50 basis... The central questions are just those on which
> Moslems and Hindus must disagree: e.g. (a) Defence: Hindu Ministers
> will at once want to Indianize in communal proportions (b) Tariff:
> Hindu ministers will want high protection for industries, which are
> mainly in Hindu hands, to the deteriment of the Moslems who are
> more confined to poor agriculturalists than the Hindus.[136]

Such caveats were urged upon Jinnah in May 1946, when he
judged the disadvantages of a temporary union to be worth the
prize of a safe passage through grouping to an eventual six-province
fully sovereign Pakistan.[137]

Jinnah's planning was undermined by the Labour Government's
beliefs that Britain's post-war interests would be best served by
immediate withdrawal, and that an orderly retreat and sound post-
imperial relations with the subcontinent would alike be best
achieved by enlisting Congress co-operation. His hopes of obtaining
more than a truncated Pakistan depended upon an extended
imperial presence of some sort. That they were no mere illusions is
revealed by the sympathies of some leading British Conservatives
and Liberals. As late as May 1947 Mountbatten's staff and the India
Committee of Attlee's Cabinet espoused a scheme that permitted
an independent India of many nations while the Chiefs of Staff
advised that if Congress rejected Dominion status then
Commonwealth membership might be accorded severally to West
Pakistan, united Bengal, and even to a maritime state such as
Travancore.[138]

Jinnah's readiness to accept, from time to time, quite different
constitutional forms as consistent with the Pakistan demand flowed
in part from the necessities of a dynamic situation, but in part, too,
from the advice proffered by colleagues. In April 1946, 470 Muslim

legislators voted for a single sovereign Pakistan of six full provinces; a few weeks later the Working Committee and the Council accepted a scheme for a Union of India; in April 1947 Jinnah endorsed Suhrawardy's plan for a 'Free State of Bengal'; two months later he accepted 'moth-eaten' Pakistan. Yet the essence of the Pakistan demand—the right to a territorial asylum, to the self-determination of the Muslim nation in the north-western and eastern regions of India—was never compromised. Certainly, Jinnah planned that the regions should include virtually the whole of six provinces, whereas in the circumstances of 1947 he was left with a Pakistan defined by religious distribution district by district. Yet that outcome lends no support to speculation that the Pakistan demand was Jinnah's bargaining counter for power in a united India, or that the Partition hoisted him with his own petard.

NOTES

1. Sir Penderel Moon, 'Mr Jinnah's Changing Attitude to the Idea of Pakistan', in A.H. Dani (ed.), *World Scholars on Quaid-i-Azam Mohammad Ali Jinnah.* (Islamabad, 1979), 267-70, p. 270.

2. L. Ziring, 'Jinnah: The Burden of Leadership', *ibid.*, 396-408, p. 407.

3. C.H. Philips and M.D. Wainwright (eds), *The Partition of India: Politics and Perspectives 1935* (London, 1970), 29.

4. N. Mansergh, *The Prelude to Partition: Concepts and Aims in Ireland and India,* The 1976 Commonwealth Lecture (Cambridge, 1978), 26, 59.

5. Viceroy's Personal Report No. 3, 17 April 1947, *TP*, x, 165.

6. Mountbatten to Sir Stafford Cripps, 9 July 1947, CAB 127/139, PRO.

7. E.g., Clement Attlee's draft memoirs. ATLE 1/13. Churchill College. Cambridge: Mountbatten on Nehru and Patel in letter to Cripps, 9 July 1947, loc. cit.; Moon to J.McL, Short, 2 Sept. 1946, CAB 127/150, PRO; H.V. Hodson, *The Great Divide Britain-India-Pakistan* (London, 1969), 217-18; L. Collins and D. Lapierre, *Freedom at Midnight* (London, 1975), 101; S. Gopal, *Jawaharlal Nehru: A Biography, I* (London, 1975), 257: Tara Chand, *History of the Freedom Movement in India*, IV (Delhi, 1972), 574.

8. K.B. Sayeed, 'The Personality of Jinnah and his Political Strategy', in Philips and Wainwright, *op. cit.*, 276-93, esp. 282.

9. *Ibid.*, 293, Dr Ian Copland more recently observed that Jinnah 'remains an engima' ('Islam and Political Mobilization in Kashmir, 1931-34,'. *Pacific Affairs*, 54 (1981), 228-59).

10. E.g. Tara Chand, *op. cit.*, IV, 321ff.

11. See Moon, 'Jinnah's Changing Attitude', loc. cit., for an analysis of such arguments.

12. E.g. S.R. Mehrotra, 'The Congress and the Partition of India', in Philips and Wainwright, *op. cit.*, 188-221, p. 216; A. Seal, 'Imperialism and Nationalism in India', J.A. Gallagher, G. Johnson and A. Seal (eds), *Locality, Province and Nation: Essays on Indian Politics, 1870-1940* (Cambridge, 1973), 1-27, p. 24.

13. For studies of mobilization, see Copland, 'Islam and Political Mobilization', loc. cit., esp. 228-31, 257-9.

14. Cited in H. Bolitho, *Jinnah: Creator of Pakistan* (London, 1954), 70.

15. A. Jalal and A. Seal, 'Alternative to Partition: Muslim Politics Between the Wars', in C. Baker, G. Johnson and A. Seal (eds), *Power, Profit and Politics Essays in Imperialism, Nationalism and Change in Twentieth Century India* (Cambridge, 1981), 415-54; Moore, *The Crisis of Indian Unity*, 1917-40 (London, 1974).

16. Z.H. Zaidi, 'Aspects of Muslim League Policy, 1937-47', in Philips and Wainwright, *op. cit.*, 245-75, esp. 250-7. See also J.A. Gallagher, 'Congress in Decline: Bengal, 1930 to 1939' in Gallagher, Johnson and Seal, *op. cit.*, 269-325, esp. 307-12.

17. Lady Mountbatten wrote to her husband of Miss Jinnah in April 1947: 'Like Mr Jinnah, she has, of course, a persecution mania...' (TP, x. 388), M.I. Chagla, a useful, witness believed that she injected an extra dose of venom into Jinnah's diatribes against the Hindus (*Roses in December* (Bombay, 1973), 119). For recollections of Jinnah see also the works of Kanji Dwarkadas.

18. L. Brennan, 'The Illusion of Security: the Background to Muslim Separatism in the United Provinces'. *Modern Asian Studies*, 18 (1984), 237-72.

19. Azim Hussain, *Fazl-i-Husain: a Political Biography* (Bombay, 1946), 265.

20. Cited in Bolitho, *op. cit.*, 113-14.

21. See D. Pandey, 'Congress-Muslim League Relations, 1937-39: "The Parting of the Ways", *Modern Asian Studies*, 12 (1978), 629-54.

22. Brennan shows that in the UP 'for the first time since 1909, the Muslim elite seemed to have no leverage in the new institutions of government', many of the gains of the past thirty years seemed to be vanishing or at least under threat', and 'the foundations they had fought so hard to build were shown to be straw' (*op. cit.*, 231).

23. Prasad to Patel, 11 Oct. 1938, B.N. Pandey (ed), *The Indian Nationalist Movement, 1885-1947: Select Documents* (London, 1979), 127-8.

24. R.G. Coupland, *Report on the Constitutional Problem in India*, II, 3 vols Oxford, 1942-3, pp. 167-78.

25. Jinnah's presidential address to Muslim League at Patna, 26 Dec. 1938, Jamil-ud-din Ahmad (ed.), *Speeches and Writings of Mr Jinnah*, 2 vols (Lahore, 1960 edn), I, 67-81.

26. *Ibid.*, 80.

27. *Ibid.*, 139.

28. *Ibid.*, 36, 139, 184.

29. *Ibid.*, 116.

30. The earliest X-ray photograph in the Quaid-i-Azam archives at Islamabad (QAP) is dated Lahore, 26 Oct. 1936.

31. Cripps-Geoffrey Wilson diary of visit to India, 15 Dec. 1939 (in possession of Mr Maurice Shock).

32. Coupland's Indian diary. 1941-42, 17 Jan. 1942, Rhodes House Oxford.

33. *Ibid.*, 8 Apr. 1942.

34. A. V. Alexander's diary, 4 Apr. 1946, Churchill College, Cambridge.

35. Cited in Hodson, *op. cit.*, 217.

36. The following account of the Karachi conference draws heavily on A.K. Jones, 'Mr Jinnah's Leadership and the Evolution of the Pakistan Idea: The Case of the Sind Provincial Muslim League Conference, 1938', in Dani, *op. cit.*, 180-92.

37. Gazdar to Jinnah, 10 July 1937, cited in Ziring, 'Jinnah', loc. cit., 406.

38. Alhaj Mian Ahmad Shafi, *Haji Sir Abdoola Haroon: A Biography* (Karachi, n. d.).

39. Address of 9 Oct. 1938, cited in Jones, 'Mr Jinnah's Leadership', loc. cit., 183.

40. See Jinnah's Osmania University speech, 28 Sept. 1939, Ahmad, *Speeches and Writings of Mr Jinnah*, I, 87; Cripps-Wilson diary, 15 Dec. 1939; 'Two Nations in India', sent by Jinnah to *Time and Tide* on 19 Jan. 1940 and published 9 Mar. 1940.

41. *Statesman*, 11 Oct. 1938, cited in Jones, 'Mr Jinnah's Leadership', loc. cit., 186-7.

42. *Statesman*, 14 Oct. 1938, cited in Mehrotra, 'The Congress and the Partition', loc. cit., 207.

43. *Pioneer*, 15 Oct. 1938, cited in S.S. Pirzada (ed.), *Foundations of Pakistan: All-India Muslim League Documents*, 1906-47, 2 vols (Karachi, 1970), II, xix.

44. Zaidi, 'Aspects of Muslim League Policy', loc. cit., 261.

45. Pirzada, *op. cit.*, II, 306-24.

46. *Ibid.*, 321.

47. *Ibid.*, xx-xxi.

48. Shafi, *Haji Sir Abdoola Haroon*, 139.

49. Haroon's correspondence with Aga Khan in Nov.-Dec. 1938, in Shafi, *ibid.*, 137-42. For the Aga Khan's own notion of a 'United States of Southern Asia' see 'Scheme of His Highness Sir Aga Khan as modified by Sir Fazl-i-Husain, January 1936', *ibid.*, 118-21, and Jalal and Seal, 'Alternative to Partition', loc. cit., 445-9.

50. Shafi, *op. cit.*, 150-1.

51. Haroon's introduction to Latif's *The Muslim Problem in India* (Bombay, 1939), v-viii.
52. *Ibid.*; *The Cultural Future of India* (Bombay, 1938); *A Federation of Cultural Zones for India*, Secunderabad, 20 Dec. 1938; *Statesman*, 30 Mar. 1939.
53. Pirzada, *op. cit.*, II, 153-71.
54. Cited and discussed in Coupland, *Report*, II, 199-201.
55. Hafeez Malik (ed.), *Iqbal: Poet-Philosopher of Pakistan* (New York, 1971), appx, 383-90.
56. Ahmad Bashir to Jinnah etc., 22 Mar. 1939, QAP, file 96.
57. *Ibid.* See also Ahmad Bashir letter to a newspaper. 7 Apr. 1939, *ibid.*
58. Ahmad Bashir to Jinnah, 21 Oct. 1939, *ibid.*
59. Ahmad Bashir's letters to Jinnah and an account of the Pakistan Majlis appear in Sarfaraz Hussain Mirza (ed.), *Tassawar-e-Pakistan Say Qarardad-e-Pakistan Tak* (Lahore, 1983).
60. Sikandar Hayat Khan, *Outlines of a Scheme of Indian Federation*, Lahore, 30 July 1939. See also Sikandar's speech in *Punjab Legislative Assembly Debates*, 11 Mar. 1941 (in V.P. Menon, *The Transfer of Power in India*, London, 1957, appx I, 451-67). For another Punjabi scheme published in Lahore in summer 1939, see 'A Punjabi' [? Miyan Kifayat Ali] *Confederacy of India*, pub. by Sir Muhammad Shah Nawaz Khan of Mamdot.
61. Ahmad Bashir, 'Sir Sikandar Hayat's Scheme' and 'Sir Sikandar's Federal Scheme', *Civil and Military Gazette*, 5 and 27 Aug. 1939.
62. Syed Zafarul Hasan and Muhammad Afzal Husain Qadri, *The Problem of Indian Muslims and its Solution*, Aligarh Muslim University Press, 14 Aug. 1939.
63. Printed commendation by Amiruddin Kedwaii, Umar Uddin Zafar Ahmad Siddiqi, Masud Makhdum, Dr Zaki Uddin, Dr Burhan Ahmad Faruqi, Jamil-ud-din Ahmad and Muddassir Ali Shamsee, n.d., but attached to similarly printed address by 'The Authors', d. Sept. 1939, QAP, file 96.
64. Viceroy's statement, 18 Oct. 1939, in M. Gwyer and A. Appadorai (eds), *Speeches and Documents on the Indian Constitution 1921-47* (London, 1957), II, 490-3.
65. Ahmad Bashir to Jinnah, 21 Oct. 1939, loc. cit. See also extract from his letter to Nehru, 6 Dec. 1939, in S. Gopal (ed.), *Selected Works of Jawaharlal Nehru*, X (New Delhi, 1977), 420 n.
66. Gandhi, 'Opinions Differ', *Harijan*, 11 Nov. 1939, reported in *Statesman* (Delhi), 12 Nov. 1939. Gandhi was replying to a private letter from 'M.A. of Aligarh' (see *Collected Works of Mahatma Gandhi*; LXX (New Delhi, 1977), 332-4.
67. Typescript document, 4 pp., QAP, file 96.
68. 'Confidential Note for the President', nd, *ibid.*
69. Haroon to Hon. Sec. A.I.M.L, 2 Feb. 1940, *ibid.*
70. C. Khaliquzzaman, *Pathway to Pakistan* (Lahore, 1961), 223-4. Khaliquzzaman grossly exaggerates his own role, though in March 1939 he

had proposed to the Secretary of State a vague scheme for three or four separate federations of provinces and states under a small central co-ordinating body (*ibid.*, 205-7); Marquess of Zetland, '*Essayez*' (London, 1956), 248-9. See also below, pp. 125-6.

71. AIML session, 22-4 Mar. 1940, Pirzada, *op. cit.*, II, 325-49.

72. At the time Liaquat Ali Khan rightly said that the term 'territorial readjustments' connoted a Muslim claim to Aligarh and Delhi, an interpretation questioned by Pirzada in the light of later events (*ibid.*, xx-xxi).

73. See above, n. 70, and below, pp. 125-6.

74. See his speech of 11 Mar. 1941 (see n. 60).

75. See Pirzada, *op. cit.*, II, xxii—xxiii; Philips and Wainwright, *op. cit.*, 29.

76. Mansergh, *op. cit.*, 27.

77. Still, the Associated Press of India reported that as Jinnah spoke 'there were many in that huge gathering of over 100,000 people who remembered the Mohammed Iqbal, the poet of Islam, the animator of the idea of Pakistan' (Pirzada, II, 327). Jinnah later wrote of Iqbal: 'His views were substantially in consonance with my own and had led me to the same conclusions as a result of careful examination and study of the constitutional problems facing India and found expression in due course in ... the Lahore resolution ...' (Malik, *op. cit.*, 384-5).

78. For the discussions see Gowher Rizvi, *Linlithgow in India. A Study of British Policy and the Political Impasse in India*, 1936-43, (London, 1978), 129ff.; K. Veerathappa, 'Britain and the Indian Problem (September 1939-May 1940), International Studies, VII (1966), 537-67.

79. Cited in D. Pandey, 'Congress-Muslim League Relations', loc. cit., 647.

80. Prasad to Nehru, 12 Nov. 1939, B.N. Pandey, *op. cit.*, 137-8.

81. Resolutions of AIML Working Committee, 15-17 June 1940, QAP, file 95. See also Coupland, *Report*, II, 243.

82. Sikandar to Jinnah, 31 May 1940, QAP, file 21; Coupland, *op. cit.*, 241.

83. Viceroy's statement of 8 Aug. 1940, Gwyer and Appadorai, *op. cit.*, 11, 504-5.

84. Liaquat to Jinnah, 28 July 1941, QAP, file 1092.

85. Allegations of dictatorship remain prominent in Partition historiography (e.g. Collins and Lapierre, *op. cit.*, 103; Tara Chand, *op. cit.*, IV, passim). Hodson wrote that Jinnah 'displayed his authority ... imperiously' in Aug. 1941 (*op. cit.*, 89).

86. E.g., May 1944 speech, Ahmad, *op. cit.*, II, 47-50.

87. Press statement, *Statesman*, 19 Feb. 1941.

88. E.g., Nov. 1940 and Apr. 1941 speeches, Ahmad, *op. cit.*, I, 184-5, 259.

89. *Statesman* (Delhi), 18 Feb. 1941.

90. Menon, *op. cit.*, 451-67.

91. Pirzada, *op. cit.*, II, 359-71.

92. Menon, *op. cit.*, 105.

93. Coupland's Diary, 2 Feb. 1942.

94. *Ibid.*, 17 Jan. and 2 Feb. 1942. Coupland assumed these sessions in his own 'Agency Centre' scheme (*Report*, III, 82).

95. Memo. on Pakistan, 21 Mar. 1942, Coupland's Diary, 269-70.

96. Declaration as published, 30 Mar. 1942, *TP*, i, 456.

97. Resolution of League Working Committee, 11 Apr. 1942, *ibid.*, 606.

98. See my *Churchill, Cripps, and India, 1939-45* (London, 1979), 88 and n. 4; *TP*, i, 380, 392, 393. The Cripps Mission file (802) in the QAP is 'embargoed'.

99. Coupland's Diary, 185, 214.

100. *Ibid.*, 221-2.

101. Working Committee resolution, 11 Apr. 1942, loc. cit.

102. Ahmad, *op. cit.*, 1, 582-6.

103. For further expressions of the idea, see *ibid.*, I, 383, 409, 477, 567-8.

104. See Richard Casey to Wavell, 11 Sept. 1944, TP, v, 13, 79; East Pakistan Renaissance Society, *Eastern Pakistan: Its Population, Delimitation and Economics Calcutta*, Sept. 1944. As early as 11 June 1940, Prof. A. Sadeque, Professor of Economics and Politics at Islamia College, Calcutta, sent to Jinnah a proposal for dividing India into Pakistan, Hindustan and 'Greater Bengal' (QAP, file 106).

105. Pirzada, *op. cit.*, II, xxx.

106. See my *Churchill, Cripps, and India*, 132-5.

107. See my *Escape from Empire; The Atlee Government and the Indian Problem* (Oxford, 1983), 18-31.

108. E.g., interview of 8 Nov. 1945, Ahmad, *op. cit.,* II, 230-3.

109. Pirzada, *op. cit.*, II, 512-13.

110. *TP*, vii, 71, 82.

111. *Ibid.*, 126.

112. *Ibid.*, 82.

113. See Ahmad to Jinnah, 29 May 1946, QAP, file 1092.

114. *TP*, vii, 303.

115. E.g., M.I. Qureshi (joint secretary of the League's Planning Committee) to Jinnah, 31 May 1946, QAP, file 1092.

116. M.A.H. Ispahani, 'Factors Leading to the Partition of British India', in Philips and Wainwright, *op. cit.* 330-59, pp. 348-50.

117. Aurangzeb Khan to Jinnah, 19 May 1946, QAP, file 12; Ahmad to Jinnah, 29 May 1946, loc. cit. See also typed lists of 'Advantages' and 'Disadvantages', nd; Liaquat to Jinnah, 21 May 1946; Prof. A.B.A. Haleem (Aligarh) to Jinnah, 23 May 1946; all in QAP, file 12.

118. *TP*, vii, 469.

119. Jinnah to Wavell, 8 June 1946, *ibid.*, 473.

120. For elaboration see my *Escape from Empire*, 124-44.

121. See, e.g., Jinnah's bitter complaint to Attlee and Churchill, 6 July 1946, *TP*, viii, 68.

122. See, e.g., *TP*, ix, 153.
123. E.g., Churchill to Jinnah and Simon to Jinnah, both 11 Dec. 1946, QAP, file 21.
124. *TP*, x, 229.
125. *Commons' Debates*, 12 Dec. 1946, cols. 1362-70; 20 Dec. 1946, cols. 2341-52. See also K. Dwarkadas, *Ten Years to Freedom* (Bombay, 1968), 195-6.
126. See Sir W. Monckton to Templewood, 15 Jan. 1947 and reply, 16 Jan. 1947, T.C.
127. *TP*, ix, 440; x, 105, 165.
128. *Ibid.*
129. *Ibid.*, 256. See also 276, Annex. I.
130. *Ibid.*, 229. See also 227-8, 264. Cf. the common Pakistani belief that Jinnah saw Suhrawardy's scheme as a heresy (eg. M.A.H. Ispahani, *Quaid-e-Azam as I Knew Him* (Karachi, 1967 edn), 257-8). For relations between Jinnah and Suhrawardy over the scheme from Feb. 1947, see Ziring, 'Jinnah', loc. cit. A draft scheme for a 'Free State of Bengal', d. 4 June 1947, appears in QAP, file 142.
131. See my *Escape From Empire*.
132. See also A.K. Brohi, 'Reflections on the Quaid-i-Azam's Self Selection as the First Governor-General of Pakistan', and S.M. Burke, 'Quaid-i-Azam's Decision to become Pakistan's First Governor-General', in Dani, *op. cit.*, 289-306. Cf. Mountbatten's simple explanation in terms of Jinnah's vanity and megalomania, and Congress suscpicions of Jinnah's fascist intentions (above, nn. 6-7).
133. In May 1949 three of Pakistan's governors, the three chiefs of staff, and 470 military officers, were still British.
134. For Gandhi see his *Autobiography: the Story of My Experiments with Truth* (Ahmedabad, 1927), and S.H. and L. Rudolph, *The Modernity of Tradition* (Chicago, 1967), Pt. II ('The Traditional Roots of Charisma: Gandhi').
135. Appeal for 'Day of Deliverance', 2 Dec. 1939, Ahmad, I, 98-100.
136. Coupland's Diary, 17 Jan. 1942.
137. See, e.g., M.L. Qureshi to Jinnah, 31 May 1946, loc. cit.
138. *TP*, x, 387, 416.

5

Jinnah and the Making of Pakistan
Ian A. Talbot

The worldwide Islamic Revival of the 1970s has overshadowed the attempts made by Muslims earlier in the century to unite religious and political authority. Muslims led the revolt against the colonial west throughout much of the Middle East, Africa and South and South-East Asia. In India especially, the Muslim urge to political power was clearly demonstrated. As British rule there drew to an end, many Muslims demanded, in the name of Islam, the creation of a separate Pakistan state. Its emergence in August 1947 remains one of the major political achievements of modern Muslim history. It resulted mainly from the efforts of one man, Mohammad Ali Jinnah.

The Muslims of British India were not a united community. They were divided by ethnic background, language and sect. The main ethnic division was between the descendants of the Arab and Turkish invaders of India and those whose ancestors had been converted from the indigenous Hindu population. There was no common Muslim language in India. Instead, Muslims shared with their Hindu neighbours the main regional languages—Bengali, Punjabi, Gujarati and Tamil. Rivalries between the Sunni and Shia sects of Islam were another factor limiting Muslim unity. Many Muslims also shared economic interests with their Hindu counterparts, particularly the cultivators of the Punjab and the large landowners of the United Provinces known as the *taluqdars*. Finally, as the British introduced elected councils and assemblies in the twentieth century, a division of political priorities and interests emerged between the Muslims who lived in regions such as the Punjab and Bengal, where they formed a majority of the population, and those who inhabited areas such as the United Provinces, where they were outnumbered by the Hindus. In these circumstances Jinnah's uniting the Muslims behind the demand for Pakistan in the 1940s was an outstanding achievement.

Despite this remarkable accomplishment, Jinnah remains an enigmatic and controversial figure. Although he began his career as a respected leader of the Indian National Congress, he ended it as its most implacable opponent. Although he was not a devout Muslim, he demanded in the name of Islam the creation of Pakistan. Although he could not speak most of the main Indian Muslim languages, he captivated audiences of millions during the campaign for Pakistan.

Jinnah's background and his character are almost as enigmatic as his political motivations and the reasons for his success. His family background is obscure: little is known other than that he came from a merchant family of recent converts to Islam which had settled in Karachi. There is even uncertainty about his date of birth, although he always maintained that it was on Christmas Day, 1876. Throughout his life Jinnah was a remote and inscrutable figure. He had no true friends and was rarely seen relaxed and off guard, whether in private or in public. The final Viceroy of India, Lord Mountbatten, felt far more at ease with the sociable Jawaharlal Nehru, who was Jinnah's leading Congress Party opponent. Jinnah's inscrutability and stubborn support for his Pakistan demand frequently frustrated Mountbatten during the series of meetings which took place between them early in April 1947. After one marathon session during which Jinnah appeared not to have been listening to any of his arguments, Mountbatten wrote in exasperation that 'Jinnah must be a psychopathic case'.

When Jinnah was sixteen, his father sent him to London to study law. He pursued his studies at Lincoln's Inn with great devotion. Whilst in London, he met several Indian politicians including Dadabhai Naoroji, MP for Central Finsbury and leading member of the Indian National Congress. It was during this period that Jinnah acquired the English manner and appearance and the belief in the effectiveness of parliamentary democracy which were to become his political hallmarks.

Jinnah returned to India in 1896 as a qualified barrister. He faced three years of uphill struggle before he established himself as Bombay's leading Muslim lawyer. It was only when his career was thus assured that he entered politics. His first appearance was at the 1906 Calcutta session of the Congress in which he acted as private secretary to its President, Dadabhai Naoroji. There he established links with several Congress leaders, most notably with the influential Gopal Krishna Gokhale, whom he accompanied on a visit to England in April 1913; by that date Jinnah had emerged as one of the leading Muslim figures in the Congress and was regarded by many as its future leader.

Until 1913 Jinnah had steered well clear of the main Muslim political organisation, the Muslim League. This had been founded in 1906 in order to safeguard Muslim political rights. Its outlook was conservative and loyal to the British and it reflected in the main the priorities of the Muslim educated élite of the United Provinces, from where it drew its leaders and its greatest support. Elsewhere in India it had little influence. In April 1913 Jinnah agreed to lead the Muslim League in the hope of bringing its views into line with the Congress. He arranged its 1915 session to coincide with the Congress' and played a leading role in the negotiations which took place between the two parties. They resulted in the famous Lucknow Pact of 1916, the only occasion in modern Indian history in which the Muslim League and the Congress came to a voluntary agreement about the political future of India. The Pact granted the Muslims many of the safeguards which they had demanded, including separate electorates and 'weightage' in the Legislative Councils of those provinces in which they formed a minority of the population. However, despite the hopes which it raised, the Lucknow Pact had only a temporary effect on Muslim-Hindu relations.

It only represented the agreement of the tiny political élite of the two communities and was therefore vulnerable to the emergence into politics of new social groups and classes. Jinnah and many others who believed in a liberal constitutional approach to the communal and national issues, felt ill at ease when Gandhi launched his first Civil Disobedience Campaigns against the British in the aftermath of the First World War. Jinnah refused to abandon his traditional approach to politics and resigned from the Indian National Congress shortly after Gandhi had gained control of it at the December 1920 Nagpur session.

The new political environment created by the British constitutional reforms of 1919 represented, however, a far greater setback to Jinnah's career than Gandhi's temporary radicalisation of Indian politics. As a result of the Montagu-Chelmsford reforms, such subjects of provincial administration as education, local self-government and public works were transferred to the control of ministers responsible to elected assembly members. This system, known as dyarchy, offered great opportunities for politicians with strong local support. For those like Jinnah, who had no landed or tribal powerbase, it spelt disaster: throughout his career he had operated at the All-India level of politics; under dyarchy, however, real power and influence lay at the local level. For a time he attempted to soldier on as leader of an independent group in the Central Assembly and as a broker between the powerful local Muslim politicians and the Congress during constitutional negotiations. Even this role was denied him after the rejection of his proposals by the Congress and the all-party scheme produced by Motilal Nehru in 1928. His mediatory role was increasingly taken over by Mian Fazl-i-Husain, the Punjabi Muslim leader whose strong provincial powerbase and membership of the Viceroy's Executive Council gave him much greater authority in negotiating on behalf of the Muslims.

Jinnah settled once more in London in 1931, determined to retire from politics and to concentrate on his legal career. He was only left in peace, however, until 1933 when Nawab Liaquat Ali Khan, his future right-hand man and Premier of Pakistan, visited him in his Hampstead house. Liaquat stressed the Indian Muslims' need for Jinnah's experienced leadership. Jinnah was given a further indication of the importance which was attached to this in October 1934, when the Muslims of Bombay elected him in his absence as their representative for the Central Legislative Assembly. However, it was not these entreaties which decided Jinnah to return but rather that the 1935 Government of India Act presented him with an opportunity to regain his former influence. Jinnah arrived back in Bombay in October 1935. Within twelve years he was to become the Governor-General of an independent state of Pakistan.

Numerous questions arise concerning Jinnah's role in the Pakistan movement. How did he make the transition from being an able debater in the refined atmosphere of the Central Legislative Council to that of the *Quaid-i-Azam*, the great leader beloved throughout the thousands of villages of Muslim India? Did he create the desire for Pakistan within the Muslim community or merely guide it, using his legal talents to plead its case before the British and the Indian National Congress? Did he really believe in the possibility of achieving Pakistan at all, or was his demand for it merely a bargaining counter which he adopted to safeguard Muslim rights as British rule drew to its close? Finally, was he in control of events or was he merely swept along by the tide of an Islamic revolution?

The opening of government and private archives in India, Pakistan and Britain has enabled historians to answer at least some of these questions which so perplexed Jinnah's contemporaries. The picture which emerges of him is not that of a charismatic leader guiding his people to the promised land, but rather that of an able, single-minded political tactician who took full advantage of the dramatic political changes which occurred after India's entry into the Second World War.

In 1937 elections were held throughout India for control of the autonomous provincial assemblies which had been created by the 1935 Government of India Act. Despite its reorganisation by Jinnah, the Muslim League won only 109 out of the 482 Muslim seats. This stemmed from its poor showing in the two major centres of Muslim population, the Punjab and Bengal. It had fared dismally in the former province, losing all but one of the eighty-six Muslim constituencies to the Unionist Party. The Unionist Party owed its success to the support of the large landowners who controlled the votes of the overwhelmingly rural electorate. Sikander Hayat Khan had succeeded Mian Fazl-i-Husain as its leader in 1936. Like his late predecessor he used his strong provincial powerbase to dominate All-India Muslim politics. Jinnah wisely recognised his own dependence on the Punjabi leader by allowing him to control the Muslim League organisation in his province from October 1937 onwards, in return for his support in national politics.

By 1939 the Muslim League had considerably increased its influence, thanks to the blunders of the Congress, whose success in the 1937 elections had enabled it to form ministries in seven of India's eleven provinces. For the first time large numbers of Muslims came under Hindu rule. The provincial Congress governments made no effort to understand and respect their Muslim populations' cultural and religious sensibilities. The Muslim League's claims that it alone could safeguard Muslim interests thus received a major boost. Significantly it was only after this period of Congress rule that it took up the demand for a Pakistan state, although the idea of separate Muslim homeland in north-west India had been aired by the poet Sir Muhammad Iqbal as early as 1930 and the actual word 'Pakistan' had been coined in 1933 by Rahmat Ali, a Cambridge undergraduate. (The word 'Pakistan' is made up of the initial letters of Punjab Asghania—the North-West frontier province—Kashmir and Sind, and the ending stan—land. Pak, an Urdu word, also means spiritually pure, or clean.)

The outbreak of the Second World War transformed this undergraduate dream into an issue of practical politics: the war not only accelerated the British departure from India but built up the Muslim League into a position of equality with the Congress. Just one day after the declaration of war, Jinnah was invited to see the Viceroy, Lord Linlithgow, on an equal footing with Gandhi. When Linlithgow made his statement on war aims on 18 October 1939, he dubbed the Congress a Hindu organisation, whilst implicitly accepting the Muslim League's claim that it spoke for all India's Muslims. The Viceroy's famous 1940 August Offer declared that the British,

could not contemplate the transfer of their present responsibility for the peace and welfare of India to any system of Government whose authority is directly denied by large and powerful elements in India's national life.

The Cripps Mission which arrived in India in March 1942 to offer India self-government in return for wartime support went even further to meet Jinnah's demands and conceded in theory the future partition of India. The Muslim League's rise in importance stemmed not only from the British Government's genuine desire to secure communal co-operation before it embarked on further constitutional reform, but also from its need to create a counterweight to the Indian National Congress which refused to co-operate with the war effort. Jinnah adroitly exploited to the full the fortuitous circumstances in which the Muslim League now found itself: it grew in importance following the resignation of the Congress Ministries in October 1939 and the growing wartime confrontation between the Congress movement and the British. Their repression of the Quit India movement which Gandhi had launched in 1942 shattered the Congress' organisation and resulted in most of its leaders spending the final three years of the war in jail.

Jinnah was thus free to concentrate on consolidating the Muslim League's position and, most important of all, to move against his rivals in the Punjab who stood in the way of Pakistan. Despite the impatience of many of his supporters there, Jinnah waited until April 1944 before moving against the Unionist Party. By biding his time he was able to take maximum advantage of the divisions which Sikander's sudden death in December 1942 had created within it. He was also able to fully exploit the Unionist Government's increasing wartime unpopularity. Large numbers of its traditional rural supporters transferred their loyalty to the Muslim League from 1944 onwards. Their exodus was hastened by Jinnah's political success at the expense of Gandhi in September 1944 and the Viceroy Lord Wavell in July 1945: he manoeuvred Gandhi during their negotiations in Bombay into accepting the Partition of India in theory; at the July 1945 Simla Conference he successfully resisted all Lord Wavell's efforts to include a Unionist in the proposed Interim Government.

The Muslim League thus approached the crucial 1946 elections in the Punjab in a greatly strengthened position. By the end of 1945 it had captured the support of a third of the Unionist Party's Assembly members. It included in its ranks most of the leading landlords and rural religious leaders. They all controlled large numbers of votes which, for the first time in 1946, were placed at the Muslim League's disposal. The League was thus able to secure victory in all but a handful of the rural constituencies, and it repeated this success throughout the subcontinent. Although more research is required before it can be fully explained, particularly in the other major centre of Muslim population in Bengal, at the time Jinnah maintained in 1946 that the Muslim community's support for Pakistan had been affirmed.

In fact many of those who had voted for the Muslim League had done so more out of personal loyalty to its candidates than out of support for Pakistan. Indeed, what Pakistan stood for in 1946 was by no means clear. Many of the Muslim League's recent converts from the Punjab, for example, hoped that the concession of Pakistan in name would be the means of approximating most nearly to a united India in fact. Jinnah had deliberately said little about where Pakistan's boundaries would lie, or about the form of government it would have. He was perceptive enough to realise that only if the Pakistan scheme was kept vague could it appeal to all sections of the Muslim community. He thus concentrated almost solely on winning the acceptance of Pakistan in principle.

Although the Muslim League's victories in 1946 owed as much to local discontents and loyalties as the widespread support for the Pakistan demand, Jinnah succeeded in convincing both the Congress and the British that he had been given a mandate on this issue. This 'confidence trick' must rank as one of his greatest political achievements. In the constitutional negotiations which followed the elections Jinnah made full use of his strengthened position. His success was greatly assisted by the continued blunders of the Congress leaders. Their greatest mistake occured in June 1946, when they rejected the Cabinet Mission's proposals for a federal solution to India's communal problem, after Jinnah and the Muslim League had already reluctantly accepted it. Although Jinnah seemed prepared to agree to less than a fully sovereign Pakistan, provided Muslim interests were safeguarded, the Congress leadership appeared intent on hastening its emergence through its own errors. Once the Cabinet Mission had failed, the partition of India became virtually inevitable.

The final year of British rule was not a happy one for Jinnah: he believed that the new Labour Government and the new Viceroy, Lord Mountbatten, favoured the Congress Party. His anger at the British invitation to Nehru in August 1946 to form an Interim Government led him to abandon his strictly constitutional approach to politics. His calling for direct action by the Muslim League resulted in horrific communal riots in Calcutta on 16 August. The violence quickly spread to other areas and by the end of the summer India appeared on the brink of civil war. In the tense months of negotiations which followed Jinnah appeared even grimmer and more determined than usual. Agreement was not finally reached until 3 June 1947: the Pakistan which emerged from it was not the big Pakistan of Jinnah's dreams but a 'moth-eaten Pakistan' shorn of the rich agricultural districts of the East Punjab and of Calcutta and West Bengal. Although he could not have realistically expected to achieve more, Jinnah was so bitterly disappointed that he would not record his acceptance in writing but merely nodded his assent in the presence of the Hindu and Sikh leaders.

Once the plan for 3 June had been agreed, Lord Mountbatten carried out the final complex arrangements with lightning speed. India and Pakistan received their freedom at midnight on 14 August 1947. That same day violent communal clashes broke out in the Punjab. They continued until November by which time at a conservative estimate 200,000 people had died and five-and-a-half million had been made homeless.

The massive influx of refugees added to the problems which faced the Pakistan Constituent Assembly as it attempted to secure agreements with India over the division of the subcontinent's assets and administrative services and as it negotiated for the accession of the surrounding Princely States. Most of this burden fell on Jinnah who, besides being Governor-General, acted as President of the Constituent Assembly and final authority in Muslim League matters. He also assumed responsibility for the newly created ministry of State and Tribal Affairs. He was by now seventy and appeared frailer and more emaciated than ever. In June 1948 his doctors ordered him to leave Karachi for the healthier climate of Ziarat in Baluchistan. He insisted however on returning to Karachi to take part in the opening of the State Bank of Pakistan. The summer heat proved too much for him and he was forced to return almost immediately to Quetta. There he showed signs of improvement, but following an attack of influenza and bronchitis, complications set in. On 12 September 1948, Pakistan awoke to the news that its founding father had died peacefully the previous evening.

Many writers have argued that if Jinnah had lived longer, Pakistan would not have suffered from the political instability which has dogged it since independence. Jinnah certainly stood head and shoulders above his successors as a national leader. Nevertheless, Pakistan's political weakness had its roots in the way in which the Muslim League had won power in the main centres of Muslim population. It had mainly functioned there as a grand coalition of the leading landlord factions. Once Pakistan had been achieved, their traditional rivalries surfaced once more. This led to the Muslim League's rapid decline as it was also handicapped by the lack of popular powerbase in these areas. The disintegration of the Muslim League was accompanied by a general decline in Pakistani political life which soon became sunk in corruption and factionalism. Even if Jinnah had lived longer it is unlikely that he could have done more than delay its onset.

Despite Pakistan's post-independence problems, Jinnah's place in history is assured because of his supreme contribution to its creation. He is still revered in Pakistan as the Quaid-i-Azam whose charismatic leadership enabled the Muslim community to achieve its goal of an independent homeland. His achievement in fact was far greater than such Pakistani propaganda can easily admit. For the Muslims of British India were not a nation awaiting only Jinnah's leadership to assert this fact. Nor was Pakistan swept into existence by the tide of an Islamic revolution. Rather, Jinnah manipulated the popular appeal of Islam and the political conditions created by the Second World War and the British departure from India in order temporarily to unite most Muslims behind the demand for Pakistan. In reality, however, this remained the priority only of a small Muslim élite.

6

The Jinnah Story
Francis Robinson

The life of no man, not that of Mahatma Gandhi, not that of Jawaharlal Nehru, is so entangled with the nationalist politics of British India as that of Muhammad Ali Jinnah. Consider its span. In the 1890s he was helping Dadabhai Naoroji in his campaign to become the first Indian Member of the British Parliament. In the 1900s he entered the Imperial Legislative Council as the representative of Bombay's Muslims. In the 1910s he was a member of both National Congress and Muslim League and principal negotiator of the Lucknow Pact for Hindu-Muslim unity. In the 1920s, 1930s and 1940s he was involved in promoting the Muslim League interest at all stages of constitutional reform, becoming its Quaid-i-Azam or Great Leader, who alone commanded the Muslim platform throughout the transfer of power negotiations. Consider his impact. He was regarded by all concerned as the man primarily responsible for the division of British India into two sovereign states at independence. Then, consider the extent to which his career is beset by seeming paradox. He is the ambassador of Hindu-Muslim unity who ends up dividing India. He is the man of avowed secular habit who presides over the realization of a religious ideal. He is the advocate of Pakistan who leaves open to the end the possibility of a united India, indeed, shows interest in being its first prime minister.

For much of the time since Jinnah's death in 1948 we have had little fresh evidence to help us unravel these paradoxes. Unlike Gandhi and Nehru, he wrote no autobiography. He left no intimate diaries. There were no confidences from close friends; they were so few. There were no indiscretions from members of his family; they remained tight-lipped. The assumed needs of state-making, moreover, conspired to preserve and to project a cardboard image of the man. For India he had to be the malevolent force, as played in the Attenborough film *Gandhi*,[1] who seduced Muslims into rending the sacred fabric of the motherland. For Pakistan he had to be the leader of genius and increasingly the good Muslim, who, almost as the Prophet had done thirteen centuries before, led the faithful to the promised land where they might live under the holy law. It has not been easy to gain a satisfactory idea of what Jinnah was trying to do, or why he was trying to do it.

In recent years, however, enough new evidence has become available to make possible a major reassessment of his career, indeed, to enable us to resolve some of its paradoxes: there are the twelve volumes of British documents relating to the transfer of power which were published between 1970 and 1982, the 80,000 pages of Quaid-i Azam papers which are deposited in the National Archives of Pakistan, and the archives of the All-India Muslim League which are slowly being made available. Stanley Wolpert and Ayesha Jalal are the first to attempt major reassessments. Wolpert examines the whole life, Jalal the last most important part.

Wolpert draws together much detail about Jinnah's life which makes him, in his earlier years at least, seem more human than he has done. The boy was a young rip who cut school to gallop his father's Arab stallions in the desert. The young man was still enough of a rip to get arrested for pushing his friends around in a cart on the Oxford-Cambridge boat race night. Like many barristers he was a thwarted thespian who was good enough to sign a contract with a Manchester repertory company and dreamed of starring in Romeo and Juliet at the Old Vic. When he did get to play Romeo it was opposite Ruttie, the spirited and precocious daughter of a Parsee millionaire twenty-five years his junior. Wolpert makes us constantly aware of how the fortunes of this ill-fated match and those of Jinnah's political career were intertwined, from the high point of its announcement after his triumph of the Lucknow Pact, through its deterioration in the early 1920s together with that of his political life, to Ruttie's death at the end of the decade and his complete withdrawal from politics. In the same way he keeps us continually alert to the progress of Jinnah's degenerative lung-disease from the late 1930s, the toll it took of his resources, the effort it demanded to keep up appearances, until the very struggle itself seemed to fuel his concentration of effort and to focus his will to win. Thus Wolpert paints a life which moves from hope in youth, to brilliant success in middle age, to declining years spent striving to salvage some kind of victory out of defeat on several fronts, personal and physical as well as political.

Wolpert's vision of Jinnah's political progress is strictly conventional. The paradoxes of the Quaid's career are not serious enough to make him pause for thought. So Jinnah begins as the Muslim Gokhale, opposing the Muslim League and separate electorates and working for Hindu-Muslim unity. Although harried from the centre of the political stage at Nagpur in 1920, he continues to strive for some form of Hindu-Muslim agreement, most notably as Indians begin to negotiate the next stage in the devolution of power from 1926 to 1928, and as they face up to the meaning of the new rules for politics between 1934 and 1937. This endeavour, however, is wrecked by the Congress victory in the general elections of 1937; now the Congress is strong enough to ignore both him and his League. Jinnah must revive the League or die. At the Lucknow session of 1937, therefore, he devotes himself completely to the Muslim cause. At Patna in the following year he declares Congress to be nothing but a 'Hindu body'. Then, sixteen months later, at the famous Lahore session of March 1940 he makes clear, so Wolpert tells us, that 'partition ... was the only long-term solution to India's foremost problem'. He 'lowered the final curtain on any prospects for a single united independent India'. From that moment Jinnah's determination was fixed; he was set on his seven-year campaign to realize the sovereign state of Pakistan. Evidence to the contrary is either ignored or explained away. It is a vision which should cause little offence to those bred in the traditional historiography of the Islamic republic.

Wolpert's analysis of Jinnah's motivation is less conventional and makes a real contribution. He emphasizes, as others have done before, his vanity, his ambition, his need to play the starring role. His contribution is to show these characteristics continually at work in his career. The centrepiece of the analysis is the study of his interaction with Gandhi. Wolpert makes a good case for Jinnah being obsessed with the Mahatma. It was Gandhi who robbed him of his starring role when he pushed him off centre stage at Nagpur; this was, Wolpert tells us, the most bitterly humiliating experience of his public life '... the searing memory of his defeat at Nagpur [was] permanently emblazoned on his brain'. It was Gandhi who destroyed the ideals of Hindu-Muslim unity with which the Congress began; 'Mr Gandhi,' Jinnah told the Muslim League in 1938, turned 'the Congress into an instrument for the revival of Hinduism. It was Gandhi, Jinnah told a Peshawar audience in 1945, who made no sacrifices in 1920-21 and 'ascends the *gaddi* [throne] of leadership on our skulls'. Here Wolpert adroitly emphasizes the connection between Jinnah's deepest personal grievances and the Muslim cause. The message is that Congress rejected Jinnah in 1920 and continued to do so afterwards. Most of his subsequent actions can be seen as motivated by the need to extract compensation for that rejection. As his old friend, Kanji Dwarkadas, perceptively remarked, after meeting him sick and depressed in December 1946, 'He wanted to keep the fight on because he was badly handled and treated and abused by the Congress leaders ... his self-esteem, his pride, and his feeling of being personally hurt had embittered him.' This is convincing stuff. It goes well with other observations regarding Jinnah's intense psychic drive, Mountbatten's 'psychopathic case'. It dovetails nicely with Robin Moore's recent perception of the identity between Jinnah's feeling of rejection and persecution by Congress and the Muslim sense, although Moore would have done better to talk of the Urdu-speaking Muslim sense, 'of persecution by the Congress denial of their achieved status'.[2]

This contribution acknowledged, Wolpert's *Jinnah* is, nevertheless, a disappointment. On flicking through the pages it seemed to promise much. The subject needs accessible books which can take the fruits of the considerable research devoted to South Asia to a general reading public. Here, perhaps, was a good candidate for the task. But, although the book begins and ends well, it loses the reader for several chapters in a maze of constitutional comings and goings. Then, there is Wolpert's treatment of facts: Mohamed Ali was not an 'alim (p. 34), Mazharul Haque did not die in 1921 (p. 39), Abd al-Hamid was not Ottoman Caliph in the 1910s (p. 52), Shaukat Ali was not an 'alim (p. 52), Abul Kalam Azad did not come from Delhi (p. 63), the Moplahs did not riot against Hindus after the abolition of the Khilafat in 1924 (p. 83) and so on. This is too slapdash to breed confidence. Then, there are those patches in the prose. Consider this: 'Jinnah was the 'idol of the youth', and 'uncrowned king of Bombay'. Raven-haired with a moustache almost as full as Kitchener's and lean as a rapier, he sounded like Ronald Coleman, dressed like Anthony Eden, and was adored by most women at first sight, and admired or envied by most men.' Or this: 'Silently, patiently, passionately they waited till Ruttie would attain her majority at eighteen and married just a few months after that, as soon as the last legal obstacle could be slashed aside by Jinnah's invincible courtroom sword.' It is all a matter of taste, of course, but while such mush might draw a few readers from the Georgette Heyer market, one fears that it may well deter others.

The major criticism of Wolpert, however, is that he offers us so little sense of the hard play of power, especially in the years from 1940 to 1947. Given the huge quantity of records newly available in Britain and in Pakistan it is surprising, for instance, that he does not now come to question the purpose of the Lahore resolution or wonder about Jinnah's response to the Cripps offer. It is surprising, too, that he does not show us how consistently weak Jinnah was in relation to the political bosses in the Muslim majority provinces, and how hard he had to work in papering over the cracks in order to present a veneer of unity at the centre. Moreover, because he gives us so little idea of the extent of Jinnah's political weakness, he cannot really tell us the full extent of his political achievement. But, given all the new materials available, it is the more surprising that Wolpert perceives not one single limitation in the orthodox understanding of Jinnah's strategy. He does not see that there may now be hard evidence for the old speculation that the Pakistan demand was less an aim than a bargaining counter, that there might be something in the idea that partition into two sovereign states was for Jinnah less a triumph than a disaster, that it might, in fact, be possible to unravel some of the paradoxes of Jinnah's career. Indeed, Wolpert does not see that when the Quaid seems to doubt the desirability of partition in his first speech to the Constituent assembly of Pakistan, as he himself notes, he might be speaking from his heart, or better put, from the veiled recesses of his mind.[3]

Ayesha Jalal shows us just how much Wolpert failed to see. To be fair, her portrayal of Jinnah's political career up to 1937, although it concentrates more on the structure of opportunities than on the interaction of personalities, does not differ greatly. She identifies Jinnah as a constitutionalist and a nationalist whose prime aims were to assure Muslims a safe position as India moved to independence and to assert himself as their sole spokesman. His natural talent was for the affairs of council chamber and committee room at the centres of all-India politics, so when from 1917 the national movement became increasingly extreme in its forms of action, and from 1920 politics became focused on the provinces, Jinnah found his style out of keeping with the times while there was no longer any stage on which he could play. Politically isolated for the next decade and a half, except for the years 1926-28, he found no opening until 1934 when Muslims from the minority provinces begged him to revive the Muslim League. From then on Jinnah aimed to broaden the basis of League support and to come to terms with the Congress at the all-India level. He and the Congress High Command had a joint interest in destroying both the power of the provincial politicians in their various regional bastions and that which the 1935 Government of India Act gave the British at the centre. The strategy was wrecked by the League's failures and the Congress's success in the general elections of 1937. Now Congress leaders made it clear to Jinnah that they had no need to deal with him or his League. He could, if he wished, join them on their terms.

It is in her understanding of Jinnah's strategy after 1937 that Jalal comes to differ radically from Wolpert. She sees him continuing to pursue a Muslim future within India, and not moving quickly to a decision that the future must be found outside it. Most men after a defeat like that of 1937, she reflects, would have thrown in the towel. But Jinnah, that master of the 'long slow game' sets out once more to build a position of strength from which he could negotiate at the centre with both the British and the Congress. He gained some help as the powerful leaders of the Muslim majority provinces found that they needed someone to represent their interests in Delhi. He gained more when, after the outbreak of the second world war, the British came to appreciate the value of strengthening Jinnah's position as the representative of all India's Muslims at the centre. In this context Jinnah gave new form to his strategy. His presidential speech to the Muslim League session at Lahore, March 1940, asserted that the Muslims were a separate nation on the Indian subcontinent. The session's first resolution announced the League's aim to achieve sovereign and autonomous Muslim states in the northwestern and eastern zones of India. Jinnah was suggesting in the speech and by means of the resolution, later known as the Pakistan resolution, that because there were two nations in India, the transfer of power would necessarily involve the dissolution of British India's unitary structure of central authority, and that any reconstitution of that centre would have to take account of the League's demand that the Muslim majority provinces should be grouped to form a separate state. This was not the end that Jinnah actually sought, merely a means to ensure that his voice was heard when the final constitutional arrangements of independent India came to be negotiated. It should be seen, as Jalal puts it,

> as a bargaining counter, which had the merit of being acceptable (on the face of it) to the majority province Muslims, and of being totally unacceptable to the Congress and in the last resort the British also. This in turn provided the best insurance that the League would not be given what it now apparently was asking for, but which Jinnah in fact did not really want. (p. 57).

From 1940 to 1946 Jinnah developed his strategy with growing success. By 1942 the Cripps Mission was using the terminology of Pakistan and implicitly accepting the two-nation idea. By 1946 most of Muslim India had swung behind the demand for Pakistan demonstrating its support in the sweeping victories of League candidates in the general elections of 1945-46. The Congress, moreover, although it denied the two-nation theory to the end, was unable convincingly to refute it either on the streets or in the ballot box. Throughout Jinnah kept Pakistan's precise form vague, its territories were always undefined. Throughout he managed to play the emotive communal card and undermine independent leaders in the Muslim majority provinces without having to face up to its implications of a partition of Bengal and the Punjab. Then, in May 1946, the Cabinet Mission proposed a three-tier system with compulsory grouping of provinces as the basis for India's constitutional future. Jinnah was offered the prospect of victory in the 'long slow game' he had played from such a weak hand. Here there was the means by which he could discipline the Muslim provinces and bring them into the Indian union on his terms. Jinnah was offered, as Jalal puts it, his 'Pakistan'. This was not, of course, how the Leaguers saw it; the Cabinet Mission did, after all, explicitly reject their Pakistan. Jinnah could only persuade them to accept the Mission's proposal if it was seen as a step towards their Pakistan and if there was the proviso that the League should join no interim government without parity with the Congress. At this point, 6 June 1946, Jinnah may well have come closest to winning his game. Within days, however, the prospect of victory began to fade. The Congress refused to enter an interim government based either on parity, or some version of it. The British refused to impose a settlement.

'The last thirteen months of British rule,' declares Jalal, 'saw the tragic collapse of Jinnah's strategy.' He strove desperately to salvage something from the wreckage but as the months passed he had less room for manocuvre. His followers demanded their Pakistan more and more vociferously; the outbreak of appalling communal rioting underlined their case and the need for settlement. The British wished to leave as soon as they could but were concerned to leave behind them a government strong enough to help to protect their interests in the Indian Ocean region. The Congress wished to take power as soon as possible and they, too, were concerned to take

over a strong centre from which they would be able to command
independent India. The common interest with the British, which
the League had shared during the war, had now shifted to the
Congress. At the same time, Jinnah was forced to face up to the
fundamental contradictions in his strategy. His Pakistan was
enshrined in the groupings of existing provinces proposed by the
Cabinet Mission; his two-nation theory was a weapon designed to
carve out for the League a share of power, an equal share if possible,
at the centre of an independent India. But, as the British searched
for ways to transfer power to a strong centre, and the Congress
sought ways of achieving one, the attractions of giving Jinnah what
he asked for, as opposed to what he really wanted, became
overwhelming. And so the two-nation theory came instead to be
the 'sword' which cut Jinnah's Pakistan down to size. The principle
of national self-determination which he had loudly asserted for the
previous seven years came to mean that India's great northwestern
and northeastern provinces of the Punjab and Bengal would be
partitioned according to the religions of their peoples. In the end
'it was Congress that insisted on partition. It was Jinnah who was
against partition.' Power was transferred to two centres. The Quaid
was left to savour the irony of becoming the idolized founder of a
state whose birth he had long fought to prevent.

What an extraordinary game of poker Jalal lays before our eyes!
How deftly Jinnah plays his weak hand over many years! How close
he comes to success! How tragic is his failure! By enabling us to
peep at Jinnah's cards and by pointing out to us the tricks he was
really trying in order to win, Jalal reveals the inner coherence of a
career spanning half a century in politics, and more particularly the
single-minded purpose which marks its last decade. Those paradoxes are now resolved. Jinnah never deserted his early attachment
to Hindu-Muslim unity; his strategy was designed to achieve some
form of it in the India of the future. There was no disjunction
between a secular ideal. There was no flagging in his zeal for a
united India; his Pakistan was never meant to divide it. In some
fine analytical set pieces, moreover, Jalal reveals the logic of Jinnah's
twists and turns in the complex negotiations surrounding the
transfer of power. We understand more fully the wording of the

Lahore resolution. We see how his plans were far more fundamentally threatened by the Cripps offer than those of Congress. We feel for him when the Cabinet Mission proposals tease out the contradictions between his rhetoric and his purpose. We perceive the continuing attempts to preserve his strategy in his many shifts and ploys from June 1946, when Congress refused to enter the interim government, down to his May 1947 demand for a corridor through Hindustan to connect the two halves of Pakistan, and his June 1947 proposal that the constituent assemblies of the two new states should both meet in Delhi.

It is hard to believe that this is a first book. A novel thesis is brilliantly sustained from beginning to end. The understanding of politics is mature, the exposition sophisticated, the tone almost unnervingly confident. The style may well jar on some: 'inwardness' is too favourite a word; the prose strains obtrusively for effect; there is that superior and knowing Cambridge air—'full-time worker (almost a contradiction in terms in the enervating climes of Bengal)', big Punjabi families knew 'when expediency demanded them to be turn-coats—an old Punjabi tradition, alive and well to this day'. Such aspects of voice and attitude, however, should not keep readers from a book which transforms the widely held understanding of the role of Jinnah in the making of Pakistan, and does so with a sureness of touch and a depth of scholarship that should quickly establish it both as the orthodox academic interpretation and its author as a scholar of unusual gifts. As a piece of historical revisionism, as an analysis of action in high politics, as a narrative of a dramatic moment when great men played for high stakes, it compares well with the best post-war work of its kind, for instance, Maurice Cowling's *1867 Disraeli, Gladstone and Revolution: The Passing of the Second Reform Bill* (Cambridge, 1967).

It should be understood, however, that this book ventures no more than a treatment of high politics. It concentrates on analysing Jinnah's political strategy and on explaining how Pakistan happened. It has no interest in Jinnah's relationship with his community except to assert that 'his use of the communal factor was a political tactic, not an ideological commitment'. It is not concerned to explain why growing numbers of Muslims should clamour for a Pakistan which many saw as some form of Islamic state. It is innocent of any serious investigation of Indo-Muslim political thought. When it comes to the Congress and the British we are told enough for the main thrust of the argument to make good sense, but no more. The image we are given of the Congress, for instance, is that it wanted the British to go quickly, to inherit a strong centre and to shut the League out; we are given no understanding of how the interactions of people, interests, ideas and events might have fashioned such policies. This limited focus of historical explanation has undoubtedly assisted lucid exposition of Jinnah's strategy, but by the same token it should be clear, as Jalal would be amongst the first to admit, that the full-scale epic of partition, the history of the interplay of men and forces which brought about the division of India, still has to be written. This is not to belittle Jalal's work, merely to give it context. Her achievement, moreover, must be rated favourably against that of Wolpert. She has enriched our understanding of Jinnah's role in one of the great events of the twentieth century; he has added, amid an interpretation of Jinnah's politics in which Jalal reveals we cannot have much faith, to our knowledge of the man. Five distinguished US academics pen puffs of fulsome praise on the jacket of Wolpert's book. Had Professors Keddie, Embree, Rahman, Furber and Palmer had the advantage of reading Jalal's book, they might have couched their comments in more Judicious terms.

One further observation is appropriate. Nearly two decades ago the late Jack Gallagher and Anil Seal planned a five-volume series devoted to the interplay of imperialism and nationalism in South Asia from the 1870s to the 1940s. The plan did not work out as intended; such grand plans rarely do. Nevertheless, we can now see a way in which Gallagher and Seal, together with some of their pupils, have brought this plan to a partial fruition. The process begins with Anil Seal's *Emergence of Indian Nationalism* (1968) and Gordon Johnson's *Provincial Politics and Indian Nationalism* (1973). It continues with Richard Gordon's 'Aspects of the History of the Indian National Congress with reference to the Swarajya Party' (sadly unpublished), Tom Tomlinson's *Indian National Congress and the Raj* (1976) and David Page's *Prelude to Partition* (1982). The imperial backcloth is sketched in Jack Gallagher's *Decline, Revival and Fall of the British Empire* (1982), and the process finds a conclusion of a kind in Ayesha Jalal's *Sole Spokesman*. In these seven works, although it should be said that the so-called Cambridge school has produced others which bear upon the theme, there is the history of that interplay of imperialism and nationalism with an emphasis on high politics from the foundation of the Congress to independence. There is also something more which looks towards the present. There is an analysis of the development and early working of India's multi-level political-system. With the publication of Jalal's book historians are nicely poised to study the further development of that system in the politics of India and Pakistan.

NOTES

1. The film was in part financed by the Government of India.
2. R.J. Moore, 'Jinnah and the Pakistan Demand', *Modern Asia Studies*, 17, 4 (1983), p. 535.
3. In a speech, apparently extempore, Jinnah's words were: 'any idea of a United India could never have worked and in my judgement it would have led us to terrific disaster. May be that view is correct; may be it is not; that remains to be seen.' Wolpert, *Jinnah*, p. 338.

7

Political Cohesion in Pakistan: Jinnah and the Ideological State

Alan Whaites

The issue of cohesion in several guises has dominated analyses of Pakistan since 1947. The ethnic, feudal and religious factors which have provided ammunition for political scientists for nearly fifty years ultimately revolve around the ability of a cohesive state to survive its myriad constituent parts. The dramatic social and economic changes which have taken place within the country since independence are moving this discussion onto another plain,[1] but the debate should not be seen as limited to the practical socio-political realities of modern Pakistan. The issue of cohesion is partly a question of the country's primordially heterogeneous context, and partly one of the ethos and ideology of the state itself. It is the cohesiveness of this latter element and recent challenges to Pakistan's ideological underpinnings which form the subject for this paper.

The ideological basis of the Pakistani state is a familiar subject matter for any of its school children. The state itself promulgates the idea of ideological roots which culminated in the Pakistan Movement. This is ideology in its simplest sense; a basic ideal and a choice of conscience rather than a state based upon geographic or ethnic features. The claim to be a product of theory rather than ethnicity or geography stems from Pakistan's foundation upon the personal decisions (through referendums and tribal councils) of its original citizens, some of whom (in Punjab and Bengal especially) placed the founding theory before ethnicity itself. While religion, another primordial element, was the key to this founding theory, the state was not based on an ideal of religious zealotry. The 'ideology' of Pakistan was not Islam itself, but rather the belief that Muslims and Hindus were intrinsically too different in culture and beliefs to allow the former to thrive as a minority within a state dominated by the latter.

This ideology of the 'Two Nation Theory' from its inception was more compelling as a determinant of 'external' relations for Muslims than it was for internal issues. Its immediate purpose was to offer an explanation of the position of Muslims vis-à-vis their Hindu neighbours. The question of intra-Muslim differences, particularly regarding ethnicity, was less clearly defined. Hence, the attempt to use the Two-Nation Theory as a continuing and substantive argument for a single Muslim state has seemed for some to hold little legitimacy in the wake of Pakistan splitting into the two states of Pakistan and Bangladesh in 1971. But, despite their apparent weaknesses, the ideological origins of the former remain a factor which colours its continuing life. As this paper will show, 1971 did not entirely end the relevance or controversy surrounding the Pakistan ideal. Indeed, academic discussion as to the real intentions of the Pakistan Movement, coupled with the publication of new sources such as *The Jinnah Papers*, are likely to continue to add fuel to the debate.

Ideological underpinning: motives and causes

The debate surrounding the ideological underpinnings of Pakistan has had two crucial elements. Firstly, the issue of the real motivation and intentions of the Muslim elite of those provinces in which Muslims were a minority (a question often phrased in the language of class-interest) and, secondly, the underlying cause for the rapid conversion of the Muslim elite of those provinces in which Muslims formed a majority to the cause of an independent Pakistan. The question of the real intention of those who called for Pakistan in 1940 was raised quickly after the Lahore Resolution was passed, causing doubts amongst the British and the Indian National Congress almost up to the eve of independence. Four years after the original demand for Pakistan, correspondence between Viceroy of India, Lord Wavell, and Governor of Bengal, Richard Casey, indicated a common belief that the idea of a 'Pakistan' state was no more than a bargaining counter.[2] The suggestion that the proposed state was a ruse to force concessions from the Congress has become increasingly popular.[3]

The suggestion that the elite of the 'Muslim minority provinces' acted from a selfish class-interest and pursued a deliberate policy of bluff is matched by doubts over the commitment of the majority provinces to the Pakistan ideal. The 'Muslim majority provinces' have been seen as less drawn to Pakistan by principle than pushed towards it by an anti-centralist fear. This article argues that the Two Nation Theory was a more powerful force in the minds of the Muslims of the minority provinces than were the elite interests which have been often ascribed to them. It goes on to use contemporary and more recent sources to suggest that by 1946-1947 the beliefs underpinning Pakistan had converged with the interests of the majority provinces to provide a genuine ideological commitment to Muslim, as opposed to local, self-government. Once exposed to the post-independence competition of other identities and loyalties, these centripetal forces have been often strained, although finally not broken.

Inevitably the focus of the Pakistan debate has been the period 1937-1945. The period after the watershed elections of 1937 witnessed a hardening in the position of the Muslim League (ML) and a fundamental change in its relations with the majority provinces. The changing nature of Muslim politics from 1937 onwards must be placed within the context of underlying Muslim perceptions. There is evidence to suggest that from the elites down to the village level these perceptions were increasingly ones of deep misgiving, whether well-founded or not, towards Congress. In the turbulent political world of pre-independence Indian politics, this realisation was still a long way from a coherent, united policy. For Jinnah, the task was to hold together a group which was unified in the call for Pakistan but divided by deep-set factional differences and the ambition of local politicians, a dichotomy that continues to fuel scholarly debate today.

The roots of communal politics

Some commentators believe communalism to be a product of modern politics. For them, India's colonial experience with its impact on communications and socio-economic structures, 'called for new ways of seeing one's common interest'.[4] Economic competition amongst the expanding middle-class led to short-termism, a concentration on economic opportunity, and a new correlation between communal and class divides: 'Above all, communalism developed as a weapon of economically and politically reactionary social classes and political forces'.[5] This view sees self-interest as the source of the growth in communal division, with group elites manipulating group symbols to facilitate the defence of their position and privileges.[6]

In marked contrast is the view of those, including Jinnah, who suggested that Muslim-Hindu tensions predated British rule. The debate over symbol manipulation has sometimes detracted from the issue of real, underlying community perceptions. Although theologically and ethnically diverse, all Indian Muslims with access to religious teaching would have heard at Friday prayers the principles (passed down from the earliest caliphates) of the unity and paramountcy of Islam.[7] This meant that, for many, Islam represented the primary means of self-definition. Some, such as Mohammad Ali, could separate their commitment to Islam and India,[8] but this was by no means the norm given the powerful belief structure which characterises Islam, determines Muslim social behaviour and substantially defines Muslim conceptual analysis.[9] If a sense of nationhood is integral to Islam,[10] then Muslims in both the Mughal and British periods had to come to terms with other groups within India as well as with the Muslim world.[11] Thus, the basis of the pre-independence communal divide in divergent culture and identity can be detected in earlier periods of South Asian politics. In the Mughal period, a pan-communal example is provided by the Emperor Akbar who sought to accommodate Islam to its majority environment through the building of alliances and the blurring of boundaries. But the difficulty of this position was symbolised by the backlash unleashed in the reign of Aurengzeb.[12]

Modern India also has underlined these tensions with its own
differences on the issue of how to analyse the Mughal period as
shown, for example, by the pre-independence slogan 'a thousand
years of foreign rule', differing views on Shivaji and, more recently,
the history textbook controversy of the late 1970s. All are reminders
of the belief of many Indians that Muslim rule was all alien rule
and indicate a rejection of the notion of pre-colonial communal
harmony.

The Muslim elite

In the period following Mughal rule, communal tensions were
reflected in a new environment, often with less obvious but still
equally real consequences. The arrival of an overseas colonial power
forced Indian Muslims to try to adjust to the loss of political power
which transformed them from historic conquerors into a potentially
marginalised minority. The impact of the conversion from symbolic
rulers to a minority was made greater by the belief of some leaders
that Muslims could not accept theologically the legitimacy of any
future majority Hindu government.[13] The response brought to the
fore figures such as Shah Waliullah who worked to rid Islam of its
Hindu accretions. Others, notably Sir Syed Ahmed Khan, sought
to reconcile Islam to the West by accommodating much of the
change the colonial period brought to India. Both movements were
very different expressions of a perceived need to re-assert Muslim
identity.[14]

Perhaps the most marked decline in social, economic and
political fortunes during the colonial period was that suffered by
the Muslims of the United Provinces (UP), a trend exacerbated by
the end of Urdu hegemony.[15] It is difficult to disentangle the extent
to which the development of Muslim politics was purely a response
to economic and political marginalisation on the part of a few,
rather than a product of more widely felt communal anxieties.
Despite these difficulties, the class-interest perspective as a blanket
explanation should not be taken too far. From a class-bound
position, the establishment of the Muslim College at Aligarh was

a tool in the defence of the interest of narrow and struggling social class. Yet, for Sir Syed, the Muslim elite was only one factor in the wider communal context and Aligarh meant much more than just a socio-economic fightback by a single class. Sir Syed's concerns, and those of the founders of new seminaries such as Nadwat al-'Ulama, were motivated by the feeling of a nation being in danger: 'Is it possible that ... two nations—the Mohammedan and Hindu—could sit on the same throne and remain equal in power?'[16]

Despite Sir Syed's articulation of a sense of division between Hinduism and Islam, it is realistic to assume that inevitably at least a few of those who followed the ML's banner were led by their assessment of personal self-interest and, as shown below, this was something which Jinnah clearly understood. Even so, by 1937, the elite of the minority provinces had potentially as much to lose as to gain from the call for Pakistan. From 1937 onwards, the communal debate reached a point where the elite leadership saw Pakistan in terms of the loss of Muslim political presence and leverage in the minority areas. Many, such as Liaquat Ali Khan, were to lose their fortunes with Partition. The loss of both property and human resources pointed to the lack of a Pakistani bourgeoisie at independence.[17] A further limit to the impact of elites is that such groups are constrained and influenced as much by group symbols as they are able to manipulate them.[18] Political culture is not a one-way street in which elites are able to mould mass opinion according to their own interests whilst remaining devoid of the sentiment and loyalties stirring their fellow group members. Elite families faced their own unique pressures from appeals to group identity and history. For many their own personal links with that history was likely to be more ascertainable and their families more imbued in the myths of their own pasts.

Equally, the Muslim elite, particularly that of the UP and minority provinces, could not be divorced from the long-standing tensions of communal life. Despite centuries of being specially proximate, the two communities had nevertheless retained a rigid distance.[19] As events unfolded after 1937, the attitudes of the Muslim elite will have been reinforced by the visible effects of conflict. Jinnah could not, for example, escape the conclusions of the communal violence in Bihar.[20] He himself presided over the relief fund established to assist its victims, and his personal correspondence shows a constant flow of letters and donations coming to his attention. Lower profile but more everyday acts against Muslims at the local level also were brought to Jinnah's attention by those who saw him as the natural recipient of complaints and pleas for assistance.[21] Such events must have had a profound effect, not only on Jinnah himself but also on those Muslim business leaders who in their efforts to be charitable may have gained an insight into the abuses suffered by poor Muslims.

Yet Muslim self-identity was more than simply a mask for class competition. Jinnah recognised and rejected the class element, and he himself was viewed with distaste by many amongst the traditional Muslim elite.[22] On his return from self-imposed exile and before the great upsurge in League membership, he commented that the ML was composed 'mostly of big landlords, title-holders and selfish people who looked to their class and personal interests more than to communal and national interests.'[23] During the years that followed, Jinnah and his own clique largely were to disempower those he saw as motivated by class. From his return onwards, the ML was to be driven by Jinnah's vision for all India's Muslims, serving national rather than elite needs. The class factor was simply a form of leverage to be used in the furtherance of this cause.

That Jinnah's own vision was based on communal identity rather than class and that this vision found its expression in the objective of Pakistan can be seen both in the substantive comments of his speeches and also in the changing nature of his concerns. Interestingly, after 1937, Jinnah's time was devoted less to cultural icons of the minority provinces, such as Aligarh, and more to issues affecting the potential for state-hood, such as Muslim banks and companies.[24] It has been suggested that his own decision to purchase property in India in 1945 cast doubt on his commitment to the goal of an independent Pakistan, while Jinnah's comments offer little support for this view. What can be assumed is that he had little premonition either of the speed with which independence would come or of the poor relations with India which would follow.

Jinnah did have a vision of the nature of the new Pakistan as a democratic and plural state. However, this view was premised on continuing close relations with India, with a border relationship akin to that today of Canada and the USA.[25] The bloodshed of Partition and the chaos of Kashmir were factors that lay in the distance. Nonetheless, it was not unreasonable of him to anticipate that independence itself would take place over a time-frame sufficient to ensure the preparation of the agencies of state. His belief in the need for such groundwork was demonstrated by the work of ML committee, the commissioning of a review of 'Pakistani' agriculture, and the establishment of the Federation of Muslim Chambers of Commerce.[26] It was typical of the predicament faced by Jinnah throughout this period that such groups had neither the resources nor the prestige sufficient to motivate and unite the competing and divided Muslim leadership of the majority areas.

Reacting to a Congress future

If elite interests were not the primary driving force behind the rise in communal politics then the underlying Muslim-Hindu tensions described earlier must be seen as a major contributory factor.

ML and Muslim opinion cannot be seen in isolation of wider political factors. Communal concerns sparked by the development of wider 'nationalist' politics, an area largely out of the control of the Muslim elite were very important. Most prominent amongst these was the development of Congress and the not unsurprising use of Hindu reference-points in the communication of the need for an independent India. Jinnah himself commented that India's Muslims and Hindus were inspired by different histories and one community's foes was the other's heroes.[27] Given the depth of cultural distance between the largely Hindu leadership of Congress and much of Muslim India, it is unsurprising that Congress itself during its long history sent ambiguous signals. To many Muslims, the formative nationalist agitation of B.G. Tilak, inspired by Hindu imagery and chauvinism foretold of an independent India ruled by Congress. Gandhi's own use of Hindu religious symbolism as a means to bridge the gulf between the organisation's Westernised elite and the Hindu masses appeared to be a powerful expression of Congress's roots.[28]

Despite its use of Hindu imagery, Congress remained keen to retain a cross-communal domination of Nationalist politics. Even the Khilafat Movement and its message of Muslim distinctiveness and unity was able to work under the Congress umbrella. Yet, although allied to Congress, the movement's powerful use of the symbolism of a pan-Islamic polity inevitably served to underline the divisions between Muslim and Hindu. The ability of Congress to retain considerable Muslim support into the late 1930s and, to a lesser extent, beyond was helped also by the initially poor organisational skills of the ML and its delay in pursuing a serious policy of expansion outside UP. Indeed, the history of the ML was often marked by its reactions to events rather than pro-active initiatives, a characteristic exacerbated by considerable internal division.

The application of Muslim political thought to the specific situation of Indian Muslims and their relations with their Hindu neighbours seemed a somewhat distant concern to the majority provinces within the context of third party rule: 'They did not feel so threatened by the Hindu and Sikh communities as did their brethren elsewhere in India'.[29] The watershed for Muslim politics and the Pakistan movement was the outcome of the 1937 elections. The impressive performance of Congress, coupled with the failure of the ML to capture significant popular Muslim support outside UP and Bengal, raised the prospect of Muslim marginalisation in Indian politics. The fear of Congress domination was given important psychological force by its refusal to enter into coalition with the ML in UP.[30] The majority provinces were now forced to take politics at the national level seriously, giving rise to a concern for a stronger voice at the centre.[31]

For the majority provinces, the recognition that they needed a spokesman in Delhi reflected genuine fears at the prospect of a

Congress-led India. This concern emanated less from an immediate understanding and acceptance of the Two Nation Theory (an issue which seemed minor where Muslims were a majority), than from a deep-seated distrust of the centre itself. Anti-centralism was not surprising in areas which in many ways (other than security) were touched lightly by the details of the British Raj. The late occupation of the north-west majority areas by the British and the relative isolation of eastern Bengal made the majority provinces wary of any centralised authority.

For some time it was a straight-forward 'anti-centralist' analysis of majority province motivation which dominated British thinking. Wavell himself believed local patriotism might overcome the Pakistan idea and, as late as August 1945, the viceroy's policy rested on Pakistan being a minority province issue. By autumn of the same year, however, the colonial administration began belatedly to realise the growing impact of Pakistan within the majority areas.[32] The key failing of British analysis was to lose sight of the conceptual change which the imminence of independence brought for many in the majority areas. It was the prospect of Congress power at the centre that enabled the majority provinces to think of themselves in minority terms on a national basis, a conceptual shift forced on minority province Muslims a century before.

The realisation of their 'relational' position to Hindu India was not something which the majority provinces were left to discover for themselves. Jinnah was central in communicating the Two-Nation Theory in a way which made it immediately relevant. The ML entered into a series of pragmatic and shifting relationships in its search for support in the majority provinces but was not inconsistent in its essential philosophy. The ideological mission of the ML was served by using provincial fears to assert implicitly that it was the fundamental separateness of Hindus and Muslims that created the anti-centralist feelings of the majority areas. The sensitivities of the provinces offer evidence that the possibility of central Congress rule touched a nerve in Muslim India which could be articulated using the medium of this narrow ideological agenda.

Jinnah's first priority was to take advantage of the fears held in the majority provinces to gain the credibility he and the ML needed for negotiations with the British and Congress. But it also necessitated a change in the ML's own emphasis; as its separatist ideology hardened so too did its political stance become more focused. Prior to 1937, the ML was to a large extent the vehicle for UP Muslims' concerns about ensuring guarantees for Muslims within a Hindu India. This was true to the extent that at the Round Table Conference of 1931-1932, Jinnah was prepared to negotiate away the principle of separate electorates so dear to the majority provinces.[33] Now, however, as the wider Muslim community sought to secure their 'national' future, the focus shifted as the interests of the majority provinces and the leadership of the ML converged on the idea of a separate, independent state for Indian Muslims. This convergence of views was to provide the underpinning to Jinnah's end-game strategy.

Pakistan as bluf?

The view that converging Muslim interests led to Jinnah embracing the logic of an independent Pakistan as the practical embodiment and culmination of the Two-Nation Theory in 1937 is rejected by those who argue that he never abandoned his primary aim of securing the future of the minority Muslims in a united India. Ayesha Jalal, for instance, argues that Jinnah used the idea of a separate Pakistan as bargaining ploy to 'avoid the logic of arithmetic'[34] and help establish the principle that Muslims had to be treated as a separate nation. For Jalal, Pakistan was not an ideological goal but a bluff which, in turn, not only failed but so matched the wishes of the majority provinces that eventually Jinnah's hands became tied.

Yet Jalal's argument rests on an area only tangentially explored in her work; that is, the genuineness of Jinnah's conversion to the Pakistan ideal after 1937. By taking Jinnah in isolation, she misses the fact that he was joined in his realisation of the need for an effective separation by lifelong Congressmen.[35] The forces which provoked the majority provinces to consider the communal issue similarly might have convinced Jinnah and others that the safeguards they sought could not be guaranteed in a Congress India. The shock of 1937, the intransigence of Congress, and the wider decline in communal relations offer some logic for taking Jinnah at close to face value. Jinnah's own actions and words point to an evolution in his own perceptions, as he moved from identifying himself as a demographic to a geographic leader.

While Jalal fails to accept the effect of the political environment on Jinnah's changing analysis, Akbar Ahmed seeks to go beyond the immediate pressures to suggest deeper, more personal changes in the ML leader's thinking.[36] For him, Jinnah's conversion to the idea of an independent Pakistan depended crucially on the influence of the poet Iqbal. Given the changing speeches and habits of his later life, it is highly plausible that Iqbal's influence led Jinnah to a deeper personal appreciation of Muslim identity.

End game

It is clear that Jinnah, like many of his colleagues, had envisaged Pakistan as comprising all of the provinces of Punjab and Bengal, particularly as this would provide Hindu and Sikh minorities to counter the Muslim minority in India. But the logic of Partition was self-determination for minorities and this meant a truncated Pakistan, whatever the objections of the peoples living in the affected regions.

> Undoubtedly large numbers of Muslims in both Punjab and Bengal had not in 1946 fully grasped the implications of Pakistan for their region. But they were not merely manipulating religion for their own purposes. There was widespread and sincere support for the Pakistan demand which went well beyond the privileged elite of Muslim voters in 1946.[37]

Efforts of ML workers combined with its fleeting hold on the provincial elites in the cause of communal solidarity meant that the momentum for Pakistan became unstoppable.[38] The mandate Muslims handed Jinnah in 1946 made it impossible for him to impede the progress towards the new state even if he had wished to.

The problem for Jinnah was that the chaos of majority province politics and his weak relationship with their governments limited his ability to plan adequately the future of Pakistan. He had no choice but to try and secure an agreement on some centralised functions, at least for a limited period, in the hope that this would lessen the burden of creating a new state from the chaos of a disorganised nation. Jinnah was also frustrated by the British. Muslim needs, in the run-up to Partition for a slow transition and a division of India overseen by a neutral and fair intermediary arguably were denied to him.[39] Jinnah's willingness to pursue the possibility of a limited federal arrangement to the end must be seen as a response to the mammoth problems of seeking immediate independence.

Strategy versus ideology

The pressures Jinnah faced in making the Two-Nation Theory fully understood by both minority and majority province Muslims and in uniting them behind the cause of Pakistan restricted the further development of the country's ideological underpinnings during their most crucial phase. Jinnah personally cannot be criticised for failing to articulate a vision of how a modern, Muslim state should be governed. As has been mentioned above, he did seek to initiate structures and also to outline broad principles, including democratic ideals, for Pakistan. The outlining of this vision was, however, often submerged by the constant work of defending Muslims interests at the centre whilst also mobilising support in the provinces.

Going beyond the issue of Muslim identity as an ideological premise in order to address fundamental issues of socio-political relationships in a Muslim context therefore became a sketchy process. A dependence solely on a sense of primordial unity at independence rather than a nuanced, shared vision created a potential for future social fissures.[40] The deepening of the Two-Nation Theory into a workable ideology to guide internal relations as well as those with the Hindu majority was therefore an essential strategic project which was neglected by the overstretched and overworked leaders of the ML in the last days of British rule. By 1947, the ideological legacy remained a small number of powerful speeches by Jinnah himself, but no fully articulated and binding framework for Pakistan's future.

Equally serious was the organisational weakness of the ML. For ideologies to retain momentum and cohesion, some form of institutional vehicle explicitly charged with achieving sufficient power to make the ideological beliefs real is usually created. The ML, however, was primarily a campaigning, organising force centred around a short term goal: Pakistan. This history made the movement susceptible to the temptation of trying to represent a diverse range of beliefs at the local level. The ML in Punjab almost certainly presented a very different picture of Pakistan to that offered by local activists in Bengal. Following independence, Jinnah did not consolidate the ML as a political force centred on his vision of a democratic, socially just Pakistan. Instead, the pressures of state institution-building led him to relinquish ML duties to concentrate on those of Governor-General.

Conclusion

The realities of pre-independence Muslim politics—particularly factional struggles at the provincial level coupled with the desire by the British to have a speedy transfer of power left Jinnah and the Muslims of India with an unenviable choice: a united India with no parity and a Congress constituent assembly, or a truncated Pakistan lacking any of the preparations which might be expected for a newly independent state. The decision to opt for Pakistan was the culmination of the growth in conviction from 1937 to 1947 that Partition was the best safeguard for the Muslim nation of India. The evidence that Muslim politics were ever an expression of purely 'class' concerns is arguable at best. But from 1937 onwards, there is little to suggest that the ML and its leadership were thinking in anything other than communal terms. Indeed, the evidence would suggest that, for many, the Two-Nation Theory had become a powerful conceptual force given weight by the articulation and vision of Jinnah.

The key to the process which transformed Pakistan from an extremist student ideal to a popular demand lies firstly in the more developed fears of many minority province Muslims. Those who gathered around Jinnah did not represent the totality of minority province views, but they did encompass a large number who were caught by Jinnah's idealistic vision. Secondly, the transformation was a product of the shift in conceptual thinking by those in the majority provinces. Jinnah realised before they did the importance of Pakistan (within or without a federal all-India structure), but he also saw that it was the natural corollary of the provinces' own demands for freedom from a Congress/Hindu centre. However, his precarious position in relation to figures such as Khuhro, Hidayatullah, Suhrawardy, Nazimuddin, Sikander and Daultana left him unable to translate their common concerns into firm proposals. Jinnah's great victory was in capitalising on the events after 1937 to overcome the factional feuds long enough to secure an independent future for the majority of Muslim Indians.

NOTES

1. Alan Whaites, 'The state and civil Society in Pakistan', *Contemporary South Asia*, Vol. 4, No. 3, November 1995, pp. 229-254.
2. See the letters: 'Richard Casey to Lord Wavell, 17/12/44'; and 'Lord Wavell to Casey, 1/1/45', in Z.H. Zaidi, *The Jinnah Papers (Volume 1, Part 2)* (Islamabad: National Archives of Pakistan, 1993), pp. 489-493.
3. See, for instance, Ayesha Jalal, *The Sole Spokesman* (Cambridge: Cambridge University Press, 1983).
4. Bipan Chandra *et al.*, *India's Struggle for Independence* (New Delhi: Penguin 1989), p. 402.
5. *Ibid.*, p. 407.
6. See, for instance, Paul Brass, 'Elite groups: symbol manipulation and ethnic identity among the Muslims of South Asia', in D. Taylor and M. Yapp, *Political Identity in South Asia* (London: Curzon Press, 1979).

7. Andrew Rippin, *Muslims, Their Religious Beliefs and Practices, Volume 1: The Formative Period* (London: Routledge, 1990), pp. 56-73.
8. Richard Symonds, *The Making of Pakistan* (London: Faber and Faber, 1950), p. 43.
9. Judith M. Brown, *Modern India: The Origins of an Asian Democracy* (Oxford: Oxford Umversity Press, 1991) p. 28.
10. Francis Robinson, 'Islam and Muslim separatism', in Taylor and Yapp, *op. cit.*, Ref 6, pp. 78-107.
11. Peter Hardy, *Partners in Freedom and True Muslims* (Lund: Studentlitteratur, 1971), p. 24.
12. The position of the two rulers is contrasted in Akbar S. Ahmed, *Pakistan Society* (New Delhi: Oxford University Press, 1988), pp. 5-14.
13. See Robinson, *op. cit.*, Ref 10, p. 87; and Brown, *op. cit.*, Ref 9, p. 29.
14. See also Akbar S. Ahmed, *Jinnah, Pakistan and Islamic Identity: The Search for Saladin* (London: Routledge, 1997), pp. 41-56.
15. Symonds, *op. cit.*, Ref 8, p. 26.
16. *Ibid.*, p. 31.
17. Hamza Alavi, 'Formation of the social structure of South Asia under the impact of colonialism', in Hamza Alavi and John Harriss *et al.*, *South Asia* (London: Macmillan, 1989), p. 18.
18. Robinson, *op. cit.*, Ref 10, p. 81.
19. Brown, *op. cit.*, Ref 9, p. 28.
20. 'Bihar Report ', *The Jinnah Papers, op. cit.*, Ref 2, pp. 45-64.
21. See, for instance, a letter of 20 February 1947 discussing events at Mehark Taluka. *The Jinnah Papers, op. cit.*, Ref 2, p. 8.
22. Ahmed, *op. cit.*, Ref 14, p. 64.
23. As quoted in Brown, *op. cit.*, Ref 9, p. 303.
24. See *The Jinnah Papers (Volume 1, Part 1), op. cit.*, Ref 2, pp. 22-57, 393; and *Volume II*, p. xxxviii.

8

Between Myth and History
Ayesha Jalal

Pakistan's impeccable record in commemorating the landmarks in its national struggle has not always been matched by an ability to coherently explain their historical significance. Sixty-five years since its adoption by the All-India Muslim League, the Lahore Resolution remains mired in contentious debates among historians of South Asia as well as the protagonists of provincial versus central rights in Pakistan.

Not surprisingly, most Pakistanis are no nearer understanding how the would-be *magna carta* of their territorial statehood relates to their citizenship rights, far less squares the circle of the multiple conceptions of nationhood articulated by Muslims in the pre-independence period.

The Resolution's claim that Indian Muslims were not a minority but a nation was raised on behalf of all the Muslims of the subcontinent. Yet the territorial contours of the newly created homeland for India's Muslims in 1947 left almost as many Muslim non-citizens outside as there were Muslim citizens within. Even after the creation of Bangladesh in 1971 administered a rude shock to the official narratives of national identity, the contradiction between claims of nationhood and the achievement of statehood was never addressed, far less resolved. The silence has been a major stumbling block in Pakistan's quest for an identity which is consistent with the appeal of Islamic universalism as well as the requirements of territorial nationalism.

Instead of treating the Lahore Resolution as an issue of metahistorical significance, an analytically nuanced history of the circumstances surrounding its passage can make for a stronger and more coherent sense of national identity. Discussions about the historical significance of the Resolution have concentrated more on the political implications of the transformation of the Muslim minority community in India into a 'nation' rather than on the ambiguities surrounding the demand for Muslim 'statehood'.

A close analysis of the historical content and actual content of the Resolution, however, suggests that there was no neat progression from an assertion of Muslim nationhood to the winning of separate statehood. My book *The Sole Spokesman: Jinnah, the Muslim League and the Demand of Pakistan* (Cambridge, 1985) delineated the uneasy fit between the claim of Muslim 'nationhood' and the uncertainties and indeterminacies of politics in the late colonial era that led to the attainment of sovereign 'statehood'. Instead of grasping the salience of the argument, some historians and publicists on both sides of the 1947 divide have interpreted this as implying that the demand for a Pakistan was a mere 'bargaining counter'. In so far as politics is the art of he possible, bargaining is an intrinsic part of that art. To suggest, as some have glibly done, that Mohammed Ali Jinnah used Pakistan as a mere ruse against the Congress is a gross distortion of not only my argument but of the actual history.

My argument in *The Sole Spokesman,* and one that I confirmed in *Self and Sovereignty: Individual and Community in South Asian Islam since 1850s* (Routledge, 2000), was that while the insistence on national status of Indian Muslims became a non-negotiable issue after 1940, the demand for a wholly separate and sovereign state of 'Pakistan' remained open to negotiation as late as the summer of 1946. A refusal to acknowledge this is a result of the failure to draw an analytical distinction between 'nation' and 'state'. More problematic has been a flawed historical methodology that takes the fact of partition as the point of departure for interpreting the historical evolution of the demand for a 'Pakistan'.

The historical backdrop of the Lahore Resolution makes plain why a claim to nationhood did not necessarily mean a complete severance of ties with the rest of India. Beginning with Mohammad Iqbal's presidential address to the All-India Muslim League at

Allahabad in December 1930, a succession of Muslims put forward imaginative schemes in the 1930s about how power might be shared between religiously enumerated 'majorities' and 'minorities' in an independent India.

In staking a claim for a share of power for Muslims on grounds of cultural difference, these schemes in their different ways challenged Congress's right to indivisible sovereignty without rejecting any sort of identification with India. Describing India as 'the greatest Muslim country in the world', Iqbal called for the establishment of a Muslim state in north-western India which would remain part of the subcontinental whole.

If even Iqbal was thinking in terms of an all-India whole, outright secession was simply not an option for Muslims hailing from provinces where they were in a minority. Virtually all the schemes put forward by Muslims living in minority provinces considered themselves as 'a nation in minority' that was part of 'a larger nation inhabiting Pakistan and Bengal'. If Muslims in Hindustan were seen as belonging to a larger nation in north-western India, religious minorities in 'Pakistan' and Bengal were expected to derive security from sharing a common nationality with co-religionists dominating the non-Muslim state.

For the notion of reciprocal safeguards to work, Muslims and non-Muslim had to remain part of a larger Indian whole, albeit one that was to be dramatically reconceptualized in form and substance by practically independent self-governing parts. Even schemes with secessionist overtones, most notably that of Chaudhry Rahmat Ali, wanted to carve out half a dozen Muslim states in India and consolidate them into a 'Pakistan Commonwealth of Nations.'

What all these schemes led to was the claim that Muslims constituted a nation which could not be subjugated to a Hindu majority represented by the Congress. Taking this a its point of departure and avoiding mention of 'Partition' or 'Pakistan', the League's draft resolution called for the grouping of the Muslim-majority provinces in northwestern and northeastern India into 'Independent States' in which the constituent unites would be 'autonomous and sovereign'.

There was no reference to a centre even though the fourth paragraph spoke of 'the constitution' to safeguard the interests of both sets of minorities, Muslim and non-Muslim. The claim that Muslims constituted a 'nation' was perfectly compatible with a federal or confederal state structure covering the whole of India. With 'nations' straddling states, the boundaries between states had to be permeable and flexible. This is why years after the adoption of the resolutions, Jinnah and the League remained implacably opposed to the division of the Punjab and Bengal along religious lines.

Historians and publicists in India have seized on the contradiction in the demand for a Pakistan based on the Muslim right of self-determination and the apparent unwillingness to grant the same right to non-Muslims living in Punjab and Bengal. Much like their counterparts in Pakistan, they have conveniently glossed over the difference between a purely secessionist demand and one aimed at providing the building block for an equitable power sharing arrangement at the subcontinental level between two essentially sovereign states—'Pakistan based on the Muslim-majority provinces and Hindustan based on the Hindu-majority provinces.

With their singular focus on a monolithic and indivisible concept of sovereignty borrowed from the erstwhile colonial rulers, scholars and students of history on both sides of the 1947 divide have been unable to envisage a political arrangement based on a measure of shared sovereignty which might have satisfied the demands of 'majorities' as well as safeguarded the interests of religious minorities in predominantly Muslim and Hindu areas.

In 1944 and then again at the time of the Cabinet Mission Plan, the All-India Muslim League at the behest of Mohammad Ali Jinnah refused to accept a 'Pakistan' based on the division of the Punjab and Bengal. It was Congress's unwillingness to countenance an equitable power sharing arrangement with the Muslim League which resulted in the creation of a sovereign Pakistan based on the partition of Punjab and Bengal along ostensibly religious lines.

Cast against its will in the role of a state seceding from a hostile Indian union, Pakistan has tried securing its independent existence by espousing an ideology of Muslim 'nationhood' over the provincial rights promised in the Lahore Resolution and dispensing with democracy for the better part of its history. It is no wonder that the claims of Muslim nationhood have been so poorly served by the achievement of territorial statehood.

Such historical insights may not appeal to the authors of the contending narratives of a Pakistani or an Indian identity. But even national myths require some resemblance to history. Charting a linear course to the winning of Muslim statehood cannot even begin to grasp the vexed nature of the problems which faced a geographically dispersed and heterogeneous community in its bid to be considered a 'nation'.

Nor can it explain why there are more subcontinental Muslims living outside Pakistan, the much vaunted Muslim homeland, in India and Bangladesh. Instead of being weighted under by opposing national reconstruction informed by the teleology of 1947, Pakistanis and Indians could craft a more accommodative future for the subcontinent by acknowledging the domain of political contingency, containing possibilities for different outcomes, that lay between the adoption of the Lahore Resolution and partition seven years later.

9

Jinnah and his 'Right Hand', Liaquat Ali Khan

Roger D. Long

Mohammad Ali Jinnah (1876-1948), the *Quaid-i-Azam* (Great Leader) and Liaquat Ali Khan (1895-1951), the *Quaid-i-Millat* (Leader of the People) were men of very different temperaments and character but they forged a close political relationship of historic proportions.[1] Jinnah was a thin, emaciated figure who gave the impression of being austere and remote. Liaquat was a portly figure with a smile always hovering on his face. Political negotiations with Jinnah could be a daunting, even frustrating, experience although a number of people have commented on his more agreeable, but rarely publicly-shown side. An exchange with Liaquat was usually an amicable and agreeable affair with laughter and jokes and wide-ranging discussion on a variety of topics as the Viceroy, Lord Wavell recorded in several entries in his diary,[2] but political opponents commented on his political skills; behind that smiling face there was the experience of a seasoned and hardened politician who had enjoyed a number of political victories as well as weathered his share of defeats. Jinnah was aloof and had developed a severe style of presentation in the law courts of India and London. Both Jinnah and Liaquat, either through temperament or training, probably both, had a legalistic turn of mind, although Jinnah was more authoritarian. In his meetings as President of the All-India Muslim League and later as the Governor-General of Pakistan he would ask for opinions and then announce his decision. Liaquat's meetings as General-Secretary of the All-India Muslim League and later as Prime Minister of Pakistan were more collegial with more open discussion. If there were any criticisms of Jinnah it was that he was too peremptory. For Liaquat it was that he was not decisive enough.[3] Both characterizations are only one side of the picture. Jinnah was the solitary leader who walked alone, or sometimes with his sister, Fatima, and after 1937 increasingly a charismatic figure distant at the top of his party, but he became highly respected by such diverse figures as the poet and philosopher Iqbal in the Punjab, the landowner Mahmudabad in the United Provinces, and the Calcutta businessman M.A.H. Ispahani.[5] Jinnah also became a highly respected and even beloved figure to millions of Muslims in the 1940s. Liaquat was the organization man, one step behind the leader but always in the picture, and at the center of activity as all the AIML committees revolved around him. Before his death, Liaquat too had become a powerful and charismatic leader. Both men were totally honest and incorruptable.

Jinnah devoted his life to politics and the service of the Muslim commnity, his law practice, and, until the end of his life, he exhibited a keen interest in his investments. Liaquat, in addition to politics and service to the Muslim community was also active in local community affairs, and he was intimately involved in educational institutions, especially in Muzaffarnagar, at Aligarh Muslim University, and at the Anglo-Oriental College in Delhi. He also loved 'gadgets of all kinds',[5] tinkered with cars, collected cigarette lighters, and loved to take photographs, owning several cameras.[6] In group photographs of All-India Muslim League meetings Jinnah can often be seen looking away from the camera or seemingly indifferent; Liaquat is always aware of the camera and looking at the lens, sometimes he is endearingly leaning forward to make sure he is in the picture. The manner in which he is focusing on the camera, it is clear he is following the whole process of taking the photograph with more than an academic interest. While he was prime minister of Pakistan, there are several photographs of Liaquat taking pictures or with a camera in his hands looking very relaxed and comfortable.[7] Liaquat was also fond of music. As a child he took music lessons. When he returned from England his mother found him to be passionately fond of music and politics.[8] As prime minister he could be induced to play the drums at diplomatic parties.

Jinnah's family was Shi'ite Khoja who had settled in Gujarat and his first language was Gujarati.[9] His father moved to Karachi and he became a prosperous businessman. Jinnah, who was the eldest of seven brothers and sisters, was educated at home by a private tutor, although he did not evince much interest in his studies. He moved to Bombay for a few months with his aunt and went to school there but returned to Karachi and was enrolled at the Sind Madressa-tul-Islam in 1887 and then, for a few months, the Christian Mission School. Jinnah was offered an apprenticeship in an office in London but his mother insisted he get married before he left. Thus, at sixteen years of age he was married to fourteen-year old Emibai before sailing for London. She died while he was in London. He arrived in February 1893 but in April joined Lincoln's Inn to study the law. In England he absorbed the liberal values he would never abandon. He petitioned Lincoln's Inn to be called to the Bar on 11 May 1896. and in July left for Bombay to begin his law practice.

Liaquat was from a nawabi family. The family, the Mandal clan, was, according to one source, although there are different versions of family history, descended from the Persian ruler Nausherwan the Just and migrated to India in the fifteenth century and served in the Mughal administration as *panchhazaris*.[10] In 1806 they had lands on both sides of the River Jumna in Karnal in the Punjab and Muzaffarnagar, Shoran, and Chitral in the United Provinces. Liaquat's family had settled in Karnal and the Nawab built a spacious *haveli* (mansion), 'Nawab Kothi' which stood near the Nawab Gate along the city wall. The family fortunes fluctuated in the nineteenth century but improved after 1857 when the Nawab sided with the British during the Mutiny of 1857. Liaquat was raised in Karnal in a spacious house near Qalandar Gate in an extended family with his grandmother, his mother and father and several half-brothers and sisters and one younger brother, and his uncle and his children.

He was educated at home and received lessons in the *Qu'ran* and *Hadith*. His mother recalled that he was a quiet boy but amiable and warm-hearted and had a great capacity for mimicking and imitating the voices of others. He took singing lessons and was also fond of dancing and theatrics. In a trait he shared with Jinnah, he also had a love of fine clothers. A graduate of Sir Saiyid Ahmed Khan's Muhammadan Anglo-Oriental College,[11] Chaudhuri Ghulam Sabir Khan, had been employed to run the *Haveli* school and he found Liaquat to be a better pupil than his younger brother and elder half-brother, the future Nawab of Karnal, Sajjad Ali Khan. For his part Liaquat was determined to go to Aligarh much against his father's wishes who believed that a nawab should not be educated at a public institution, but Liaquat was supported by his uncle, and on 15 February 1910 at the age of fourteen Liaquat, accompanied by Sabir Khan, was admitted to Aligarh. Liaquat did well at school and was a monitor of his hostel, English House, and became a cricket captain. He received a double promotion one year. After matriculating from the school he entered the college and moved into a private bungalow remaining aloof and with few friends, but he continued to sing and to play the harmonium. At Aligarh he picked up the habit of smoking and, like Jinnah, became a heavy smoker, even a chain smoker. He graduated from M.A.O in 1918 the same year his father died leaving Liaquat a rich inheritance. He married his cousin whom he had been raised with, Jehangira Begum, and they had one son who became known as Wilayat, from whom Liaquat became estranged in the 1930s. In the autumn of 1919 he was in England and on 27 October 1919 he enrolled as a member of the Society of the Inner Temple in London. In January 1920, he entered Oxford University and the following year he became a member of Exeter College. On 4 August 1921, he was awarded the Bachelor of Arts in the Shortened School of Jurisprudence and five months later, on 26 January 1922, he was called to the Bar by the Inner Temple. He returned to India toward the end of the year having travelled in Europe in the meantime. He returned to India a well-educated and well-travelled twenty-seven year old with his horizons broadened considerably. He enrolled in the Punjab High Court in Lahore but never practiced law.

In the five years after Jinnah enrolled at Bombay's high court on 24 August 1896 Jinnah's legal career, including a six-month stint as a municipal judge, took off and prospered.[12] He worked shoulder to shoulder with Hindus, Parsis, and Christians as well as Muslims but at this time joined the Isna Ashari sect of the Twelver Khojas. In 1904 Jinnah entered the political arena when he attended the annual session of the Indian National Congress in Bombay and he would attend many of the annual sessions of the Congress. In 1910 he was elected to the Legislative Council of India from Bombay for a Muslim seat, three years before he joined the Muslim League. He would remain a member of the Council, later Assembly, for most of the next thirty-seven years. Throughout that period he would maintain his liberal views and defend the interests of the Muslim community without prejudice to the rights of any other group. He was a staunch nationalist who demanded that India be independent. In 1916 he reached the pinnacle of his fame as a leader committed to Hindu-Muslim unity when he became renowned for the Lucknow Pact and was dubbed the 'Ambassador of Hindu-Muslim Unity'.[13]

After a brief unsatisfactory involvement with local politics in the Karnal Municipality, Liaquat ran for national office in 1923 by standing for election to the Legislative Assembly of India. This was the same year he joned the Muslim League. Liaquat's father attended the 1908 Annual Meeting of the League at Amritsar and his uncle, Daraz, attended the 1910 Annual Meeting, held at Delhi.[14] Liaquat ran for the Muhammadan constituency of East Punjab but lost the election. If he had won the election he would have been associated with the Punjab rather than with the United Provinces which was the case because three years later he stood as an independent for the Legislative Council for the UP from Muzaffarnagar and was elected. He remained in the Legislative Council for the next ten years. He would forever be associated with UP politics but he maintained his home in Karnal, as well as a fine home in Muzaffarnagar, his son was raised in Karnal with his wife, and he maintained his base at Karnal until he moved to Delhi in 1936. He was 'very much a Punjabi.'[15] In the UP Legislative Council Liaquat was associated with the cross-communal agricultural party based in Muzaffarnagar, the United Province Zamindars Association, Muzaffarnagar.[16] In the Council, however, he founded his own cross-communal political party, the Democratic Party, one of a number of small political parties created in the Council which was largely organised on factional rather than party lines although, in addition to communal interests, there was also a rural-urban divide. In the Council he defended landowner interests as he believed that a stable rural society was essential to the well-being of the state and he supported many liberal causes. Thus, like Jinnah, Liaquat's first experience of politics was as a non-communal politician, one who did not associate exclusively with defending Muslim interests although he was also a strong and vociferous spokesman for Muslims and Muslim institutions. In 1931, Liaquat was elected the Deputy President of the Legislative Council. This required him to chair the Council in the absence of the President. It meant that he had to be acceptable to all communities, interests, and parties in the Council. It is a measure of his stature in the UP that he was elected to this post. He was a staunch nationalist believing that India should be free, sooner rather than later, and he was also a strong believer in a non-communal approach to politics although it is in 1928 that Liaquat first appears in All-India Muslim League affairs when he sided with Jinnah over the issue of boycotting the Simon Comission and on the issue of separate electorates. He was one of the twenty-one League delegates, headed by Jinnah, to the All-Parties Convention.[17]

Jinnah had become the lawyer and friend of the Parsi Sir Dinshaw Petit and spent time at his house. There he met his daughter Ruttenbai, 'Ruttie'. Against her father's wishes they were married on 19 April 1918 when she turned eighteen years of age at Jinnah's magnificent house on Mount Pleasant Road atop Malabar Hill in Bombay after she had converted to Islam. She was twenty-four years younger than Jinnah. Their only child, a daughter, Dina, was born the following year on 15 August while they were in London. The marriage was a happy one at first but the difference in age and temperament and Jinnah's dedication to his growing law practice led to estrangement and separation early in 1928. Jinnah blamed the difference in age and personality for the failure of the marriage. On 20 February 1929 she died. Jinnah's sister, Fatima, an unmarried woman, eventually became the surrogate mother of ten-year old Dina and Jinnah's consort. When Dina married a Parsi Jinnah became estranged from his daughter.

Liaquat, too, became estranged from his wife and cousin and while he did not divorce her until the late 1930s, he married a second wife who, like Ruttie, was not born a Muslim but converted to Islam upon marriage. This was Sheila Irene Pant of the United Provinces, a Christian, and a remarkable and energetic woman who became known as Ra'ana Liaquat Ali Khan.[18] She was an educationist, created the All Pakistan Women's Association, and became Pakistan ambassador to the Netherlands and Italy. In 1978 in New York she received the United Nations Human Rights Prize. She, like Ruttie, was a modern woman but she was also highly educated in a formal sense. Liaquat met her in the late 1920s but they did not marry until 1933. After they built a magnificent house in Delhi at 10 Hardinge Avenue it became the venue of a very large number of League events hosted by Liaquat and his wife. They had two sons, Ashraf, born in 1937, and Akbar, born in 1941. Liaquat and his wife were extremely close and he wrote to her constantly on his frequent trips outside of Delhi on League business and he doted on his youngest sons. The house in Delhi was bequeathed to Pakistan and is now the official home of the Pakistan High Commissioner to India.

There were several crises in Jinnah's career that dramatically changed his political fortunes and were indicative of the way the Indian nationalist movement was being shaped by communal forces and the Indian National Congress. The first crisis was in 1919 with the ascendancy of Gandhi in the Congress and his determination to indigenize the nationalist movement which, in practice, meant to Hinduize it.[19] For Gandhi, simply replacing British officials with Indian ones, but keeping the same economic and political system, would merely perpetuate Western domination and Western values. For Jinnah, bringing religion into politics would make it difficult, if not impossible, to present a united nationalist front against imperial rule, which was the only way, he believed, that the British could be pressured to grant more freedoms and even force them to depart India. The second crisis was in 1928 with the Nehru Report. Various political groups had come together in a spirit of opposition to the all-British Simon Commission to write a constitution for India. Jinnah was not part of the committee that created the draft constitution but he attended the All-Parties Convention in Calcutta which considered the report. Jinnah, among other things, wanted one-third of the seats in the central legislature to be reserved for Muslims. He was violently opposed by M.R. Jayakar of the Hindu Mahasabha and overwhelmingly outvoted. For Jinnah, this was the 'parting of the ways'. In response Jinnah produced his own constitution for India, the Fourteen Points, but this, too, met with opposition.

Both Jinnah and Liaquat were involved with the Round Table Conference in London and their paths crossed again in London in 1933. Jinnah was invited to attend the First Round Table Conference in late 1930 as one of sixteen Muslim representatives.[20] During the conference he began to argue that the Muslims were a separate party from the Hindus. Gandhi dominated the Second Round Table Conference and Jinnah was not invited to the Third. Until December 1934 Jinnah retired from Indian politics and lived in London with his sister and daughter and tried to recover from the death of his wife. These were his years in the political wilderness. He took chambers in the Inner Temple and practiced before the Privy Council. Liaquat attended the Indian Statutory Commission which came out of the Conference. He argued that the representation of the landlords should be maintained under the new constitution. As he had argued in the UP Legislative Council, a stable rural society, he believed, was essential for the well-being of everyone in the state. The most important consequence of the trip, however, was that it was a delayed honeymoon trip for Liaquat and his new wife and together they met Jinnah at a social function in London and he invited them to visit him at his house in Hampstead, north London. Liaquat urged Jinnah to return to lead the Muslims of South Asia. His plea, as well as that of others, plus the fact that Jinnah was unsatisfied with his law practice in England and his failure to be accepted as a candidate for the British parliament, and the political opportunites provided by the working of the new constitution, the Government of India Act of 1935, convinced Jinnah to end his period of exile and sail back to India in December 1934. In 1936 he asked Liaquat to become the General Secretary of the All-India Muslim League and this began what was to become a very close relationship.

The working of the new constitution created the third crisis for Jinnah and led to his complete alienation from the Indian National Congress and its leadership. It was also a crisis that affected Liaquat directly and many other Muslim politicians. General elections were held in 1936 with the result that the Congress took office in most of the British provinces of India, most crucially in the United Provinces, considered to be the heartland of Islam in South Asia. Congress was not expected to win the elections by such a large margin in the UP and accordingly planned to include one-third of the representatives in the UP cabinet, two out of six, from the League. The League in the UP, headed by Chaudhury Khaliquzzaman and Ismail Khan, expected to be the two cabinet ministers.[21] However, the Congress triumph made any cooperation with the League or any other party superfluous. Congress did live up to its bargain of including two Muslims in the cabinet, headed by Govind Ballabh Pant, a relative of Liaquat's wife, but they were not from the Muslim League and they had to accept Congress Party discipline. This was tantamount to the liquidiation of the party and was felt to be a betrayal of Muslims and Muslim interests. Congress was triumphant and taking a hard stance in the UP.

Between May and October Liaquat had been absent from India as a member of the Indo-British Trade Commission which was negotiating a new trade agreement between Britain and India. When he returned in October 1937 he found his political positon to have collapsed. The political situation in the United Provinces had become communalised with the Congress increasingly seen as representing Hindu interests and harmful to Muslim institutions. Those politicians, including Liaquat, experienced the same thing that Jinnah experienced in 1919 as Gandhi Hinduized the Indian National Congress. As Jinnah felt himself increasingly isolated and marginalised in the 1920s so too did Liaquat and a younger generation of Muslim politicians in the late 1930s. Liaquat, for the first time, identified exclusively with the Muslim League and joined the League benches in the UP Legislative Assembly. He had been elected to the Assembly as an independent in the general elections in 1937.

Jinnah and Liaquat became closer when he joined him on the Muslim League benches in the Legislative Assembly in 1941, having been elected unopposed on 24 March, and Jinnah appointed him his Deputy Leader of the Assembly League party. Liaquat was closely involved in all the League's activities after 1938 including the creation of *Dawn* newspaper, begun as a weekly in 1941 and a daily in 1942. Such was the close political alliance between the two and the personal relationship that developed, that in 1943, Jinnah publicly called him 'my right hand'. Liaquat, for his part, was also involved in the successful campaign to bring the faculty and students of Aligarh Muslim University behind the League and the demand for Pakistan. Jinnah asked Liaquat to accompany him to the Simla conferences and in 1946 he appointed him, as one of the League representatives, the Finance Member of the Indian government. Liaquat also accompanied Jinnah to London in 1946 for negotiations with the British government. In 1947 Jinnah asked Liaquat to become the Prime Minister of Pakistan.

After Jinnah's death on 11 September 1948 Liaquat remained devoted to Jinnah's memory. He sought a biographer who would write an authoritative life. At first Liaquat wanted Beverly Nichols to write the biography but when he declined he turned, or was referred to, Hector Bolitho, a New Zealander who was a well-known literary figure and biographer. Bolitho was looking forward to talking with Liaquat about Jinnah but Liaquat was assassinated before Bolitho visited Pakistan. Undoubtedly his book would have been enriched by insights Liaquat could have provided. Nonetheless, Bolitho's book is a major contribution to our knowledge of Jinnah's early life. In addition to his travels in Pakistan for interviews with people who knew Jinnah, Bolitho also travelled to India and was able to record details about his life in Bombay that would have been lost without his intervention. He also travelled to Leeds to try and find details about Jinnah's attempt to become a Labour Party Member of Parliament but he was unsuccessful. Bolitho often met with opposition from people in Pakistan as he recorded in the journal and notebook he kept of his research in India and Pakistan. Some resented a foreigner writing this account of the founder of the nation. He was often frustrated with this lack of cooperation although he was warmly welcomed by Liaquat's wife, Ra'ana, who gave him every cooperation she could.[22] Bolitho's account of Jinnah's early life has never been expanded and even Wolpert, in the best single 'life' available on Jinnah, relied on Bolitho for leads and for much of his information in the early chapters of the book. It is highly regrettable that Liaquat was unable to be intereviewed for his views and recollections of Jinnah, for Jinnah never had a more devoted follower nor one, apart from his sister, Fatima, who observed him closer over a considerable period of time and was closeted with him for such a long period, but Liaquat's wife did leave behind an account of Jinnah as she saw him. She must have formed her opinion of him both from personal observations and discussions with Liaquat. This is also hinted at in the discrete correspondence between Liaquat and his wife. She recorded her memory of him in an undated memo:

He was a man of high principles and there was no bluff in him. He had nothing in common with the masses and yet they acknowledged him as their leader and followed him…Mr Jinnah was reserved and aloof and gave the impression of being haughty and conceited, but once you got to know him he was human. He could sit for hours and relate amusing tales of his high school and college days…He knew the value of money since he had earned every penny of it. He spent generously on his clothers, carpets, furniture, etc. but refused to subscribe to any funds—a peculiar trait indeed!…He was not given to entertaining and was not very social at parties, but whenever we invited him, he let himself go and got into the spirit of the function—he even cracked jokes with the guests. All by himself he was human—but that wasn't very often!…His eyes were sharp and searching and only the honest could look him straight in the eye or even to attempt to argue with him…He was a dictator to the fingertips—dare anyone disagree with him…He was very secretive and suspicious and hence could not make many friends…He was very English in his manner and way of living. Breakfast meant marmalade!…He was very fond of an oriental fruit called guava—he swore that it purified the blood! Whenever he stayed with us, I made it a point of having guavas in the house...He didn't know much about food and often what he termed good, I thought was rather poor...He was most dramatic in his speech and the monocle helped to give him the necessary atmosphere to put it across. The long tapering index finger often pointed at the guilty, the bang on the table, the monocle put on and off, the voice raised and lowered all helped to spice it up...Such was this man who could talk for hours at a public meeting to crowds of people who didn't know any English in pin drop silence.[23]

The relationship between Jinnah and Liaquat was a close one both professionally and politically. They worked closely together for ten years. It was, however, by no means a relationship of equals. Apart from the difference in their ages which established a natural hierarchy there was also the question of Jinnah's personality which did not welcome familiarity. In addition, there was the question of Jinnah's health. Only he and his sister Fatima knew exactly how ill and weak Jinnah was at times and how much Jinnah's public speeches weakened him. We know from Fatima Jinnah's autobiography that they exacted a terrible toll.[24] In 1941 in Madras he collapsed and his speech had to be postponed. That he kept up the pace he did was nothing less than a testament to his extraordinary will-power and determination.[25] Great men are often difficult to deal with and Jinnah was not an easy man to work with. His ill health and lack of energy had its impact on his relationships. During the years of the Second World War he spent many weeks and months resting and recovering from his illnesses. It was this ill-health and the sheer volume of work connected with a national political party gaining adherents by leaps and bounds that made Jinnah delegate more work to Liaquat and the Committee of Action but he insisted on being fully informed of everything that was going on with the League.

One of the things which made working with Jinnah more difficult for Liaquat was that Jinnah did not always keep him fully informed of his whereabouts and his activities. Liaquat and League workers went to considerable lengths to give full publicity to Jinnah's activities but numerous times Liaquat had to ask Jinnah where he would be and what he would be doing. The Indian press was exceedingly vigorous and gave great coverage to Indian political leaders and it was important for Jinnah's image that he be seen being greeted by large numbers of people when he arrived at a train station. This required coordination on the part of Liaquat as he organized League workers so he needed to know exactly what Jinnah's schedule was. Dawn did an especially effective job in giving publicity to Jinnah, his activities, his whereabouts, and his statements and speeches. In addition, Liaquat was responsible for getting Jinnah's speeches published.

There were two issues that came up between Jinnah and Liaquat. The first may or may not have caused any misunderstanding between the two, the second certainly did. The first was over the 'Desai-Liaquat Pact' or the 'Desai-Liaquat Formula', as dubbed by the press, but entitled 'Proposals for formation of Interim Government at the Centre'. In the autumn of 1944 Bhulabhai Desai,[26] the leader of the Congress in the Legislative Assembly of India, and Liaquat talked about some interim arrangement for the central government and a reconstruction of the Governor-General's Executive Council. Liaquat informed Desai that the League's position was the one stated in their resolutions and he was sure that the League would consider any proposals. He said these were his personal opinions and nothing could be done until they received the approval of Gandhi and the Congress leadership at which time he would refer them to Jinnah. In January 1945, on the day Liaquat left for a tour of South India, Desai gave him some proposals and asked him to keep them confidential. Liaquat did so. Over the next several months there were rumours that a pact had been made. Liaquat insisted there was no pact, merely proposals, and eventually released a copy of the proposals to the press to try to clear the air.

In Bombay Jinnah told the press he knew nothing about the pact and was reported to be annoyed with Liaquat.[27] However, Jinnah did not remove Liaquat from his position in the League, kept him as one of the executors of his will, and appointed him the prime minister when Pakistan was created. If there was a difference between Jinnah and Liaquat over the pact it is not reflected in their correspondence nor evident in their known behaviour. There was a great deal of comment about the pact at the time and a number of accounts have been written about it. Liaquat's motives were called into question. In a widely consulted volume in its time, the *Cambridge History of India*, stated, 'The view of Liaquat Ali Khan was that it was very necessary for the Muslim League to come to some understanding with the Congress because the British were likely to leave India any moment and the rigid attitude of Mr Jinnah and Mahatma Gandhi was not desirable. His view was that the younger men should make an attempt to solve the deadlock and that is why he entered into a Pact with Bhulabhai Desai.'[28] In a diatribe against Liaquat, Shaukat Hyat Khan wrote that Liaquat was motivated by the fact that he had been informed that Jinnah only had a few days to live and the pact was 'personal insurance for him...just to please the Indian National Congress.'[29] The written evidence for the views of Liaquat expressed in the *Cambridge History* and in Shaukat's autobiography is nonexistent. From everything we know about Liaquat they are so far from the truth as to be unbelievable. Liaquat had little use for the Congress and its leaders and he was totally loyal to Jinnah.

The second issue that came up was a real one and led to Liaquat's offer to resign his prime ministership. The issue, however, did not concern Liaquat and Jinnah but came about due to Liaquat's wife, to whom Liaquat was devoted. Liaquat wrote to Jinnah in longhand at the end of December 1947:

Personal & Confidential

Karachi
27.12.47

My dear Quaid-i-Azam,
    My wife has related to me what you told her last night at your dinner. I am sorry to learn that she has incurred your displeasure for some unknown reason. She could not possibly have done anything to merit such strong criticism and condemnation as for you to say that she was impossible and that she was digging her own grave.

For the last twelve years since I have had the privilege of working with you in close cooperation both of us have always had the highest regard for you and my wife has always tried her best not to do or say anything which would in any way injure the cause which is so dear to all of us. On the contrary she had made every endeavour to conform to the best of our Islamic principles and when the emergency arose she willingly did what was in her power to help.

A Prime Minister's wife can not live in a vacuum. She has to take her due place in the life of the nation and on account of the opinion which you seem to have of her it becomes very embarassing and difficult for both of us to do our duty in the position which she, as the Prime Minister's wife, and I, as the Prime Minister occupy.

You are the architect of Pakistan and as such I feel that it is but fair that you should have only such persons round you in building it up who can command your complete confidence and goodwill.

I would never dream of doing anything which would in any way injure Pakistan in the slightest degree, but as everyone knows that my health has not been too good for the last two months, my slipping out quietly will not create any misunderstanding or difficulties.

I wish to assure you that I am not writing this letter with any bitterness but out of the deep regard that I have for you.

Yours sincerely,
Liaquat Ali Khan[30]

This was such a serious breach between Jinnah and Liaquat that a memorandum was written which recorded the event. It was penned by Liaquat's wife's close English friend, Kay Miles:

This draft letter of Liaquat's requires a little background note: (1) Begum Sahiba's reputation as a social leader & social service worker was being steadily strengthened & enhanced. As the result of the <u>finesse</u> with which she handled her position as the Prime Minister's wife, and of the tremendous work she was doing for the refugees both personally & through the Women's Voluntary Service she had organised for this purpose.
(2) This quite unnecessarily made Miss J bitterly resentful & jealous, although nothing was *ever* done to detract from her respect & position as the Quaid-i-Azam's sister. On the contrary, out of respect & personal affectation & friendship for Mr J, & knowing the lady's temperament & mental & physical disabilities, every possible effort was made to

avoid any kind of friction or unpleasantness. This was to no purpose, so far as Miss J was concerned, for in her growing jealousy & possessive attitude towards her brother, she steadily poisoned the mind of an already tired & sick man, whom she was also steadily trying to shut away from his friends & colleagues.

(3) The actual incident which gave rise to Mr J's remarks to Begum Sahiba was her non-acceptance of a glass of sherry (which she dislikes) when she sat near him at his birthday dinner party. Then he quoted an incident which had taken place just previously at a dinner party in the then Sind Governor's House where Mr & Miss J were the guests of honour, & which had been brought to his notice by Miss J, with her own rendering of the facts. What had actually happened was that when an A.D.C. had requested Begum Sahiba to sit near Miss J, she suggested that some other ladies, who did not often get it, be given the opportunity to do so on this occasion.

(4) Begum Sahiba naturally resented such remarks, especially as there was so much personal friendship & respect for Mr J, by both herself & her husband. Liaquat sent in the resignation contained in this draft the following afternoon. Immediately upon receipt of it Mr J phoned Liaquat, expressed his great shock & requested him to come over to G.G.'s House that same night.

Mr J. was most upset at the threat to a personal friendship & political partnership which had weathered so many storms, & had been built up on a solid foundation of mutual respect and affection. Mr J flatly refused to even consider his resignation, but Liaquat was adamant that the matter must be considered in view of the fact that he was not prepared to continue in office under such unjust aspersions on his wife, & with the lack of stable confidence which this incident revealed. They talked the whole thing out that night, Mr J maintaining that he had merely spoken as a father out of his affection for Begum Sahiba, & requesting Liaquat to promise him that neither Begum Sahiba nor Miss J be allowed to come between them in their friendship.

(5) In her jealousy against Liaquat, Miss J, by insinuation & statement, tried to make believe that her brother was prepared to get rid of Liaquat—it was not a fact.[31]

Jinnah and Liaquat enjoyed a remarkable political relationship.[32] Liaquat was closely associated with one of the great political figures of the twentieth century. Like many of the people who came in touch with Jinnah he held him in the highest regard, with devotion, and with affection. Very few figures in history are credited with having created a state; Jinnah is one such man. Liaquat was the closest ally of Jinnah in the creation of Pakistan. It is hard to imagine the creation of Pakistan in 1947 without Jinnah; it is equally difficult to envision the establishment of the state without a cadre of League workers in establishing Jinnah as the revered and undisputed leader of the All-India Muslim League and the sole spokesman for the Muslims of South Asia. None was more important or more central to that campaign than Liaquat. Together in their different ways they were responsible for the creation and the preservation of Pakistan.

NOTES

1. The best and most authoritative complete 'life' of Jinnah is Stanley Wolpert's *Jinnah of Pakistan* (New York: Oxford University Press, 1984). On the life and career of the most eminent biographer of Jinnah see Roger D. Long, 'Charisma and Commitment: Stanley Wolpert and South Asian History', in Roger D. Long, ed., *Charisma and Commitment in South Asian History: Essays Presented to Stanley Wolpert* (New Delhi: Orient Longman, 2003), pp. 6-35. Hector Bolitho's *Jinnah: Creator of Pakistan* (London: John Murray, 1954), researched shortly after Jinnah's death, is still a very important source. Sharif Al Mujahid's *Quaid-i-Azam Jinnah: Studies in Interpretation* (Karachi: Quaid-i-Azam Academy, 1981) is also a useful study. For a description of these and other studies see the chapter 'Mohammad Ali Jinnah (1876-1948)' in Roger D. Long, *The Founding of Pakistan: An Annotated Bibliography* (Lanham, MD: The Scarecrow Press, 1998). The best account of the career of Liaquat Ali Khan is Muhammad Reza Kazimi, *Liaquat Ali Khan: His Life and Work* (Karachi: Oxford University Press, 2003).
2. Penderel Moon, ed., *Wavell The Viceroy's Journal* (Karachi: Oxford University Press, 1997), pp. 206, 413 and passion.
3. This was the view of Shaista Suhrawardy Ikramullah who said in a personal interview in Karachi on 4 September 1996 that there was so much excitement at the creation of Pakistan in the early years and an eagerness to get things done right away, including the writing of a constitution, that she and other young people were disappointed at the slow progress the government was making.
4. See the correspondence between Jinnah and Ispahani in Z.H. Zaidi, ed., *M. A. Jinnah-Ispahani Correspondence, 1936-1948* (Karachi: Forward Publications Trust, 1976).

5. According to his second wife, Ra'ana Liaquat Ali Khan, in an interview at Karachi.

6. Unfortunately he liked 2 1/4 inch slide film on glass and the images have deteriorated with time and crumbled away. I am very grateful to Liaquat's youngest sons, Ashraf and Akbar, for showing me the photographs of the family in their possession and I am also exceedingly grateful to them for their assistance in my research on the life of their father.

7. These photographs are in the possession of Liaquat's two youngest sons, Ashraf and Akbar.

8. As she recorded in an interview for *Dawn* 21 October 1951, p. 7, after his assassination.

9. This account of Jinnah's early life comes from Stanley Wolpert, *Jinnah of Pakistan* (New York: Oxford University Press, 1984), Chapter 1, p. 4.

10. Lepel H. Griffin and Charles Francis Massey, *Chiefs and Families of Note in the Punjab*, Vol. 1 (Lahore: Punjab Government Press, 1909), pp. 29-30. I have dealt with various aspects of the life and career of Liaquat Ali Khan in a number of publications such as in 'The Early Life of the Quaid-i-Millat Liaquat Ali Khan', *Journal of the Pakistan Historical Society* 32, 4 (1984): 269-274, 'Liaquat Ali Khan: From National Agriculturist Party to Muslim League' Ph.D. Dissertation, UCLA, 1985, 'Liaquat Ali Khan and the Background to the Demand for Pakistan', *Proceedings of the Sixth International Symposium on Asian Studies, 1984* (Hong Kong: Asian Research Service, 1984); *'Dear Mr Jinnah': Selected Correspondence and Speeches of Liaquat Ali Khan, 1937-1947* (Karachi: Oxford University Press, 2004), and in a forthcoming biography.

11. On the life of Sir Saiyid Ahmed Khan see Hafeez Malik *Sir Saiyid Ahmed Khan and Modernization in India and Pakistan* (New York: Columbia University Press, 1980) and also Peter Hardy, *The Muslims of British India* (Cambridge: Cambridge University Press, 1972), pp. 67 ff.

12. For the period 1896 to 1910 see Wolpert, *Jinnah of Pakistan*, Chapter 2.

13. *Ibid.*, pp. 46-49.

14. Muhammad Saleem Ahmad, 'Liaquat Ali Khan: An Appraisal', *The Concept*, 2, 8 (August 1982), p. 19.

15. According to Shaista Ikramullah in a personal interview in Karachi on 4 September 1996.

16. Peter Reeves has produced the most authoritative study of landlord organizations and politics in the United Provinces. See his *Landlords and Government in Uttar Pradesh: A Study of their Relations until Abolition* (Bombay: Oxford University Press, 1991).

17. *Indian Annual Register*, Vol. 2, July-Dec. 1928, p. 397.

18. See F.D. Douglas, *Challenge and Change: Speeches by Begum Ra'ana Liaquat Ali Khan.* (Karachi: All Pakistan Women's Association, nd) and Mehr Nigar Masroor, *Ra'ana Liaquat Ali Khan-A Biography* (Karachi: All Pakistan Women's Association, nd).

19. Stanley Wolpert first wrote about this in 'Congress Leadership in Transition: Jinnah to Gandhi, 1914-1920' in B.N. Pandey, ed. *Leadership in South Asia.* (New Delhi: Vikas, 1977), pp. 653-666. Numerous books have been written on Gandhi. The most useful on the early life of Gandhi are still those written by Judith Brown. See her *Gandhi's Rise to Power: Indian Politics 1915-1922* (Cambridge: Cambridge University Press, 1972), and *Gandhi and Civil Disobedience: The Mahatma in Indian Politics 1928-34* (Cambridge: Cambridge University Press, 1977). See also her 'life' of Gandhi, *Gandhi: Prisoner of Hope* (New Haven, CT: Yale University Press, 1989). Stanley Wolpert has also produced a fine life in *Gandhi's Passion: The Life and Legacy of Mahatma Gandhi* (New York: Oxford University Press, 2002).

20. See Wolpert, *Jinnah of Pakistan*, Chapter 10 for Jinnah's actitivities and residence in London during the years 1930 to 1933.

21. Abul Kalam Azad, *India Wins Freedom*, Calcutta, Orient Longman, 1959 pp. 160-62.

22. Bolitho's journal and his notes for the book as well as his correspondence are located at the Ames Library at the University of Minnesota. I am grateful to the Ames Library for arranging accommodation for me to stay at the university facilities for a few days in order to consult the Bolitho Papers and I am grateful for their permission for a copy of the papers.

23. Long, *'Dear Mr Jinnah'*, p. 314.

24. Fatima Jinnah, *My Brother*, edited by Sharif Al Mujahid (Karachi: Quaid-i-Azam Academy, 1987).

25. See the Jinnah Papers for an example of Jinnah's extensive activities in 1947 in Z.H. Zaidi, ed., *Quaid-i-Azam Mohammad Ali Jinnah Papers.* Vol. 1 (Islamabad: National Archives of Pakistan, 1993-).

26. On the life of Desai see M.C. Setalvad, *Bhulabhai Desai* (New Delhi: Ministry of Information and Broadcasting, Government of India, 1968).

27. *Wavell: The Viceroy's Journal*, p. 114.

28. H.H. Dodwell, ed., *The Cambridge History of India*, Vol. VI (New Delhi: S. Chand, nd), pp. 673-674. The section covering 1919 to 1969 was written by the Indian historian V.D. Mahajan.

29. Sirdar Shaukat Hyat Khan, *The Nation that Lost Its Soul (Memoirs of a Freedom Fighter)* (Lahore: Jang Publishers, 1995), pp. 174-175.

30. The corrected draft of this letter is in the Liaquat Ali Khan Papers and the original is in the Quaid-i-Azam Papers, National Archives, Islamabad.

31. Ra'ana Liaquat Ali Khan Papers.

32. A relationship that was unfairly and poorly shown in the Akber Ahmed film, *Jinnah*. The controversial film was badly conceived and scripted. As great a film *Gandhi* by Richard Attenborough was, *Jinnah* was a disappointment and a failure. The incredible opportunity to make a film for the ages was lost. It will not come back any time soon.

10

Jinnah: The Role of the
Individual in History*
Sharif Al Mujahid

During the last decade of his life, Mohammad Ali Jinnah (1876–1948), the founder of Pakistan, was the most misunderstood man in Indian politics. He generated violent opposition and excited implacable hostility among those opposed to India's partition. He was criticized, condemned, pilloried and maligned as no one else was. Yet throughout his life and after his death, he was the recipient of manifold and magnificent tributes, some of them even from those vehemently opposed to him.

In evaluating the life and work of a politician, a statesman or a public leader, it is customary to take into account what his contemporaries thought of him and his work, in the first instance. But tributes, especially paid on one's death, though providing some clues and insights into hypothesizing one's place in history, are yet more or less a conventional or routine affair. Hence, they cannot always be taken at face value. More so, because 'there is no reliable correlation between historical significance, measured by the effect of action on events, and historical fame, measured by acclaim or volume of eulogy.'[1] And, as events would have it, this lack of correlation between historical significance and historical fame is particularly true in the case of Jinnah.

Even so, it is worthwhile to identify what finds the most frequent mention and the greatest emphasis in the tributes paid to him. It is, above all, the 'unique' nature of his leadership and achievement. This must, however, be qualified by a rather paradoxical phenomenon: the sharp divergence between most contemporary observers and writers on the one hand and historians on the other as to how 'decisive' his role was in the creation of Pakistan. Their opinions, though covering a wide range, may yet be summed up in two, interrelated questions. Did Jinnah create the social and political forces that had ultimately brought Pakistan into existence? Or, did he merely canalize, however adroitly and adeptly, those impelling forces that were already in high momentum—in momentum towards a definite destination? While historians proffer the latter view, contemporary observers take the former one.

I

Historians, whether because of their wide-ranging scholarship and long insight into history or, more particularly, because of a general tendency among them to interpret events in terms of a deterministic approach, are usually prone to explain contemporary events within the framework of the outworking of historical forces and ideological factors—forces and factors long embedded and enmeshed in a country's or a nation's history, in its body-politic. More specifically, some historians tend to hold that Pakistan was somehow in the 'womb' of history,[2] that its emergence was inescapable and inevitable,[3] that it would have come anyhow, or somehow, whether there was a Jinnah or not to lead the movement to a successful culmination. At the other end of the continuum are contemporary observers and journalists, as well as those involved one way or another in the developments which led to Partition and the emergence of Pakistan. Not only do they rate Jinnah as being the critical variable in its emergence, some, like Leonard Mosley even regard Pakistan as a 'one-man achievement'.[4] More important: they doubt whether, without him at the helm of Indo-Muslim affairs in that epochal decade of 1937–47, Pakistan could have become possible, even remotely. And this assertion, sweeping as it may sound, is sought to be buttressed with an array of arguments, at once solid and convincing. H.V. Hodson, Constitutional Advisor to the Viceroy and Reforms Commissioner with the Government of India (1941–42), and the author of perhaps the most authoritative British account of the last decade of the Raj, has brilliantly summed up the case for this viewpoint. In *The Great Divide* (1969), he says:

> Of all the personalities in the last act of the great drama of India's re-birth to independence, Mohammad Ali Jinnah is at once the most enigmatic and the most important. One can imagine any of the other principal actors…replaced by a substitute in the same role—a different Congress Leader, a different Secretary of State, a different representative of this or that interest or community, even a different Viceroy— without thereby implying any radical change in the final denouement. But it is barely conceivable that events would have taken the same course, that the last struggle would have been a struggle of three, not two, well-balanced adversaries, and that a new nation state of Pakistan would have been created, but for the personality and leadership of one man, Mr Jinnah. The irresistible demand for Indian independence, and the British will to relinquish power in India soon after the end of the Second World War, were the result of influences that had been at work long before the present story of the single decade begins: the protagonists on this side or that of the imperial relationship were tools of historical forces which they did not create and could not control, pilots of vessels borne by winds and tides set in motion long before they took the helm. Whereas the irresistible demand for Pakistan, and the solidarity of the Indian Muslims behind that demand, were creations of that decade alone, and supremely the creations of one man.[5]

To this telling evaluation of the sheer magnitude of Jinnah's accomplishment on the Indian political landscape may be added the *Economist's* verdict on the measure of his achievement on the scale of the universally recognized prodigious achievement of Bismarck (1815–98), the maker of modern Germany:

> In a recent poll the Germans voted Bismarck the greatest of all time. On any standards they were wrong, for even in the same genre Quaid-i-Azam Mohammad Ali Jinnah stands higher. It took Bismarck the same seven years, from the Schleswigh-Holstein war to the treaty of Frankfurt, to create the German Empire as it took Jinnah, from the Lahore Resolution of 1940 to Independence Day, to make Pakistan.

But Bismarck started with all the advantages: a hundred-year old nationalism, the Prussian Army and Civil Service, the Ruhr, 15 years of experience of high office, and youth enough still to have 20 years as Chancellor before him in 1879. Jinnah began with nothing but his own ability and the disgruntlement of a religious minority in which he was only an unobservant member of the most heretic sect, at an age so great that he only survived his creation by one year and without any experience of public office until he nominated himself Governor-General.[6]

What the *Economist* had hinted at was explicitly spelled out by Edward Hallet Carr in his Trevelyan Lectures at Cambridge in 1961. To Carr, Bismarck 'rode to greatness on the back of already existing forces'.[7] In contrast, Jinnah had precious little in terms of extant resources to start with in 1940. Which, *inter alia*, means that he had created the social and political forces that called Pakistan into existence—a viewpoint attested to by Hodson on the basis of the respective ground realities in 1937 and 1947.

Viewed on a theoretical plane, the two viewpoints presented by (mostly) historians and contemporary observers above represent respectively the alternatives in the age-long controversy between the social determinists and the 'Great Man' theorists.[8] In essence, the issue may be summed up thus: which one plays the pivotal role in the making of an historical event—the circumstances that give rise to a character or the character itself?

By any criterion, the creation of an altogether new nation of Pakistan out of the body politic of undivided India was an historical event of lasting significance in the post-war world. In the making of such an event, it may be argued, as does F.J.C. Hearnshaw, that both character and circumstance are equally critical,[9] if only because without their interacting on and mutually effecting one another all the while, the final configuration of events, and the integration of interests, could never be produced.

In the first instance, it is true, circumstances make the character what it is, and what it tends to become. Applied in the case of Jinnah, this premise may be spelled out as follows. Jinnah's rise to supreme Muslim leadership in 1937 may primarily be attributed to three factors, two historical and one personal. On the conceptual plane, the Muslim cause was in search of a standard bearer, and on the empirical plane, the Muslim people were in search of a leader. And on the personal plane, if Jinnah had not done the sort of things he had actually done during the previous thirty-three years of his public life and had not identified himself with, if not established, a distinctive style of leadership in Muslim politics, he would not have risen to the summit of Muslim leadership during 1937–39, much less been accepted as such during the 1940s.[10] This means that even while giving rise to a character at any given juncture, circumstances must also be fortuitously complemented by the personal traits and accomplishments of the character itself.

But while conceding an equally critical role to circumstances in the making and emergence of an historical character, it needs to be noted that the character, once it has emerged on the scene, begins to play an increasingly critical role: he moulds, shapes, and exploits to the utmost the circumstances he inherits to suit, advance and achieve his ultimate purposes and objectives. Interpreted thus, circumstances cannot by themselves endow a historic character with personal traits—elements provided from within—that would enable it to rise to the occasion, help solidify and crystallize the scattered and even somewhat disparate historical forces, cause a new integration by harmonizing them with each other and by bringing about their confluence and configuration, and finally, work through a series of bold decisions and heroic actions. And this more balanced approach is commended by some historians in evaluating the measure of achievement of those credited with changing the course of history. Speaking of Napoleon, for instance, Christopher Herold remarks,

> ...in spite of the prodigious amount that has been devoted to the man and his times, there is still little general agreement as to whether Napoleon is more important as a product and a symbol...of circumstances that were not of his making, or as a man, who, pursuing his own destiny, shaped circumstances that governed the course of history. Like all great men, Napoleon was both, of course...[11]

The same may be said of Jinnah.

II

This composite approach considers man 'as a creator of his environment, as well as a creature of it'.[12] Hence, it represents an advance over the Social Darwinists' notion that regards man as 'a creature of his environment, whether natural or social'. The basic formulation of this latter concept, as enunciated by Karl Marx (1818–83), runs as follows:

> Men make their own history, but they do not make it just as they please; they do not make it under circumstances chosen by themselves, but under circumstances directly encountered, given and transmitted from the past. The tradition of all the dead generations weighs like a nightmare on the brain of the living. And just when they seem engaged in revolutionizing themselves and things, in creating something that has never yet existed, precisely in such periods of revolutionary crisis they anxiously conjure up the spirits of the past to their service and borrow from them names, battle cries and costumes in order to present the new scene of world history in this time-honoured disguise and this borrowed language.[13]

Karl Marx wrote this in 1848. Twenty-one years later, on 16 April 1869, Bismarck, the Iron Chancellor, would reiterate the same concept in his famous address to the North German Reichstag:

> ...we can neither ignore the history of the past nor create the future ...My influence on the events I took advantage of is usually exaggerated; but it could never occur to anyone to demand that *I should make history*....We cannot make history: we must wait while it is being made. We will not make fruit ripen more quickly by subjecting it to the heat of a lamp; if we pluck the fruit before it is ripe we will prevent its growth and spoil it.[14] [To this Bismarckian analogy we would return later.]

Those who give primacy to environmental determinants and challenges are not only the orthodox Marxists whose foremost spokesman was, of course, Marx himself, and to a lesser degree,

Georgi Plekhanov (1856–1918) and Leon Trotsky (1879–1940). This school also includes most of the later eighteenth century, and almost all of the notable nineteenth century philosophers, historians and social scientists (such as Hegel, Spencer, Guizot, Mignet, Augustin Thierry, and Tocquiville), as also Freud and Toynbee in the twentieth century. This general tendency among practically all of the notable social scientists during the past two centuries has led them to begin with society and 'to create man in its image'. To redress, to some extent, the imbalance created by this monistic approach, the importance of achievement motive in shaping the course of history needs to be recognized. Hence, argues David C. McClelland, the role of 'achievement motivation in society' must be conceded its due place. In effect, it means that in explaining historical phenomena, 'the motives of the men affected by an environmental change or a social institution'[15] must also be taken into account.

Opinion may, of course, differ, even sharply, about the relative weight assigned to circumstances and the character—i.e., about the measure of criticality conceded to a character—in the making of an historical event. But unless the environment is characterized by certain 'determining tendencies', circumstances alone, unmatched by the character, cannot create an event.

For instance, despite the intrepidity Christopher Columbus (c.1446–1506) displayed, and the hardships he underwent in discovering America, he was not the critical variable in that discovery. This was because certain determining tendencies in the social and economic history of Europe in the late fifteenth and early sixteenth century made it incumbent that the quest for a short passage to India succeed, sooner or later. Indeed, Columbus himself died in the belief that he had discovered eastern Asia, and Amerigo Vescuppi (1454–1512), a Florentine, had to rediscover America after Columbus in 1499, in recognition of which the continent was named after him. And these determining tendencies which pointed towards and ensured the discovery of America were 'the nascent technological facilities of nascent capitalism, the desire to exploit more intensively the markets of the East, [and] the quest for a short passage to India'.[16] Hence, in this case certain 'determining tendencies' characterizing the environment, rather than the character himself, were primarily responsible for creating an historical event.

Now going back to the Bismarckian analogy of plucking the fruit when it is ripe, i.e., of securing what the events have prepared for us, one may profitably turn to Georgi Plekhanov, who, though 'one of the foremost theoreticians of orthodox Marxism', yet makes provision for 'great men' playing a significant role in historical development:

...every act of 'securing' [he argues] is also an historical event... [because] nearly every historical event is simultaneously an act of 'securing' by somebody of the already ripened fruit of preceding development and a link in the chain of events which are preparing the fruits of the future.[17]

III

Applied to the case of Pakistan, it may, therefore, be contended that whatever the strength, the momentum and the intensity of historical forces working towards Pakistan, without the matching of the character—in this case, that of Jinnah—with the circumstances, it could not have come the way, nor at the time, it did. More so, because 'few statesmen have shaped events to their policy more surely than Mr Jinnah',[18] to quote *The Times* (London). And he shaped them superbly and adroitly towards the emergence of Pakistan. In other words, Pakistan was not the product of the ineluctable movement of events on a historically predetermined course, but the process of choice, above all, by Jinnah. This explains why underlying everything that has been said or written about Jinnah is the central theme of his achievement of Pakistan.

The critical role of achievement motivation in society may also be explained and buttressed by a close examination of the implications of the 'womb' theory in respect of Pakistan. This theory was succinctly summed up by Leon Trotsky, while explaining the role of Lenin (1870–1924) in the coming and culmination of the Russian Revolution (1917).[19] He takes cover under a Spencerian stance—viz., 'that a man and his period had to be considered together and that both were determined by the antecedent state of culture'.[20]

That this line of argument is rather fallacious may be seen from the application of the Trotskyian formulation to the role of Jinnah in the making of Pakistan. Could it, then, be said that Jinnah was not an 'accidental element' in the historical development of Muslim India and that both Jinnah and his party (i.e., the Muslim League; f.1906) were a product of the whole past of Indo-Muslim history? It could not, for it would tantamount to a tautology. A tautology because had Jinnah and his party not strived for Pakistan, and having strived, had failed to accomplish it they would still have been a product of past Indo-Muslim history in the same way as Sayyid Ahmad Shaheed (1786–1831) and the Mujahideen movement (1820s–1860s) or Mohammed Ali (1878–1931) and the Khilafat Movement (1920–22) were, although both encountered failure in the end. By the same token Maulana Abul Kalam Azad (1889–1958) and the Jamiat-ul-Ulema-i-Hind (f.1919) could also be termed as a product of past Indo-Muslim history, although both Azad and the Jamiat stood for a composite Hindu-Muslim nationalism and a united India, and were deadly opposed to partition.

Hence, the more relevant and the more critical question here is not whether Jinnah and his party were a product of the historical past of Muslim India—which, of course, they were—but whether his party could have become what it did during 1937–47 but for the 'accidental element' of Jinnah and the rather spectacular but unexpected twist he gave to the course of Muslim politics since 1937.

Not to speak of the non-League Muslim leadership, even the past role of the Muslim League did not hold out such a prospect. Nor even the general demeanour of an important segment of its leadership during 1937–47 which seemed always prone to striking out a compromise with the Indian National Congress (f.1885), more or less on the latter's own terms. Even Jinnah's past role as a 'waxing' Congress leader (1913–20), as an 'ambassador of Hindu-

Muslim unity' (1915–20), as one of the foremost advocates of Indian freedom *per se*, as the author of the Delhi Muslim Proposals (1927), and as a Muslim leader striving for a national, rather than a Muslim, consensus till 1929, and seeking to evolve a compromise formula acceptable to both Hindus and Muslims even as late as 1935 (in the Jinnah-Prasad talks), and 1938 (in his correspondence with the Congress leaders), all of which, of course, could also be put down as a natural product of the recent historical past of Muslim India—even this multifaceted, though intrinsically integrated, role of Jinnah fails to provide any significant clue as to which of the alternative paths of development presented to Muslim India at the moment (1937–47) he would take. Not to speak of 1937, even in the middle 1940s, Pakistan's emergence could not have been predicted on the basis of available historical evidence as the only likely alternative of future development of Indo-Muslim history.

Indeed, even as late as May–June 1946, with the authoritative government pronouncement against Pakistan in the Cabinet Mission Plan (1946),[21] whatever the political forces and conditions at work, the alternative path of a united India seemed the more likely and the more imminent choice, and it was Jinnah alone who made the critical decision that led Muslim India directly to Pakistan within a year, and transformed the rather remote possibility of an independent Muslim homeland into an actuality. Hence, while both Jinnah and the Muslim League were, indeed, a product of the whole past of Muslim India, Pakistan was not so much a product of that past as the product of one of the most 'event-making' figures in modern history in the Sydney Hook sense.[22] Thus, Jinnah's presence was necessary; at least as far as the calendar date of Pakistan's emergence was concerned.

Hook makes a fine distinction between an 'eventful' and an 'event-making' man:

> The *eventful* man in history is any man whose action influenced subsequent developments along a quite different course than would had been followed if these actions had not been taken. The *event-making* man is an eventful man whose actions are the consequences of

outstanding capacities of intelligence, will, and character rather than accident of position.

While 'both the eventful and the event-making man appear at the forking points of history', the event-making man 'also helps, so to speak, to create' a fork in the historical road. Hook puts down Emperor Constantine as an eventful man, and Caesar, Cromwell and Napoleon as event making.[23]

Of relevance here is, also, what Alfred Broachard said about the criticality of Kemal Ataturk in the making of modern Turkey:

> Without Napoleon, without de Gaulle, there would still be a France. Without Washington, there would certainly be the United States. Without Lenin, it is certain that there would be the Soviet Union; but without Ataturk, it is certain that there would have been no Turkey.[24]

Turkey had, of course, had a territorial, political, cultural and ethnic existence in history for over five centuries before Ataturk transformed it into modern Turkey in 1923. In contrast, Pakistan fell even below the category of middle nineteenth century 'Italy', Metternich had so disparagingly characterized as a mere 'geographical expression'. Pakistan was not even such an expression barely fifteen years before its emergence. There was a 'nation' called Turkey for several centuries, but there was none called Pakistan before 1947. Hence, if Ataturk's presence in the 1920s was so critical to the making of modern Turkey, how much more critical should have been Jinnah's presence in the 1940s in the emergence of Pakistan, and without any sort of historical prototype?

Given the Waliullah (late eighteenth century), the Mujahideen (early nineteenth century), the Aligarh (late nineteenth century), and the Khilafat (early 1920s) legacy on the Muslim side and that of the Hindu Mela (1867–70), Prarthana Samaj (f.1867), National Society (f.1870), Arya Samaj (f.1875), Gaurakshini Sabhas (f.1883), Tilak (1856–1920), Malaviya (1861–1946), and Gandhi (1869–1948) on the Hindu side, the demand for Pakistan (1940) is, of course, understandable as a culminating point of the 'natural evolution' of the 'separatist' tendency among Muslims in response to Hindu exclusivism and ethnocentrism on the one hand, and of the process of alienation from the (predominantly Hindu) Congress on the other; but certainly not its realization without the presence of an event-making man.

And this especially because, despite the existence of certain centrifugalist tendencies in the Indian polity since the beginning, the rise of the British in the nineteenth century gave that polity a definite swing toward centrepetalism—e.g., a common official language, common administrative, judicial and educational systems, integrated multi-tiered communication and economic systems encompassing the entire subcontinent, and the spectacular rise of a pan-Indian press, of political parties, and social, cultural, religious and other bodies. Thus, especially since Queen Victoria's (1819–1901) proclamation of 4 November 1858, the trend towards uniting and integrating the various strands into a single-unit polity had gained an almost irreversible momentum.

At the most, the historical situation during the 1937–47 decade presented and permitted, if at all, two major alternative paths of development, though not of equal weight, for Muslim politics:

(i)   going along with the Congress' viewpoint, if not actually merging the Muslim League into it or accepting for it a satellite status; and

(ii) striking out an independent line, though not necessarily in opposition to the Congress.

These alternative paths were presented at least on seven different but specific occasions (1937, 1939, 1940, 1942, 1944, 1945, and 1946). But on no occasion did Jinnah waver, and each time he chose for himself and for Muslim India the path towards establishing Muslim religio-political identity on a constitutional plane—the path concretized since 1940 in the Pakistan platform. And this he did whatever the toils and labours, whatever the trials and tribulations, whatever the circumstances and consequences. It is true that Jinnah did accept the Cabinet Mission Plan initially

(June 1946). But his acceptance, though genuinely sincere at the time, was primarily motivated by two overriding reasons:

(i) the original Plan, as elucidated in the Mission's (supplementary) Statement of 25 May, contained 'the seeds of Pakistan', providing for a somewhat limited Muslim religio-political identity but complete autonomy and the substance of power for the Muslim majority provinces in a confederal India; and

(ii) it had held out the prospect of these provinces opting for a sovereign Pakistan after a decade, if the proposed confederal arrangements failed to work to their satisfaction.

But the two provisions—viz., compulsory grouping of Muslim majority provinces in the northwest and northeast into Groups B and C respectively, and the centre being confined to Defence, Foreign Affairs and Communications—which contained these seeds and held out this prospect—were sought to be scuttled by Pandit Jawaharlal Nehru's (1889–1964) interpretation of the Plan,[25] compounded by Gandhi's exhortations to Assam to revolt against grouping and not to enter Group C.[26] And, for sure, this interpretation and these exhortations amounted to a gross distortion of the original Plan, negating not only the Muslim claim to a religio-political identity and to political parity with Hindus, but also recklessly jeopardizing the prospect of the establishment of a confederal structure at the centre. Hence, Jinnah's twin decisions during the middle if 1946—first to accept and then to reject the Plan—could not be termed contradictory since both stemmed from the same underlying principle: to ensure power for Muslims in their majority areas.

It has been argued that given the legacies referred to above, Pakistan would have inevitably come, sooner or later. But this is one of those 'ifs' in history about which no sure prediction could be made. It is rather hard to say with any measure of confidence that a united Indian government with an overwhelming Hindu majority, once entrenched in power, would have conceded the right to self-determination to the 'Pakistan' areas. But what is easier to predict is that, as in the recent past, New Delhi could and would have easily found a Malik Khizr Hayat Khan Tiwana (1900–75) here and a Sheikh Abdullah (1904–82) there to provide her with a plausible justification to keep the 'Pakistan' areas under permanent Indian 'occupation'.

IV

Historical fatalism lays down that 'before the great man can remake his society, his society must make him'.[27] This is the classical exposition of the role of environment vs. the Great Man proffered by Herbert Spencer (1820–1903). Characteristic of him is his rather exaggerated stress on the role and effect of environment, leading him to deny, on the one hand, that 'great men create social and political institutions' and to maintain, on the other, that 'their rise was not a matter of deliberate choice at all'.[28] But this mechanistic and monistic approach has long proved fallacious. So also the concomitant view which regards personal traits as being merely incidental to leadership or which sees leadership chiefly in terms of the situation.[29]

But since, even according to Marx, men make history, 'the activities of individuals cannot help being important in history', nor can the individual be declared a *quantite negligeable*,[30] says Plekhanov. He has shown how the accidents of private life, i.e., the personal traits of an individual such as talent, intelligence, knowledge, resoluteness, and courage, or otherwise, have markedly influenced the course and outcome of events. For instance, despite the brilliant victories achieved by the French army during the Austrian War of Succession (1741–48), France got nothing out of the peace of Aix-la-Chapelle (1748) because 'Louis XV, as he said, was fighting as a king and not as a merchant'. If only Louis XV had not taken up such a posture, France was in a formidable position to compel Austria to cede fairly extensive swathes of territories in what is now Belgium, leading to a different course of political and economic development of France. Likewise, it has been said, had Louis XV been less lascivious and more moralistic, or had he submitted less to his favourite i.e., Madame Pompadour's influence, or alternately, had she refrained from interfering in politics, events would not have turned out so unfavourably for France during the Seven Years' War (1756–63), nor would France have lost the major part of her colonial possessions in America and India as a result of the war.[31] Again, during Napoleon's campaigns, his most distinguishing trait—viz., his military genius—shines forth. For instance, French armies were almost always defeated or immobilized whenever Napoleon entrusted their command to other officers.[32] In recent times, Dean Acheson, Secretary of State during the Truman Administration (1946–53), has shown how the flow of events were impeded or channelled by the individual personalities involved.[33] And, according to Patrick Morgan, 'Henry Kissinger in office was reportedly more impressed by the role of personalities than was Henry Kissinger the scholar'.[34] In a reported statement in early 1970s Kissinger had confessed,

> I tended to think history was run by impersonal forces ... But when you see it in practice, you see the differences that the personalities make. The overtures to China would not have worked without Chou En-lai. There would have been no settlement in the Middle East without Sadaat and Golda Meir and Dyan.[35]

In that sense, but at a higher level, Jinnah was the right man at the right place and at the right time—just as William Pitt the Elder (1708–88) and Winston Churchill (1874–1965) in England. By far the most striking case is that of Winston Churchill which clinches the point at issue. He was fortunate in 1940, but not in 1915—at the time of the ill-fated Gallipoli campaign. But to say so does not mean that these persons merely happened to be there at the right time. Neither Pitt, nor Richelieu, nor Churchill, and by the same token, nor Jinnah was merely a great, or merely an eventful, man in that sense. For them, greatness was something that involved 'extraordinary talent of some kind and not merely the compounded luck of being born and of being present at the right place at a happy moment'.[36] For it called for the right place and the right time to be fortuitously compounded by the critical variable of these persons being *also* the right men.

To say this is, however, not to underrate by any means the importance of the fortuitous conjunction of the right place and the right time. Rather, the contrary. To quote Carr, 'Had Bismarck been born in the eighteenth century—an absurd hypothesis since he would not then have been Bismarck—he would not have united Germany, and might not have been a great man at all'.[37] Indeed, 'men can and do make their own history', but *only* under certain conditions and *only* when these conditions are ripe for heroic action. Their 'ideals, plans, and purposes' may be

> causally rooted in the complex of conditions, but they take their meaning from some proposed *reworking* of conditions to bring them closer to human desire.... It is difficult to give a satisfactory account of what happened, how it happened, and why, without striking a plausible balance between the part men played and the conditioning scene which provided the materials, sometimes the rules, but never the plots of the dramas of human history.[38]

Hence the contention that a historic personality such as Jinnah is fashioned by his environment, the cultural milieu of his times, and by the ideological tradition he had inherited, and more importantly, by the way he reacts to that environment, to that milieu and to that tradition, and by the way he moulds and utilizes them to suit, serve and advance his purposes. That is, to quote William Delthy, he 'represents a type of interaction in which the individual receives influences from the historic sphere and is molded by these particular influences, while he in turn exerts his influence upon the historic level'.[39] In this sense, Jinnah's contribution was to synthesize the various dominant ideological strands in Indian Islam at this stage, the synthetic product being the all-embracing ideology of Pakistan. Indeed, in terms of a visionary approach, personal talent, political and intellectual leadership, organizational skill, resolute action, and concrete achievements, Jinnah had given at least as much to the formulation of the concept of Pakistan as he had received influences, legacies and 'supports' from the historic realm—legacies and supports in terms of traditional values, political forces, ideological orientation, institutional entities, communication networks, and mass response. Indeed, in a substantial and significant sense, his individual genius served as the creative force in Indo-Muslim history at this critical juncture.

V

To Carr,

> the great man is always representative either of existing forces or of forces which he helps to create by way of challenge to existing authority. But the higher degree of creativity may perhaps be assigned to those great men who, like Cromwell or Lenin, helped to mould the forces which carried them to greatness....'[40]

And as Hodson had pointed out, Jinnah had moulded or created the forces during the 1937–47 decade that carried him to the wresting of Pakistan. Nothing brings out this striking phenomenon as the deep divergence between Nehru's 1936–37 haughty 'two-forces' dictum and the triumphant vindication of Jinnah's (and the Muslim League's) claim during the critical 1945–46 general elections. During 1936–37 Nehru had assertively spelled out the contours of his 'grand' vision of India's body politic, which in a sense was the political corollary of the late nineteenth-century Hindu cultural ethnocentrism in the early twentieth century political context. He ruled out Muslims as the third side in India's political triangle, boldly asserting that:

> Thus, in the final analysis, there are only two forces in India today—British imperialism and the Congress representing Indian nationalism ....The communal groupings have no such real importance in spite of occasional importance being thrust upon them.[41]

To which Jinnah's riposte was: 'I refuse to accept this proposition. There is a third party in this country and that is Muslim India....'[42]

And in posing this riposte, Jinnah was challenging 'existing authority' in the Carr paradigm since the Congress had been such an 'authority' on India's political landscape for a long while, and was soon to become the 'authority' at the provincial administrative level. Indeed, it did assume power, first in six and later in eight of India's eleven provinces during 1937–38.

To make good his claim, Jinnah presently breathed new life into the moribund Muslim League, and organized it methodically all the way from the top to the bottom. In particular, he extended its support base to encompass the entire subcontinent; he made its policies and programme coherent and viable; he infused enthusiasm and confidence in the rank and file; he laid out the grass-root organizational networks, built up communication channels, and fashioned a chain of command through a hierarchically structured leadership. Consequently, within three brief years (1937–40), a revitalized Muslim League, had developed into a formidable political machine under his astute leadership, with the requisite unity of command, communication networks, organizational strength, electoral clout, and muscle power to confront and counter the almost impregnable and long-entrenched Congress, both at the ballot box and on the streets.

How formidable the Muslim League had become under Jinnah's leadership may be seen from the following. Its organizational strength was confined to a meagre membership of 1,330 in 1927; its 1930 session had failed to attract initially the required quorum of 75 members; its 1931 session was attended by 120 members; it did not meet in 1932, while in 1933 infighting and factionalism led to acrimony and pandemonium at its three council meetings, and their abrupt adjournment. Its General Secretary, Sir Mohammed Yakub, proposed its merger with All Parties Muslim Conference (f. 1929) at its council meeting as 5 March 1933, and a split in its ranks led to the holding of two rival sessions at Howrah (Aziz Group) and Delhi (Hidayat Group) in October and November 1933 respectively. And what a radical transformation had the Muslim League undergone once Jinnah re-assumed its leadership on 4 March 1934. While the League session in April 1936 was attended by 200 delegates, the figure rose to 2,000 at

Lucknow in 1937. The seating capacity of the *pandal* was 5,000 at Calcutta (Special session, April 1938), 50,000 at Patna (December 1938), and over 60,000 at Lahore (1940), while the attendance at Lahore was estimated at over 100,000. The Muslim League itself officially claimed a membership of two million in 1944, as against the Congress claim of 3.2 million members in 1938.[43]

A more reliable index of the social depth the League had acquired among its constituents was its burgeoning electoral strength since 1937. In early 1937, it had secured barely 112 out of 491 Muslim seats in the 1937 provincial elections under the 1935 Act, but by 1942 it had mustered strength to a point that it commanded the allegiance of 304 out of 524 central and provincial assembly Muslim members. Equally important, between 1 January 1938 and 12 September 1942, the League won 46 (82 per cent) out of 56 Muslim seats in by-elections, and between September 1942 and mid-1945, nine out of fifteen Muslim seats, the rest going to independents and none to the Congress,[44] which, in its Rashtrapathi's 'two-forces' doctrine, had flaunted itself as 'the existing authority' during 1936–37. This meant that the League had acquired a social depth among Muslims comparable to that of the Congress among the Hindus. One immediate and more manifest result of all this was a quickening of community consciousness and the welding of Muslim solidarity, making the pan-Indian Muslim community concept and the 'third party' status claim a *fait accompli*.

The climax to this burgeoning trend towards consolidating and crystallizing the 'new' forces would come at the hustings during 1945-46. To the utter surprise of Jinnah's opponents, and even the British government, the Muslim League won 453 (i.e., 86.45 per cent) out of 524 central and provincial Muslim seats and secured 4.70 million votes—i.e., about 75 per cent vote as against its measly score of four per cent of the total Muslim popular vote in the provincial polls in February 1937. The League's share during 1945–46 came to 24 per cent of the total vote cast in all the constituencies, and since the Muslims constituted some 26.9 per cent of the total population in British India, the League's voting record was termed brilliant. The juxtaposition of the League's

1945–46 score with its 1937 figure indicates that those who voted for the League and for Pakistan during 1945–46 were the 'new' forces which had been created, or helped to be created or moulded, by Jinnah himself since 1937, as a concomitant fallout to his marathon campaign against and challenge to existing 'authority'— that is, to the entrenched Congress during 1937–47. And, all said and done, these forces carried him triumphantly to the threshold of Pakistan and of greatness.

At another level, the 75 per cent popular vote, *inter alia,* provides an index to the measure of Jinnah's success in generating an astonishing mass response. This, in the final analysis, he could if only because he was highly empathetic to Muslim yearnings, however vague and nebulous, and had opted for the Muslim *ijma* (consensus) on the issue of Muslim individuality in India's body politic. A reference to Azad would help clinch the issue at hand. As indicated by his *Al-Hilal* (1910–14) writings, Azad had received more potent and more penetrating influences from the historic realm than did Jinnah. Yet, Azad, who was initially rather staunchly oriented towards Muslim individuality in politics, opted for a composite Hindu-Muslim nationalism since the early 1920s. More surprising: he stuck to this path even after the events had forced other erstwhile Muslim 'nationalists' to feel increasingly the overriding and imperative need to strike out in favour of Muslim nationalism and nationhood. As against this singular inability of Azad to see his way through the dense jungle of Indian politics and to keep pace with Muslim consensus, Jinnah had consistently opted, after occasional fumblings, for the Muslim *ijma* (consensus), and this especially since 1929, in the aftermath of his discomfiture in selling his composite, federal-oriented Delhi Muslim Proposals, not only to the Hindu and Congress 'nationalists', but also, in particular, to his pan-Indian Muslim constituency.

And in opting for Muslim consensus, Jinnah had fulfilled a critical Hegelian test of a great man as well—a test which requires him to perceive the needs of his time and to succeed in translating them into ideology—and political action. This point has been elaborated and made more explicit in Hegel's classic formulation of the relationship of a great man to his age, which, according to Carr, has not been bettered.[45] It lays down that,

> The great man of the age is one who can put into words the will of his age, tell his age what its will is, and accomplish it. What he does is the heart and essence of his age; he actualizes his age.[46]

And as events would have it, Jinnah was highly empathetic to Muslim yearnings, and had played out that historic role superbly in the epochal decade of 1937–47,[47] whereas Azad had failed even to perceive that role for himself in respect of Muslim India. Hence, in the ultimate analysis, what made Jinnah a Jinnah and Azad an Azad at this juncture in Indo-Muslim history was the critical variable of their respective reaction to the influences from the historic realm and to the 1937–47 Muslim situation. This also explains why Muslims, much against their tradition, had disdainfully disowned a traditional *alim* (religious scholar), while enthusiastically owning a Westernized barrister. And they owned him if only because at that point of time he was the *zeitgeist* ('spirit of the times') for Muslim India in the Hegelian sense.

Surprisingly though, Iqbal (1877–1938), the sage that he was, had concluded by 1937 that Jinnah fulfilled the Hegelian test of a *zeitgeist*. 'You are the only Muslim in India today to whom the community has the right to look upto for safe guidance through the storm which is coming to North-West India, and perhaps to the whole of India', wrote Iqbal to Jinnah on 21 June 1937.[48] Jinnah had acquired the charismatic dimension when he took up a charismatic goal. That was long before the Pakistan demand was formally launched in 1940. In 1937, the supreme goal was the restitution of power to Muslims. They were then in a political wilderness, having been severely denied their due share in power by the Congress which, having opted for the melting pot solution since the Nehru Report, had offered Muslims absorption, not collaboration, and went in determinedly and doggedly for setting up exclusive one-party governments. A leader need not necessarily be charismatic by himself. Instead, he may acquire a charismatic appeal when he comes to symbolize a charismatic goal. Churchill was not charismatic at the Battle of Galilee in 1915, nor when he went into the first post-war British general elections in July 1945. He was, however, a charismatic leader of the highest calibre between 1940 and 1945 when he symbolized the stout British defiance against the deadly German plans to invade, conquer and occupy the British Isles for good. The cause he then stood for stolidly against all odds and symbolized was an inherently charismatic goal; hence Churchill got transformed into a charismatic leader, almost overnight. Likewise, Jinnah's promise to restitute power to Muslims at a time, when they had reached their nadir, transformed Jinnah into a charismatic leader.[49]

The Pakistan demand represents the crafting of a new strategy to reach this charismatic goal: the restitution of power to Muslims. 'If the UP sample [where the Muslims were denied a share in power in 1937]', notes Penderel Moon, 'was to be the pattern of Congress's political conduct, then what would be the position of Muslims when a federal government for all-India came to be formed? There would be no room on the throne of India save for Congress and Congress stooges.'[50] Thus, if Muslims cannot share the throne of India with the Hindus, then, they should create and craft a throne for themselves alone in their demographically dominant regions.

To sum up, whereas Jinnah's predecessors and contemporaries had guided the course of Indo-Muslim history, he altered it. These contemporaries included not only Muslim leaders, but, as was pointed out by Hodson, Hindu leaders and British statesman as well.[51] Indeed, to quote Kenneth Cragg, 'there are few more total and rapid reversals in history'[52] than that represented by the arrival of Pakistan. And since 'the really decisive advocacy, as well as the epitome of the causation' of Pakistan belonged to Jinnah,[53] he was what Sidney Hook calls an 'event-making', rather than an 'eventful', man: one who had helped to create 'a fork in the historical road' and left 'the positive imprint of his personality upon history—an imprint that is still observable after he has disappeared from the scene'.[54]

An imprint of one such personality upon history was delineated by Alfred Broachard when he said, 'without Ataturk it is certain that there would have been no Turkey.'[55] To John Marlowe, the re-birth of Turkey under Ataturk aborted long-term Allied plans and designs in the Middle East—'to push the frontiers of Europe eastwards to the old limits of the Roman Empire, to re-integrate the Levant into the sphere of European civilization, to recreate the Mediterranean as a European *Mare Nostrum* and so, in effect, reverse the effects of the defeat which Islam had inflicted on Christianity 1300 years before'. Moreover, 'Ataturk's successful defiance of the victorious Allies emboldened Iraqis and Egyptians to rise against the British, and Syrians to rise against the French rule' Indeed, to Marlowe, 'the long retreat of the West, which started with the Greek defeat by the Turkish revolutionary army at the battle of Sakarya [1922] on the road to Ankara is still [1964] going on'.[56] To this, one may add, it is still going on, forty-one years after Marlowe's insightful comment, with the Iranian Revolution of 1979 representing the most spectacular and the most successful defiance of the West—more spectacular and more successful in terms of social depth and societal transformation than even that of Turkey. In perspective, then, Ataturk had materially, substantially and most significantly helped to alter the course of history across the entire sprawling Middle East.

And in the case of Jinnah, the imprint is observable not only on the empirical plane in the continued existence of Pakistan, but also at the conceptual or theoretical level. In the Khalistan demand, in (Northern) Cyprus, in former Yugoslavia, in Chechnya, Jinnah's (self-determination and/or partition) paradigm has been adopted, or is being insisted upon, as the most rational, the most sensible and the least acerbic solution to thwart the permanent dominance of the numerically larger (ethnic, linguistic and/or religious) group over the smaller one(s) in a bi-or multi-national 'country'/state. Thus, such event-making men represent, as it were, an independent or 'accidental' variable in their respective cosmos, casting lengthening shadows across the corridors of history, and beyond time and space.

No wonder, in the subcontinental context, Jinnah became, as it were, the crystal in the crucible of Indo-Muslim leadership since the 1760s. And that explains why he was hailed as the *Quaid-i-Azam* ('Great Leader') during his lifetime, and as the greatest Muslim since Aurangzeb (1619–1707) after his death.[57]

NOTES

*An earlier version of this paper was published under the title, 'Jinnah and the Making of Pakistan: The Role of the Individual in History', in The *Journal of South Asian and Middle Eastern Studies*, vol. xxi: No. 1, Fall 1997, pp. 1–16.

1. Sidney Hook, *The Hero in History: A Study in Limitation and Possibility* (Boston: Beacon Press, 1956), p. 152.
2. E.g., see Aziz Ahmad, *Studies in Islamic Culture in the Indian Environment* (Karachi: Oxford University Press, reprint, 1970), p. 276; Percival Spear, *India: A Modern History* (University of Michigan Press, 1961), pp. 408–10; Walter T. Wallbank, *A Short History of India and Pakistan* ((New York: New American Library, 1963), p. 233; Richard Symonds, *The Making of Pakistan* (London: Faber and Faber, 2nd edn., 1950), p. 193, and Ishtiaq Husain Qureshi, *The Muslim Community of the Indo-Pakistan Subcontinent (610–1947)* (the Hague: Mouton and Co., 1962). Symonds was, however, a contemporary observer, and not a historian.
3. Jinnah had himself described Pakistan in such terms when he asserted that 'Pakistan started the moment the first non-Muslim was converted to Islam in India long before the Muslims established their rule'. See Jamil-ud-Din Ahmad (ed.), *Speeches and Writings of Mr Jinnah* (Lahore: Ashraf, reprint, 1964), II: 2. However, there is a fundamental difference between the approaches of Jinnah on the one hand, and the latter day historians and analysts on the other. Jinnah presented this 'womb' theory, if only to argue out the case for Pakistan in historical terms, and, moreover, to counter the most telling arguments of his detractors, who pronounced the Pakistan demand as an historical absurdity, besides controverting the facts of geography, race, language, and culture, and economic and defence requirements. Thus Jinnah enunciated this theory *before* the event, if only to endow the Pakistan demand with a historical clout, while the latter day historians and analysts adumbrated it *after* the event.
4. E.g., Margaret Bourke-White, *Halfway to Freedom* (New York: Simon and Shuster, 1946), p. 13; Editorial, 'Mr Jinnah', *The Times* (London), 13 September 1948; D.F. Karaka, 'Jinnah Told Me', *March* (Bombay), 15 September 1948; Frank Moraes, *Yonder One World: A Study of Asia and*

the West (New York: MacMillan, 1958), p. 112; Leonard Mosley, *The Last Days of British Raj* (London: Weidenfeld and Nicholson, 1961), p. 239; Penderel Moon, *Divide and Quit* (London: Chatto and Windus, 1964), pp. 37–38; H.V. Hodson, *The Great Divide: Britain-India-Pakistan* (London: Hutchinson, 1969), pp. 37–38. John Terraine, *The Life and Times of Lord Mountbatten* (London: Arrow Books, 1970), pp. 193–94; and Ian Stephens, 'The Creative Statesman', in Khalid Hasan (ed.), *Quaid-i-Azam Mohamed Ali Jinnah: A Centenary Tribute, 1876–1976* (London: Embassy of Pakistan, n.d., but 1977), p. 18. Percival Spear, Review of Hector Bolitho *Jinnah: Creator of Pakistan* in the *Twentieth Century* (London, April 1955) p. 384.

5. Hodson, *op. cit.*, pp. 37–38.
6. *Economist* (London), 17 September 1949.
7. Edward Hallett Carr, *What is History?* (New York: Vintage Books, 1961), p. 68.
8. For an exposition of the two theories, see Carl G. Gustavson, *A Preface to History* (New York: McGraw Hill, 1955), pp. 123–24.
9. F.J.C. Hearnshaw, 'The Science of History', in William Rose (ed.), *An Outline of Modern Knowledge* (London: Victor Gollanz, 1937), p. 800.
10. See Sharif al Muhjahid, *Quaid-i-Azam Jinnah: Studies in Interpretation* (Karachi: Quaid-i-Azam Academy, 1981), ch. 1.
11. J. Christopher Herold, *The Age of Napoleon* (New York: American Heritage Publishing Co., 1963), pp. 6–7. Herold seems to echo what Carr, essentially a social determinist, said at the conceptual level: 'Society and the individual are inseparable; they are necessary and complementary to each other, not opposites'. Carr, *op. cit.*, p. 36.
12. David C. McClelland, *The Achieving Society* (New York: D. Von Nostrand, 1961), p. 392.
13. Karl Marx and Frederick Engels, *Selected Works* (Moscow: Progress Publishers, 1970), I: 398.
14. Cited in Georgi Plekhanov, 'The Role of the Individual in History', in Patric Gardiner (ed.), *Theories of History* (New York: The Free Press, 1959), pp. 147–48.
15. McClelland, *op. cit.*, pp. 391–92.
16. Hook, *op. cit.*, p. 106.
17. Plekhanov, *loc. cit.*, p. 148.
18. Editorial, 'Mr Jinnah', *The Times* (London), 13 September 1948, Interestingly though, Sarvepalli Gopal (*Jawaharlal Nehru: A Biography* [Delhi: Oxford University Press, 1975], I:357), comes to a similar conclusion: '...Jinnah knew *precisely* what he wanted and where he was going' [italics for emphasis].
19. Leon Trotsky, *The History of the Russian Revolution*, trans. Max Eastman (New York: Simon and Schuster, 1932), I: 330.
20. Hook, *op. cit.*, pp. 218–19.

21. Cf. Responding to K.M. Munshi's 'Thank God Pakistan [is] out of picture' congratulatory telegram, Sardar Vallabhbhai Patel, 'the lodestar of the Congress' and the high priest of 'the sacred ideal of National Unity', wrote on 17 May 1946, 'Since many years, for the first time, an authoritative government pronouncement [i.e., the Cabinet Mission Plan of 16 May] in clear terms has been made against the possibility of Pakistan in any shape or form'. Patel to Munshi, 17 May 1947, K.M. Munshi, *Indian Constitutional Development* (Bombay: Bharatia Vidya Bhawan 1967), 1:103.

22. See Hook, *op. cit.,* pp. 154.

23. *Ibid.,* pp. 154, 156–57.

24. *Le Soir* (Antwerp), 26 March 1981.

25. See Nehru's 10 July 1946 press conference statement in S. Gopal (ed.), *Selected Works of Jawaharlal Nehru* (New Delhi: Orient Longman, 1972–82), 15: 242–43

26. See Gandhi's statements and speeches in *The Collected Works of Mahatma Gandhi* (New Delhi: Ministry of Information and Broadcasting, 1969–84), 84:162, 165, 171; 85:466; 86:228. See also Congress President (Azad) to Viceroy (Wavell), 14 June 1946, *The Transfer of Power 1942–7* (London: HMSO, 1977), VII: 939.

27. Herbert Spencer, *The Study of Sociology* (New York, 1912), p. 37.

28. Robert L. Carneiro, 'Herbert Spencer', in David L. Sills (ed.), *International Encyclopedia of the Social Sciences* (New York: Macmillan, 1968), 15: 125.

29. See Hook, *op. cit.,* ch. IV.

30. Plekhanov, loc. cit., pp. 146–47.

31. *Ibid.,* pp. 152–53.

32. Hook, *op. cit.,* pp. 100, 98.

33. Dean Acheson, *Present At the Creation* (New York: Signet, 1969), pp. 498–508.

34. Patrick M. Morgan, *Theories and Approaches to International Politics: What are we to Think* (New Jersey: 3rd edn., 1982), p. 45.

35. Cited in *ibid.,*

36. Hook, *op. cit.,* p. 155.

37. Carr, *op. cit.,* p. 67.

38. Hook, *op. cit.,* p. xiii.

39. Cited in Edgar Alexander, *Adenauer and the New Germany* (New York: Farar, Straus and Cudahy, 1957), p. 17.

40. Carr, *op. cit.,* p. 68.

41. S. Gopal (ed.), *Selected Works of Jawaharlal Nehru* (New Delhi: Orient Longman, 1976), 8: 120–21. This statement, dated 10 January 1937, meant to rebut Jinnah's third-party claim (see below), was a rephrasing and reiteration of Nehru's earlier statement of 18 September 1936 (*ibid.,* 7: 468).

42. *Star of India* (Calcutta), 6 January 1937.

43. For details and documentation, see Sharif al Mujahid, 'Jinnah and Muslim Politics' and 'Towards Pakistan' in Waheed-uz-Zaman and M. Saleem Akhtar (eds.), *Islam in South Asia* (Islamabad: National Institute of Historical and Cultural Research, 1993), pp. 438, 38, 463.
44. For details and documentation, see Sharif al Mujahid, 'Towards Pakistan', loc. cit., p. 463.
45. Carr, *op. cit.*, p. 67.
46. *Ibid.*, p. 68.
47. See above, Hodson's evaluation, note 5.
48. Sharif al Mujahid (ed.), *Ideological Foundations of Pakistan* (Islamabad: International Islamic University, 1999), p. 54.
49. For a self-contained study on the charismatic dimension of Jinnah's leadership, see Sikandar Hayat's forthcoming monograph, 'The Charismatic Leader: Quaid-i-Azam Jinnah and the Creation of Pakistan', and for an extended discussion, see Sikandar Hayat, 'Charisma, Crisis and the emergence of Quaid-i-Azam', *Journal of the Pakistan Historical Society* (Karachi), Quaid-i-Azam Number, L: 1 & 2, January–June 2002, pp. 31–46.
50. Penderel Moon, *Divide and Quit* (London: Chatto and Windus, 1946), pp. 14–15.
51. See above, note 5.
52. Kenneth Cragg, *Counsels in Contemporary Islam,* Islamic Surveys (Edinburgh: University Press, 1965), pp. 21.
53. *Ibid.*, p. 20.
54. Hook, *op. cit.*, p. 157.
55. See above, note 24.
56. John Marlowe's review of *Ataturk: The Rebirth of a Nation* by Lord Kinross (London, 1964) in *The Spectator* (London), 6 November 1964, p. 609.
57. Maulana Shabbir Ahmad Usmani's funeral oration, 12 September 1948, *Dawn* (Karachi), 13 September 1948.

11

The Lost Jinnah
Syed Jaffar Ahmed

As for the role of the Quaid-i-Azam Mohammad Ali Jinnah in the partition of India, the historians have contested each other for long. While some refer to the primacy of the historical forces—though interpreted differently—in determining the fate of the subcontinent and attributing to Jinnah the role of a mere facilitator, the others hold himself to be the primary historical force, suggesting Pakistan to be a 'one-man achievement', as Leonard Mosley argued.

It would not be wrong to say that if one does not subscribe to either of the extreme positions, and avoids interpreting the role of the deep-seated socio-political factors and that of the individuals, rather mechanically, one may conveniently comprehend the correlation between the two.

The historically evolved subjective conditions do not operate above the objective impetuses, fashioned around a particular set of people. Nor do the individuals, no matter how powerful they appear, undermine or control the processes set in motion over a long period of time.

However, the role of an individual becomes over-sized at times when he is uniquely positioned to respond to events taking place at an unusually fast pace; when, in the words of Lenin, an age starts moving at the pace of an steam engine from that of a bullock-cart.

The same happened in the case of Jinnah, who, in the eventful decade before Partition, corresponded to the fast-changing situation. What further magnified Jinnah's role was the fact that the platform of Muslim separatism which he represented had no one else to match his stature or even qualify to be his shadow. This was nicely epitomized by Beverely Nichols when he said: 'If Gandhi goes, there is always Nehru, or Rajgopalachari, or Patel or a dozen others. But if Jinnah goes, who is there?'

So if the creation of Pakistan has come to be identified so closely with Jinnah, it has this background which, compared to other contemporary situations, makes it unique too. Hence, Stanley Wolpert's oft-quoted statement: 'Few individuals significantly alter the course of history. Fewer still modify the map of the world. Hardly anyone can be credited with creating a nation-state. Jinnah did all three.'

In the context of the above, it is an intriguing paradox that Jinnah, who mattered so much in the creation of the country, has influenced so little in shaping it into what it has become today. Perhaps no country would have distanced itself from the vision of its founding fathers to the extent Pakistan has.

Jinnah certainly was not an ideology who would have left treatises on politics or economy, but he did have views and a vision about the country he had so arduously brought into being. It was this vision that was deprived of realization after his death. Tributes are showered at him regularly, his dates of birth and death are celebrated nationally, he is held at the apex of national honour, and yet he does not matter much in Pakistan. That his ideas on politics and society could be invoked in guiding the country's policies have seldom been considered seriously.

After fifty-six years of independence, where does the nation stand today? Without being cynical, one finds to one's dismay that the basic notion of nationhood missing in the country. Instead of going into the background of various cleavages in Pakistani society, one may confine oneself to the more apparent and presently the more relevant political and ideological divisions, and then to see that, apprehending these, what the Founder of the Nation had propounded to be the viable course in building a modern and egalitarian nationhood.

Today, the country, which was achieved through political and constitutional means, seems to be groping once again for the means which might help civilianize its fourth military rule. For a large part of her history the country was deprived of a constitution. A consensual and workable (though not free of weaknesses) constitution could be made only after half of the country was amputated, demonstrating what an uphill task it had been for the country's leadership to evolve a consensus.

And when the constitution was made, and at such a tragic cost, it was subjected in subsequent years to suspension or abeyance by ambitious military rulers, in cohesion with a pliable judiciary. Where would have Jinnah stood in such a scheme of things, for he was someone who had, even when he was taking on the colonial power and defying its will through his political stands, persuaded the military to abide by discipline, and not to break ranks with the government it was under oath to be loyal to.

As for the role of the military, Jinnah had the clearest of minds. Thus, while addressing Pakistan Army officers and men in Quetta on 14 June 1948, he actually read out the text of the oath which made it binding on the military men to affirm their allegiance to the constitution and the government.

He asked his audience to study the constitution and 'understand its true constitutional and legal implications when you say that you will be faithful to the constitution of the Dominion'. This is what Jinnah was saying of the armed forces' obligation to the constitution. Thirty years later, General Ziaul Haq proclaimed: 'What is constitution? A document of twelve pages! I can tear it into pieces and throw it away.'

Insofar as the ideological division in the country is concerned, one can say for sure that the menace of religious extremism and intolerance pose the biggest threat to Pakistani society today. Over the years, hundreds of religious groups and militant organizations have emerged, preferring their own versions of Islam and Jihad. Unfortunately, the militants associated with these groups are less conversant with the wider teachings of Islam and are moved and motivated by the spirit to export Islam to other regions through armed means. They are all operating with the zeal to ensure the domination of Islam over the world.

However, it must also be accepted that their aspirations alone have not put them on the path they are following, but they have been pushed and pampered by external forces as well as the country's own institutions of highest authority. The extremist groups have not only distorted the image of Islam in the world, but have also sought to divide the Pakistani society along sectarian lines because in almost all cases these groups regard their own sectarian versions as the *actual* Islam, and are not tolerant of other versions.

As a result of this, these groups have not only been engaged across the borders, in Afghanistan and Indian-held Kashmir, but have been operating against each other as well within the country. According to one study, in the last two decades about 2,000 people have lost their lives in internecine sectarian feuds and terrorist actions. The people attracted to these outfits are mostly youth belonging to the poor class who are attracted by the name of religion by these organizations in the background of the state's failure in fulfilling its responsibilities to help sustain its poor. The most unfortunate aspect of the extremist religious phenomenon is that it has been cultivated under the patronage of the state's own security apparatus.

The extremists hold a parochial worldview, making them paranoid of the 'other'. Being incapable of challenging others through dialogue or intellectual means, they hold to guns and have gradually come to hold society at large hostage. They are least bothered about what compromises the state-formation necessitates and what constitutional values constitute a democratic society. In other words, they are unable to comprehend the nature of the modern nation-state which is a political entity operating above, but not against, divergent religio-cultural identities.

The ignorance of the extremist class about the ideas of state and nationhood runs counter to Jinnah's way of thinking who held a clear position on how nations come into being and what tends to deconstruct them. In fact, Jinnah was the most notable of all Muslim leaders of his time who had understood well the dynamics of the relationship between democracy and nationalism.

Not only this, he had also applied this understanding, in a very creative manner, to the political conditions prevailing in India. By creatively interpreting the modern concepts of state craft—

nationalism and democracy, for instance—in the Indian context, Jinnah was able to realize that in a country where culturally defined political groups have the potential to become the majority or minority political groups rather permanently, there always is a need to upgrade the minority group or safeguard its interests so that the national fabric is not torn apart.

In India, the Muslims were likely to become a permanent minority in case representative institutions were introduced without safeguards for them. Therefore, Jinnah rose to take up their case. But in doing so he was pursuing a political, and not a religious, course. Jinnah did not approve of the use of religion for political purposes—a fact affirmed by his declining to participate in the Khilafat Movement, described by him as 'a false religious frenzy'.

So, if while declining to be tempted to resort to religious emotions Jinnah led the platform of Muslim separatism, it was because using religion for political purposes is one thing while upholding or supporting the political rights of a religious group is another. Jinnah pursued the latter. He sought to resolve the communal problem in India in the Indian context, but after all his efforts were frustrated, he was left with no option, but to ask for the establishment of a separate Muslim homeland. This means that Muslim separatism was not a given or a priority thing as far as Jinnah was concerned.

After the creation of Pakistan, Jinnah was mindful that the same mistake of letting the nation divide into a majority and a minority on religious lines should not be repeated. So he sought to integrate all religious communities within the framework of one Pakistan nation.

A lot has been written about his speech of 11 August 1947, but unfortunately very few have tried to understand the underlying political philosophy in it. This speech was not conducted on the spur of the moment, nor was it merely an attempt to win over the confidence of the minorities, but read in its totality, the speech is an excellent exposition of Jinnah's political thought.

Therein, Jinnah laid down his proposed strategy for nation-building in the newly born country, and his manifesto in this regard. And while doing this, he first narrated what, to him, was the cause behind the partition of India which got divided since it failed to resolve the angularities of the majority and the minority community; 'Indeed, if you ask me this has been the biggest hindrance in the way of India to attain its freedom and independence and but for this we would have been free peoples long ago. No power can hold another nation, and specially a nation of 400 million souls, in subjection; nobody could have conquered you, and even [if] it had happened, nobody could have continued its hold on you for any length of time.'

After discussing the role of the angularities of the majority and the minority in India, he referred to an opposite case of the Great Britain, where the state had been successful in resolving the divide between the Roman Catholics and Protestants by bringing an end to the discrimination between them and making them equal citizens. Jinnah said: 'Today you might say with justice that the Roman Catholics and Protestants do not exist; what exists now is that every man is a citizen, and equal citizen of Great Britain and they are all members of the nation.'

Having described the equality of citizens as the fundamental principle and a cornerstone of nationhood, Jinnah proposed his ideal for Pakistan: 'Now I think we should keep that in front of us as our ideal, and you will find that in the course of time Hindus would cease to be Hindus and Muslims would cease to be Muslims, not in the religious sense, because that is the personal faith of an individual, but in the political sense as citizens of the state.'

These statements of Jinnah sufficiently show that he wanted to see the state in Pakistan to be neutral with respect to different religious affiliations of its citizens. This could be realized if religion was accepted as personal faith of the individual. But, unfortunately, Jinnah's political philosophy could not be appreciated by those who came to the helm of affairs in Pakistan, with the result that the state increasingly indulged in matters which eroded its neutrality.

Almost all authoritarian and military regimes relied on religion and religious symbols for legitimizing themselves. The religious card was played by political leadership as well in an uninhibited manner. For a large part of the country's history, separate electorates remained on the statute book. The constitution of 1973 was the first constitution which considered it important to declare Islam as the state religion. Not only this, but it also laid down that only a Muslim could become the president and the prime minister of the country.

One may find this condition to be against the concept of neutrality of the state and the idea of the equality of citizens which, quite interestingly, is also upheld in the same constitution as a fundamental right. This was also not necessary, as with its 97 per cent or more population being Muslim, there was hardly any possibility of any non-Muslim ever obtaining these offices. The worst action of the state elite and institutions was to get into the business of creating extremist religious organizations for pursuing foreign policy and the so-called national security agendas.

With religious intolerance and extremism looming large in the country, Jinnah seems to have become irrelevant today. But he is most relevant if Pakistan wishes to emerge from its present ashes of rage and hatred.

12

American Views of Mohammad Ali Jinnah and the Pakistan Liberation Movement

Betty Miller Unterberger

14 August 1947 is a date of deep historic significance to the peoples of the Indian subcontinent. On that day the two great states of India and Pakistan achieved independence and became dominions of the British Commonwealth of Nations. In the rise of both nations, as is characteristic of most national movements, there were three principal ingredients: a community possessing distinctive characteristics, a particular set of circumstances under which that community would respond to the call of nationalism, and the leadership to coordinate the first two to produce a nation.

In both India and Pakistan the circumstances that lent the final impetus to the emergent nationalism fostered by the First World War was the outbreak of the Second World War. However, effective leadership was a sine qua non of this process. Successful national leadership customarily has had two component parts: one or more outstanding personalities to inspire loyalty, and permanent, well-organized machinery, political or otherwise, through which to develop a mass following. Nationhood for both India and Pakistan was in large measure the achievement of such a party and leader. In the case of India it was the Indian National Congress party and the internationally acclaimed Hindu Mahatma, Mohandas K. Gandhi. For Pakistan, it was the All-India Muslim League and its Quaid-i-Azam (great leader) Mohammad Ali Jinnah.[1]

Among the many responsibilities facing the United States as a result of the world leadership thrust upon it by the Japanese attack on Pearl Harbor was the problem of formulating a response to nationalism in Asia and Africa. Just as in the First World War, nationalism and the accompanying issue of self-determination presented especially difficult dilemmas for the United States, when the independence movements challenged the empires of allied nations. The problem was most difficult concerning Great Britain and its Indian empire. The American people naturally sympathized with nationalist movements that had often received their inspiration from the American revolution. Moreover, the United States was eager to win the confidence of the emerging nations by championing their cause. Yet Winston S. Churchill, Britain's wartime leader, was quick to make clear the limits within which American interference with India would be accepted. President Roosevelt might dislike Britain's imperial position, but in the face of diplomatic and military crisis he soon learned when and where American pressure might be applied.[2]

Prior to the Second World War, American public and official interest in India had been minimal. Americans knew little of Indian history, philosophy, religion, or politics, and commercial contacts between the two peoples had been slight. Yet the Indian National Congress was clearly the most advanced and certainly the most widely known nationalist movement of the colonial era, and Gandhi had become the symbol of the nationalist strivings of the Asian peoples.[3] On the other hand, both Jinnah and the Muslim League were virtually unknown in the United States until the Second World War despite Jinnah's recognition in Britain and India as one of the foremost leaders of the Indian independence movement. Actually, most Americans had little understanding of the complexities of the existing political situation in British India. They generally believed that the Indian National Congress, founded in 1885, represented the political aspirations of all the elements of the Indian population. This may be partly due to the fact that since their independence the term 'Congress' had been associated in the American mind with the national legislature that represented all shades of political opinion. The propaganda of the Congress party of India helped to strengthen this misconception.[4] American interest in Congress's position aroused the concern of both Jinnah and the Muslim League, but the League had no effective spokesman in the United States and this resulted in general American ignorance of Jinnah's position and Muslim League policies.[5] In any case, the Muslim League, founded in 1906, had been, in its formative years, a national political organization without either a nation or a national cause. It was not until the 1930s that it gradually acquired the leadership and the administrative machinery that would ultimately catapult it to victory.[6]

It was Jinnah, virtually alone, who led the Muslim League to a position from which it could force the partition of India and the creation of Pakistan. To the people who followed him, Jinnah was more than the supreme head of the state and the personal architect of the Islamic nation of Pakistan. He commanded not only their confidence but also their imagination. In the face of difficulties that might easily have overwhelmed him, he fulfilled the hope foreshadowed in the vision of the great and revered poet-philosopher, Sir Muhammad Iqbal, by creating for the Muslims of India a homeland for which they could envision the old glory of Islam growing afresh in a modern state worthy of its place in the comity of nations. Few statesmen have shaped events by their policy more surely than Jinnah. Even his critics accepted Jinnah as a great man because his actions and influence in the last years of his life changed the course of history.[7] Certainly among his people he was regarded as a modern Moses who led them to the promised land. What the ultimate verdict of history on Jinnah will be, time will decide. In the Valhalla of the Muslim world his niche is secure.[8]

But what was the American image of Jinnah? How was he regarded by the American public, the press, American officialdom, those Americans who came to know him personally? The American historian is hard pressed to find an answer to this question, for so little research has centered on US-Pakistan relations. American diplomatic historians have paid only slight attention to the role of Jinnah in the struggle for the independence of the subcontinent.[9] Moreover, Jinnah's life awaits an American biographer since fulfilled by Stanley Wolpert. Research into recently declassified official documents reveals that Jinnah was known by numerous American officials in India and was interviewed by some of the most prominent American press correspondents. What then does an examination of these materials, combined with an analysis of the American periodical and newspaper press, reveal about the American view of Jinnah?

First a brief biography is necessary. Jinnah was born on 25 December 1876 in Karachi to a commercially advanced family in a Muslim majority territory. He had attended the Christian Mission High School in Karachi, and at fifteen he was sent to England to study law at Lincoln's Inn. During his stay he seems to have stood out among the other Indian students in London. He passed his examinations in two years, and at the age of eighteen he became the youngest Indian student ever to be called to the bar. During his stay in England, Jinnah became devoted to the Western political philosophy of liberalism. Several of the Indian leaders cultivated his friendship by involving him in their political activities, especially in the successful campaign to get an Indian elected to the British Parliament. Jinnah often went to Parliament to listen to the speeches of the British leaders. His convictions about the effectiveness of the parliamentary system date from this period.[10]

Outwardly, therefore, Jinnah appeared to be largely free of more traditional Muslim influences. Furthermore, he was already a member of the Indian National Congress when the Muslim League was founded, and for many years he actively participated in the Congress party and worked for Hindu-Muslim political cooperation.[11] He also strove to make a success of his legal career. Although he was the only Muslim lawyer in Bombay at that time, he was soon recognized as the most brilliant advocate in the Bombay bar. He also became the highest paid Indian lawyer in his time. Once his intelligence was recognized, responsibilities were given to him by those who trusted his capacities. Two of the leading Congress personalities of this period, Dadabhai Naoroji and G.K. Gokhale, treated Jinnah as a friend and a possible candidate for a place of authority in the Congress party. In those days of Hindu-Muslim cooperation it seems to have been taken for granted that the young Jinnah would play an important role in the future struggle for independence from Britain. Later, Jinnah participated in the Muslim League Council session of 1912, which drafted the change in League policy and amended its constitution to include the objective of 'a system of self-government suitable to India, through Constitutional means.'[12] He agreed to join the League shortly thereafter on condition that his loyalty to the Muslim League and Muslim interests would not mean dissociation from the cause of self-government for a united India. He continued to work for educational and legal reforms to benefit the Muslims, while using his 'good offices' to bring the League and the Congress into closer harmony.[13]

Jinnah's efforts in this regard culminated in 1916 at Lucknow when he persuaded the League to meet simultaneously with the Congress and was the chief negotiator of the Lucknow Pact signed by both Congress and the League. This was the first and only complete agreement ever reached by these parties on a future constitution for India. The Muslims were to receive one-third of the elective seats of the Central Legislature and were to have reserved seats in the provinces in proportion to their population in those provinces. Congress also agreed that the Muslims should have separate electorates, both in the provinces and at the centre.[14] At Lucknow, Jinnah was elected president of the League session for the first time. He was now playing a triple role as a leader of the League, a leader in the Congress, and a member of the Imperial Legislative Council, a three-fold honour virtually unique in the annals of Indian political leadership.[15]

While League-Congress cooperation continued to a degree during the years of the First World War and immediately thereafter, gradual changes were taking place in both parties as each group mobilized for participation in the progressively greater degree of self-government being conceded by the British. As the new nationalism spread through Indian society it became more closely associated with religious symbols and alignments; increasingly, religious heritage provided spiritual and cultural roots on which to base mass indigenous national development. Also, as Mahatma Gandhi came to the fore and the Congress was converted into a more radical nationalist and mass participation party, the Congress began to lose the support of some of its political moderates, among them Jinnah.[16] Also, at the same time, the moderate and more secular national position of Jinnah fell into growing disfavour within the Indian Muslim community.[17] The launching of the Khilafat (Caliphate) movement, the objectives of which included obtaining safeguards for the Muslim holy places, and the linking of this with Gandhi's noncooperation movement both increased the religious and political consciousness of the Indian Muslim community and for a time continued Hindu-Muslim cooperation against a common foe—the British.[18] However, when the Khilafat agitation ended in 1922 many Indian Muslims felt disillusioned and more than ever in need of a separate political voice apart from the Congress. There was also, however, some reaction in favour of a return to the safer, moderate policies of an earlier day. There was only one Muslim political leader of stature in India who had remained outside the Khilafat agitation and was, therefore, undamaged by its demise, and only one all-India Muslim political organization that had not lost credibility. Both the leader and the party had a moderate reputation. At the most propitious psychological moment, the leader, Jinnah, revived the All-India Muslim League. At the Lahore League sessions in May 1924 under the chairmanship of Jinnah, the scattered branches of the League were reorganized and political support for separate electorates and guarantees of religious safeguards for all communities were reiterated.[19]

Despite its communal overtones, however, both Jinnah and the Muslim League remained basically in a middle-of-the-road political position. It should be noted that President Woodrow Wilson's ideals of self-determination and justice for all peoples had made a deep impression on the Indian subcontinent.[20] The influence of that idealism on Jinnah can best be seen at an All Parties National Convention at Delhi. There, Jinnah formulated on behalf of the 'united front' of Muslim groups gathered there his famous 'Fourteen Points.' These included the separate electorate principle and constitutional provisions to safeguard the Muslim religion and culture that remained the bases of negotiations between the Muslims and other parties for a number of years. This was Jinnah's last great effort at reconciliation of Hindu and Muslim interests.

He was bluntly reminded that he had no right to speak on behalf of the Muslims because he did not represent them. Jinnah learned the lesson that political leadership did not rest on one's forensic ability to plead a political case. It also demanded political strength, that is, actual support from the masses of people.[21]

Commentators are generally agreed that it was the success of Gandhi and his followers in taking over the direction of nationalist activities in the early 1920s that led Jinnah to abandon the Congress. He apparently was repelled by what he viewed as the irrationality and unconstitutional agitation brought into the independence movement by Gandhi's massive civil disobedience programme. For a brief period he seems to have despaired of India. He left the country, apparently for good, and set up a law practice in England.[22]

The first mention of Jinnah in the American press came with his appointment as one of the fifty-eight delegates from British India to the first Round Table conference in London, opened by the king in St. James's Palace on 12 November 1930.[23] It was at this conference that the Muslim bloc presented an ultimatum to the Hindu leaders at London, asking for separate electorates and a share in public service.[24] On that occasion, Jinnah's speech was reproduced in full in the *New York Times*.[25]

During the conference, Beatrice Barnby, in a feature article in the *New York Times*, described the hereditary feud of the two great sects of India as the chief stumbling block at London's Round Table. She wrote graphically about the antagonism and difficulties bred over the centuries by the Moghul invasion, the clashing of different races in India, and the economic differences that split the unity of those who desired peace. 'Who will give way?', she asked. 'Will the minority of Mohammedans entrust their faith to the Hindus, their hereditary enemies? Or will the Hindus with an emancipated vision grant to their former conquerors an enlarged representation?'[26]

When twenty-seven representatives were named to study the rival Indian claims in a final effort to break the Hindu-Muslim deadlock, the *New York Times* noted that Jinnah saw little hope of inducing the extremists to yield. They found it 'regrettable' that both Jinnah, the Muslim leader, and Sir Tej Bahadur Sapru, the Hindu leader, had refused to serve since they were considered the 'most reasonable and unprejudiced' members of their respective groups. If the matter were left to them, there would be an end to the religious controversy, said the *New York Times*.[27]

The clash between Hindu and Muslim interests was, in fact, deeply embedded in the history of the subcontinent and could not be overcome by mere rhetorical shibboleth. That was why the Muslim leaders were desperately trying during the twenties and thirties to find a modus vivendi under a loose federation. The growing Muslim middle class, imbued with Western ideas, was becoming increasingly conscious of the social, cultural, and historical differences between the Hindus and the Muslims. One noted scholar has characterized the development as Anglo-Muslim synthesis as distinguished from Anglo-Hindu synthesis.[28] Indeed, the terms 'Hindu nationalism' and 'Muslim nationalism' were commonly used in political treatises by eminent leaders of both communities. American scholars also noted this. As early as 1923, Claude Van Tyne had written: 'The Moslems, 70 million of them in India, are to all intent a nation and the Government had to regard them as such.'[29]

In the last week of 1930, while the Round Table conference was still in session, Iqbal, the most important exponent of Muslim nationalism in the Indian subcontinent, announced the plan for an independent Muslim state on the North-West of India in his address to the annual Muslim League session at Allahabad. Iqbal posed the central question then facing modern Indian Islam; namely, 'is it possible to retain Islam as an ethical ideal, and to reject it as a polity in favour of national politics, in which religious attitude is not permitted to play any part? This question becomes of special importance in India, where the Muslims ... [are in a minority].'[30] Iqbal insisted that the very least the Muslims and the League must demand were communal safeguards. Pessimistic about the results of the Round Table conference, he also said that 'without the British empire, the formation of a consolidated North-West India Muslim state appears to me to be the final destiny of the Muslims, at least of North-West India... The life of Islam as a cultural force in this country very largely depends on its centralization in a specified territory.'[31]

While Iqbal's proposed Muslim state apparently was to be linked to an all-India Federation, the full text of his speech as it was reported implied that denial of at least the minimal Muslim demands for communal safeguards would inevitably cause a crisis to which the Muslims would react by pursuing a course of complete political independence. At the time, however, the implication of Iqbal's speech hardly seemed to be realized by the assembled Leaguers who were still hopeful that the Muslim delegation would obtain a sufficient political settlement at the Round Table conference. Iqbal was not alone in his thinking. In the early 1930s another Indian Muslim graduate student in England, Rahmet Ali, reportedly proposed that a Muslim nation be carved from the provinces of North-West India to be called Pakistan.[32]

The failure of the British government at the Round Table conferences in 1930–32 to reconcile the Hindu and Muslim factions or to present them with reforms mutually acceptable to their separate political aspirations brought increased bitterness to both factions.[33] For Jinnah, it marked a turning point in his thinking. He later declared that it was here that he had received the shock of his life at the Hindu attitude and sentiments that led him to conclude that there was no hope of unity. Disappointed and depressed about his country, he decided to settle in London.[34] The *New York Times* reported that Jinnah had urged speedy action on Muslim autonomy to allay suspicions, directing sharp criticism at the British government's policies. It also observed that he had emerged as Gandhi's bitterest enemy at the Round Table conference and was the last of the Indian delegates left in England.[35]

Meanwhile, the League was fighting for its survival. While it had been the only continuous all-India instrument in the development of a Muslim political identity, it had in the very process of providing a platform for the various shades of Muslim political opinion been torn apart by factionalism. More important, it had gradually lost a number of its key leaders, including Jinnah.[36] Although the League was able despite severe losses of men, money, and prestige to remain an ongoing concern, it was in a degraded

state shorn of dignity and power. It was at this stage that Great
Britain was preparing for a further relinquishment of power. With
other Muslims, Jinnah believed that transfer of rule to a united
India would mean Hindu domination. On the eve of the first
election to the provincial legislatures under the Government of
India Act of 1935, the League was the only likely organization
besides the Congress to contest the elections on anything resembling
an all-India scale. Consequently, as the elections approached, the
League turned to the one leader of all-India stature best able to
direct it in its campaign. The turning point came in 1936 when
the League secured the return of Jinnah to the League's presidency.
The weight of events convinced Jinnah that the Indian Muslims
needed him and that a middle-of-the-road league was the place for
him to use his leadership potential effectively.[37] Therefore, Jinnah
returned to India and continued his parliamentary efforts to
safeguard Muslim political rights. By 1937, Jawaharlal Nehru had
become an important leader. Jinnah sought to convince him that
the Muslims were a third party in Indian politics at that time, in
addition to Congress and the British. He indicated, however, that
the Muslims were 'ready to work as equal partners for the welfare
of India,' but Nehru and the Congress remained scornful and
Jinnah's offer was ignored. While the League, in its first all-India
election effort and after only six months of active organizing and
campaigning, polled only a small percentage of the Muslim votes
cast in the elections, it reportedly won almost 70 per cent of the
seats it contested. The Congress, however, discounted the League's
political power and would not sanction Congress League coalitions
in the provinces, even where the League was strong.[35] An apparent
impasse was reached when Jinnah wrote: 'Unless the Congress
recognizes the Muslim League on a footing of complete equality
and is prepared as such to negotiate for a ... settlement, we shall
have to wait and depend upon our inherent strength which will
determine the measure of distinction it possesses.'[39] In this crucial
dilemma, Jinnah turned more and more to a series of letters that
Iqbal had written him in 1936 and 1937. In these letters Iqbal,
concerned with the economic, social, and political advancement of
the Muslims, expressed the belief that 'in order to ... solve these

problems, it is necessary to redistribute the country and … provide one or more Muslim states.'[40] Then Iqbal had made a statement to Jinnah of far-reaching significance: 'You are the only Muslim in India today to whom the community has a right to look up for safe guidance through the storm which is coming to North-West India and perhaps to the whole of Pakistan.'[41] Iqbal's statement reinforced Jinnah's personality and developing beliefs. As a dynamic leader and a champion of both civil rights and social and economic progress, he found renewed inspiration in Iqbal's ideas for utilizing his unique abilities in the service of his community. Moreover, the Muslim feeling that the new provincial governments of the Congress were acting against Muslim interests served as a catalyst not only on Jinnah himself but also on Indian Muslims generally. It is from this period that Jinnah became known as the Quaid-i-Azam, and the League actively undertook to organize all classes of Muslims on a mass scale.[42] Although scholars disagree on the reasons behind the transformation of Jinnah's personal role and the turning of the Muslim League into an organization of the masses, all agree that he succeeded to a remarkable degree in subordinating the diverse elements of the Muslim League to his control and in launching a successful mass-contact movement among the Muslims.[43]

The positions of both the Muslim League and the Congress were vitally affected by the outbreak of war in 1939. The European conflict called into question more than ever the entire existing order of things on the Indian scene. More specifically, India's declaration of war in 1939 (decided by the Viceroy alone), the promulgation of the Atlantic Charter in 1941, and Churchill's interpretation of the charter all served to unsettle Indian affairs even more. Although the Congress condemned nazism and fascism, they held that since Britain had declared war without seeking or obtaining the consent of the Indian people, the Congress could not associate itself with the war effort unless India was declared an independent nation. All members of the Congress who held official positions resigned, and the Muslims celebrated the event with a day of thanksgiving for deliverance from Hindu tyranny. The Congress used the occasion to begin its 'quit India' movement and try to force the British to grant Indian independence immediately. One result was the jailing of the Congress leadership during much of the war period. Jinnah kept the Muslim League out of that particular struggle, using the time to further strengthen League power among the Indian Muslims.[44]

Although Jinnah's effective leadership of the Indian Muslims had received little attention in the American press, by the close of 1939 the *New York Times*, in its coverage of Indian affairs, had made clear his prominence as an important if not the most important Muslim leader in all of India.[45] John Gunther, in his book, *Inside Asia*, described Jinnah as one of the most important Asian leaders, an eloquent orator whose opposition to the Hindus was bitter and inflamed. He noted that although Congress accused Jinnah of being a flagrant opportunist, Jinnah's attack on Congress had split and weakened nationalist sentiment. He described the All-India Muslim League as the Muslim analogy to Congress, though not nearly as powerful.[46] By early December 1939, *Time* magazine considered Jinnah sufficiently important to run his portrait and describe his role as 'the greatest single force for disunity in all disunited India.' Obviously unsympathetic, *Time* noted that while the great Hindus, Gandhi and Nehru, obviously worked toward an India for Indians, the leader of the Muslims usually thought first about independence for Muslims and afterward about independence for Indians. Jinnah's reasons for endorsing the British white paper of the previous month, which deferred dominion status until after the war, were described as partly political and partly religious: 'He is a minority leader, who wants both to curry favor with Britain and to avoid a 'freedom' in which Moslems are bound to worse enemies than the British.' Nevertheless, *Time* recognized the historic depth of Muslim Hindu religious and social differences.[47]

As early as 1940 the *New York Times* had made clear that before any solution to the Indian problem could be effected, not only the Congress party but also the All-India Muslim League must be pacified. They reported that Jinnah, in correspondence with Nehru, had been adamant that before the Muslims would join the Congress two steps were necessary: first, the Congress must recognize the Muslim League as the authoritative and representative organization of Indian Muslims; and second, Hindu-Muslim differences must be settled. Jinnah had described as 'unwarranted and mean' Nehru's assertion that the Muslim leader was bent on the preservation of British domination over India.[48] The *New York Times* also observed that the Muslims comprised the best part of the Indian army and the British were unwilling therefore to antagonize them. This was an argument that was to play an increasing role in American attitudes toward Jinnah and the Muslims in the next years.[49]

Although events in India were overshadowed by the war in Europe, they received increasing attention in the American press. In general, the position of the All-Indian National Congress was endorsed by liberal journals as well as traditionally pro-British newspapers like the *New York Times* and the *Christian Science Monitor*. Nehru and his views also were coming increasingly and favourably to the attention of the American public. Emphasis was placed on his support of the nationalist cause throughout Asia. Moreover, Nehru himself presented the case of the National Congress in the *Atlantic Monthly* in an article entitled 'India's Demand and England's Answer.' The India League of America also had a continuing voice in the United States in its publication of *India Today*, a brief monthly edited by Anup Singh.[50] Jinnah and the Muslim League viewed American sympathy toward the Congress's position with concern. In early March 1940 the chairman of the League's Foreign Committee called upon the American people to intercede with the National Congress on behalf of the Muslims, whom he claimed had no common interest with the Hindu majority. However, since the League had no effective spokesman in the United States, the result was continued American ignorance of the Muslim League's policies.[51]

Yet, it must be noted that two articles on Jinnah and the Muslims appeared in the periodical, Asia. One described him as an enigma, incorruptible by any outside agency but consumed by exaggerated ambition, and a person who bid fair to end, 'politically, as a victim of his own overreaching ambitions.' The second article, however, attributed the growth in popularity of both Jinnah and the Muslim League to an awakened mass consciousness among Muslims. Although recognizing Jinnah's genius in reorganizing the

Muslim League and building it into a major political organization, the author observed that the Muslim League was not fully supported by all Muslims, many of whom had serious disagreements regarding its methods and objectives.[52]

In general, therefore, American newspapers and periodicals gave little sympathetic coverage to Jinnah and the Muslim League's position or even to the League's monumental demand of 23 March 1940, the Lahore resolution, which in effect asked for the creation of Pakistan.[53] Jinnah here enunciated the demand Iqbal made ten years earlier. He announced that no constitutional plan would be workable in India or acceptable to the Muslims if it did not provide that the 'areas in which the Muslims are numerically in a majority as the North-Western and Eastern zones of India should be grouped to constitute Independent States in which the constituent units shall be autonomous and sovereign.' The resolution implied the independence of these two states from India but not from one another.[54]

Jinnah and the Muslim League viewed India not as a country but essentially as a subcontinent, dismissing the unity of India as a mere fantasy. In the past, the subcontinent had been united only under a few strong and ambitious rulers but had invariably fallen to pieces with the removal of the iron hand. It was bound to disintegrate again after the departure of the British. Nation and nationality were purely Western concepts with little relevance to the facts of Indian life, for Western democratic forms presupposed a community with an identity of interest and unity of thought that were absent in India. In the subcontinent, religion was not an individual or personal affair, as neither Islam nor Hinduism were religions in the sense in which the West understood religion. Properly speaking, they were two social codes representing two civilizations as distinct from one another in traditions and ways of life as the nations of Europe. The divergent nationalities of India would not be transformed into a nation by virtue of cornmon subjection to a democratic constitution. In constitutional usage Muslims were described as a minority, but they could not be likened to European minorities. They were a nation by any definition of the term, and party government coupled with parliamentarism would lead to their permanent servitude. No nation would be willing to accept a democratic constitution that endangered its own integrity. The Muslims, as a national group living in a definite territory, were entitled to separate statehood. Jinnah compressed these ideas in one of his best-known passages:

> Hindus and Muslims belong to two religious philosophies, social customs and literatures. They neither intermarry nor interdine ... and, indeed, they belong to two different civilizations which are based mainly on conflicting ideas and conceptions. Their aspects on life and of life are different ... Hindus and Muslims derive their inspiration from different sources of history. They have different ethics, different heroes, and different episodes. Very often the hero of one is the foe of the other, and, likewise their defeats and victories overlap.[55]

Although the American consul general at Calcutta offered little analysis of the Pakistan resolution at the time of the Lahore session, the *New York Times* quoted Jinnah's famous resolution at length, emphasizing his view that 'Hindus and Moslems brought together under a democratic system forced upon minorities can only mean a Hindu *Raj*; democracy of the kind favored by the All-India Congress High Command means the complete destruction of all that is most precious in Islam.'[56]

The *New York Times* noted that while Jinnah held that autonomous national states alone could solve the Hindu-Muslim problem, Congress was threatening civil disobedience in India by opposing the war as the next step toward completing Indian independence. Jinnah, though describing union as impossible, had indicated that 'the Islamic group was ready to give support to Britain in the European war.' Moreover, he indicated his desire to meet Gandhi and discuss plans for 'two Indias—Moslem and Hindu which are as unlike as Germany and France.' He noted: 'I feel I can speak in behalf of Moslem India and Gandhi in behalf of the Hindus but not all India as he pretends to represent.'[57]

As the American commitment to the British war effort unfolded, culminating with the passage of the Lend-Lease Act in March 1941, increasing official attention was focused on all of Great Britain's problems. In April 1941, Thomas M. Wilson, the

American consul general at Calcutta, reported extensively on
Jinnah's demands for Pakistan of the previous year. He predicted
that although the movement lacked the support of the Muslims,
the longer the constitutional issues remained unsolved the stronger
it would become. After describing the historic and literary origins
of the Pakistan idea, he noted that 'to Mr Jinnah the movement
had become almost a fetish and his efforts in its behalf take on the
coloring of a crusade—if indeed such a term properly may be
applied to an all Moslem movement!' Since in its extreme form
Pakistan divided the Muslim League not only from Congress but
also from the whole of Hindu India, Wilson believed it was hardly
likely that any British government would willingly see the country
divided in accordance with Jinnah's proposal. Wilson observed that
although for various reasons due to wartime exigencies, the demand
for 'Pakistan might be postponed or put aside, that it would be a
great mistake to dismiss it as something of decreasing or no
importance.' Moreover, he noted that 'Pakistan Day, March 23,
had been widely and enthusiastically observed by Muslims
throughout the country...'[58]

A month later Wilson reported from Calcutta that at the all-
India Muslim meeting in Madras in the middle of April Jinnah had
clarified his stand on Pakistan 'with a vengeance.' Whereas it had
been hoped that for reasons of expediency the demand for Pakistan
would be postponed, when the meeting convened Jinnah took an
extreme stand. He declared that under no circumstance would the
Muslim League 'agree to any constitution of an All India character
with one government at the center.' Moreover, Jinnah had
succeeded in his efforts to have the constitution of the Muslim
League amended to the end that Pakistan was now the avowed aim
of the League. Jinnah had stated that 'since the fall of the Moghul
Empire, I think I am right in saying Moslem India was never so
well organized and so alive and so politically conscious as now...'
Wilson observed 'that conditions in India are very serious indeed.
Differences between Hindus and Moslems could hardly be worse
and seldom have they been farther apart than they are at this
moment.'[59]

Towards the close of November 1941, *Time* magazine once again ran a portrait of Mohammad Ali Jinnah with the caption '... Tired of British Talks.' *Time* noted that the twenty-six members of the Muslim League, the 'most important political party in India after Gandhi's Indian National Congress, had walked out in a body, led by the League president, monocled, Mohammad Ali Jinnah.' The stated reason for the walkout was to protest against the way Britain and the British-run Indian government were handling the defense of India in the Second World War. But the gesture meant more than just that. Fifteen months previously India's viceroy, Lord Linlithgow, in a desperate bid for Indian cooperation in the empire war effort had established a cabinet and executive council, eight of whose thirteen members were 'distinguished and representative Indians.' Neither the Congress nor the Muslim League were consulted in the move. Both had since charged that all key jobs in the council went to Britons, and that the Indians picked were tried and true 'yes men' for the British raj. *Time* noted that when Jinnah and his followers took their walk, most observers believed it was chiefly a delayed action protest against the council. But it also seemed clearer than ever that if Britain wanted more than lukewarm cooperation in fighting the Second World War, she must do more than talk about settling India's problems.[60]

The events of 1942 infinitely strengthened the bargaining position of the Muslim League and made Jinnah a key figure in India. Although Jinnah insisted that the British government 'does not attach sufficient importance to the Moslem League,' the idea of Pakistan was recognized officially by the British for the first time during the Cripps negotiations, and opposition to the Muslim minority was given as the chief reason for not consenting to Congress's demands. Furthermore, after the imprisonment of Congress leaders due to their movement of massive civil disobedience, Jinnah rapidly began consolidating his position and increasing his number of followers among the Muslims, always by hammering away at the idea of Pakistan and backing up his words by threats of force.[61]

During the next five years Jinnah gradually came to be recognized in the newspapers and periodicals as a key figure in Indian politics, the sole boss of the Muslim League, brilliant, colourful, shrewd, incorruptible, and absolutely committed to the Muslim cause. Described as something of a paradox because of his unorthodox Muslim behaviour and his elegant Western-style dress, Jinnah was nevertheless reported as the chief obstacle to Indian independence and powerful enough to thwart the war effort if his demands for Pakistan were not considered sympathetically.[62]

In the fall of 1942, Herbert L. Matthews, the distinguished correspondent of the *New York Times*, began an extensive tour of India that produced a more balanced and objective coverage of Jinnah and his cause. Matthews clarified in his numerous reports the extent to which the United States at that time was indoctrinated mainly by the Congress picture that depicted everyone united under the Congress banner following Gandhi implicitly. The American stereotype viewed the British as faithless, hopeless, uncharitable imperialists, whose only object in India was to squeeze out her life blood and incidentally to rule by dividing the Hindus and Muslims. One's sympathies naturally went toward the Indians, the underdogs. The Americans believed that any great people or country had the right to govern themselves. They stood for democracy, the four freedoms, and the precepts of the Atlantic Charter, all of which were being denied to India. This was the view that Matthews had taken with him to India. He noted that his first step toward wisdom had been the recognition that the picture was not simple or clear, that the British had much to say on their side, that the Indians were not united, and that Jinnah, who was contemptuously dismissed in New York as a political tool of the British with little following, was one of the most important factors in the Indian situation.

After a long, patient, weary search for the truth, which led Matthews to every region of India, to ten of its eleven provinces, and to more than a dozen of its principal states large and small, Matthews discovered that the kaleidoscopic picture that had been presented to him did not conform to the reality that he found. Matthews noted: 'The strength of Jinnah and the League was a great surprise to the newcomer.' Although Jinnah had never had much of a sympathetic press in the United States, the correspondent's studies in every part of India where he pursued the question of communal tension convinced him that at least nine out of ten politically conscious Muslims in British India were with Jinnah and the Muslim League. The corollary was the overwhelming importance of communal dissension, which in the considered opinion of the correspondent was the most important factor in the Indian situation. It lay at the base of the whole political structure, providing an apparently insuperable cause of disunity. He noted that the idea of Pakistan had helped the Muslim League acquire a tremendous following, and 'it was hard to see how it could be abandoned now even if Jinnah wanted to.'[63] Matthews's reports were followed with great interest within the State Department and substantiated by military intelligence reports.[64]

American military intelligence officers in India followed Jinnah's growth in leadership and power with great interest. They were sensitive to the strength of the Muslim component of the Indian army and believed that Muslim soldiers were deeply loyal to Jinnah and opposed to Gandhi's 'quit India' movement. Therefore, because they had arrived at a critical juncture in the war effort, they were somewhat sympathetic to Churchill's position when he informed Roosevelt that although the British government was earnestly considering a declaration of dominion status after the war, granting with it the right to secede, 'we must not on any account break with the Moslems who represent 100 million people and the main Army elements on which we must rely for the immediate fighting.'[65] This position was confirmed to President Roosevelt in a secret message from Ambassador W. Averell Harriman that emphasized Churchill's information that approximately 75 per cent of the Indian troops and volunteers were Muslims and of the balance, less than half, or perhaps only 12 per cent of the total, were sympathetic to the Congress group. Because of the importance of the Muslims in the defense of India, the prime minister had clearly indicated that he would not 'take any political step which would alienate the Moslems.'[66] Given this information it was not surprising that the Near Eastern Division of the State Department agreed that 'any settlement which does not provide the Moslems with satisfactory safeguards might seriously decrease the valuable military assistance already being received from them.'[67]

American military intelligence reports from India indicated that Jinnah was proving himself to be a 'very astute leader.' While the Congress leaders were in jail, Jinnah solidified his political control throughout the Muslim areas, roaming throughout India preaching the imperative need for India to be divided and for a sovereign Muslim state to arise in Pakistan.[68] They observed that Jinnah's historic claims to Pakistan were reinforced by an examination of the history of the Mughal Empire and the Muslim relationship to it. Jinnah's strength was recognized as very real. In support of this view they noted a significant and most important incident that had just occurred; namely, that when the Congress's resolutions for civil disobedience were published, Jinnah immediately gave orders for Muslims to 'take no part in any disturbance… Not one Muslim in India entered the fray or raised his hand.'[69]

It should be noted that many Americans were concerned about Gandhi's decision to confront a Japanese invasion with his familiar nonresistance methods. At the same time, Jinnah was receiving a more statesmanlike image by his opposition to Gandhi's civil disobedience programme. With the fall of Singapore on 15 February, the remainder of Malaya, Burma, and India were left vulnerable to Japanese conquest. Colonel Louis Johnson, the president's personal representative to India, had been sent to bring about a settlement of the Indian problem during and after the unsuccessful Cripps mission. He wrote: 'Congress resolutions followed Gandhi lead of nonresistance even to Japs. Defense of India will be most difficult, if not impossible…'[70]

Actually the State Department became somewhat alarmed at the pro-Congress attitude of Johnson in his trip to India where he had indicated that since the Muslim League was being used by the British government, its approval of any plans for self-determination for India was unnecessary. In response the department had indicated that it would be detrimental to the interests of the United States to favor unduly any faction or group in India and urged Johnson not to identify himself closely with any particular political group. It held that the Indian problem should now be judged from the military standpoint.[71]

When American troops arrived in India in the spring of 1942, Gandhi bluntly denounced this action and prepared to 'unleash a large-scale 'quit India' campaign in which American as well as British forces will be urged to get out of India immediately.'[72] It was these events that had led Roosevelt to raise the entire India question again with Churchill.[73]

During the spring of 1942, John Paton Davies, Jr., second secretary of the Chinese embassy attached to the staff of General Joseph W. Stilwell who was then commanding American forces in China, Burma, and India, reported to both the general and the secretary of state his observations on the political situation in India. Davies was the diplomatic officer who later became famous for his perceptive and realistic observations on Mao Tsetung and the Communist forces in China during the latter part of the war. To Davies, Jinnah stood head and shoulders above any other leader in the Muslim League. He described him as incorruptible and a good tactician and organizer, although he reportedly lacked warmth and magnetism. Davies noted that the Muslim League had but one function—to fight for the rights of the Muslim minority. Its programme was Pakistan and little else. Jinnah had no constructive all-India programme because he was opposed to an all-India union. Davies said that Jinnah believed, and 'apparently with good reason, that Congress would not give the Muslims a fair deal.'[74] A week later, after a conversation with Jinnah in Bombay, Davies emphasized that there was a wide rift existing between Jinnah and the leaders of Congress, and that Jinnah's suspicion of Congress matched its mistrust of him. While Davies recognized the differences as being very real and extensive, he thought them not completely unbridgeable. However, he felt that the likelihood of a Congress-League rapprochement lessened with each step Gandhi took to force the Congress toward open opposition to the Anglo American war effort in India. In a confidential memorandum to General Stilwell, Davies reported that Jinnah did not wish to embarrass the British at the present and was, therefore, supporting the war effort. He noted that if Jinnah's demands were to be granted for Pakistan, he wished them to be realized now and not after the war. Jinnah had suggested that the British declare that they were prepared to grant independence immediately to India, Pakistan to the Muslims, and Hindustan to the Hindus, and that if Congress would not accept these terms Pakistan would at least be granted independence and the rest of India would remain under British rule. Such a declaration, Jinnah had remarked with a smile, would bring the Congress around to terms within two months' time.

On 21 December 1942, Davies had still another extended interview with Jinnah at his home. He found him very hospitable and as they sat before a great fire, they talked intimately and realistically. In speaking about independence and the desire for freedom, Jinnah indicated that it was no longer confined to a limited class of intelligentsia but now permeated the people of all classes. He insisted that if the British were 'sincere and honest' in seeking a solution to the Indian problem, the Indian factions could reach an agreement in no time. An orderly constitutional arrangement could be made for the two states—Pakistan and a Hindu state—that would in practice function in close harmony. Whatever immediate costs it might entail, such an arrangement would be to the longterm advantage of the British, but he implied that the British would not be sincere and honest. He pointed to the impossible goal they had set for India—a unified, democratic government. Such a thing, said Jinnah, was an impossibility in India.

Davies described Jinnah as astute and opportunistic a politician as there was in India at that time, and admirably qualified to fill the role of leader needed in the circumstances in which the Muslims found themselves. Moreover, he had skillfully exploited the apprehensions of his community and had built up the Muslim League as a disciplined organization obedient to his will. The political credo of the Muslim League and Jinnah's battle cry was Pakistan. However, he made clear that all of the discussion over Pakistan should not obscure the fact that the leaders of the League wanted to be rid of British rule. And that was true even of Jinnah. The Muslim frustration with regard to independence, he reiterated, was complicated by the very real fear of Hindo domination. In response to the rumors that the British government subsidized the Muslim League, Davies pointed out that Jinnah was generally considered to be incorruptible. While Davies agreed that the British used the League, he was convinced that they did not own it. Davies believed that the Pakistan proposal had been devised initially for bargaining purposes by the Muslim League rather than as an end in itself.[75] The Near Eastern Division of the State Department regarded Davies's observation with considerable interest.[76]

During this period another well-known correspondent, who would later achieve fame as a result of his observations on Mao Tse-tung, reported on Jinnah and the Muslim League. Edgar Snow noted that it was a policy of the British command not to make any settlement with the Congress during the war because they were convinced that 'The Moslems are our big worry. They are the people we depend upon in the army. If we make an arrangement turning over the country to the Congress—the Hindus—the Moslems might mutiny, if Jinnah told them to.' Both Davies's and Snow's observations were circulated widely in the State Department and were sent on to the president.[77] Their views were repeatedly confirmed by American military intelligence observers.[78] In June 1943 the threat and perils of mass civil disobedience in India were so feared that President Roosevelt believed that the United States should be prepared as far as possible to meet or limit the scope of that danger. To that end he decided to send a personal representative to New Delhi. He selected William Phillips, a long-time, highly respected, and distinguished career diplomat.[79]

Phillips was remarkably impressed by his visits with Jinnah. In his memoirs and personal reports to the president, he described his visit with him:

> As he entered the room I was struck by his tall and slender figure. Erect and well-dressed, he looked far more like an Englishman than an Indian. His manner was courteous and he had a natural charm. An easy and rapid talker, it was a quarter to nine before he got up to leave. We had been three and three-quarter hours in conversation. That his brilliant intellect, his ability to hold masses of people spellbound for

hours at a time, and above all his concept of an independent Moslem nation had captivated the Moslem people, was understandable.

While attracted to him personally, Phillips, although he met him several additional times, did not approve of his 'dream of severing India into separate nations.' Nevertheless, he appreciated Jinnah's statement that he could be counted on 'to do nothing to obstruct the war effort since I regard victory against Japan as essential to the good of India.'[80] Phillips had several additional interviews with Jinnah, and he, along with Davies, agreed that while Jinnah had been exploited by the British in their divide and rule policy, the frequent accusations of pro-Congress groups that Jinnah was playing the British game were unacceptable.[81]

During the closing years of the war and immediately thereafter, the State Department continued to observe and report, with deep interest, on Indian political divisions. Jinnah was interviewed on dozens of occasions by American military and diplomatic personnel. At least four extensively researched and lengthy reports were made in various areas of the State and Defense Departments particularly concerned with the problems of Hindu-Muslim disunity, the strength of the Muslim League, the political significance of partition, and the position of Mohammad Ali Jinnah. All the reports recognized Jinnah as a distinguished lawyer and politician with the capacity to attract young men to his cause and to lead them. They noted that Jinnah's legal training appeared to govern his approach to all questions, and most of his acquaintances regarded him as 'incapable of using unconstitutional means' to achieve his ends. He was described as a shrewd and calculating politician who had proved his political acumen on numerous occasions. He was a man with tremendous capacity to weigh issues and bide his time. Although recognized as ambitious, he was described as 'absolutely honest and incorruptible,' a man who had achieved his position through unique ability and single-mindedness. It was noted that through sheer personal charm he had managed to gain the confidence of the peasants, artisans, and laborers who comprised most of India's Muslim population. They saw Jinnah and the independent Pakistan proposal as the chief symptom of a communal illness that prevented India from attaining its freedom.[82]

And yet, it was not until after Jinnah's sweeping political victory at the polls in the Indian elections of the winter of 1945–46 that new policy statements regarding Jinnah and the future of Pakistan began to be considered in the State Department.[83] These elections, plus the refusal of Nehru and the Congress party to accept the interpretation of the British and the Muslim League of the cabinet's final proposals in late 1946, led to the gradual realization in America that Jinnah's dream of Pakistan appeared to be the only solution to the Indian impasse.[84]

When the British government finally secured the approval of the National Congress and Muslim League to a partition agreement, the American government and the press greeted the resolution of the Indian dilemma with relief. The State Department praised the final independence announcement and pledged American friendship with all groups. American newspapers and journals accepted Pakistan as the only possible solution.[85]

And so it was that on 10 June 1947 the American government in a press release made clear that the future constitutional pattern of the peoples of India was a matter to be determined by them alone and that whatever pattern developed, the United States would look forward to the continuance of the friendliest relations with Indians of all communities and creeds. Secretary of State George C. Marshall cabled his hope to 'have the friendliest relations with the new Pakistan state when it is established...[86]

When history was made in Karachi with the birth of the state of Pakistan and Mohammad Ali Jinnah assumed power on 15 August 1947 as governor general of the new dominion, the United States was the first nation to extend diplomatic recognition and the only foreign power to send an official delegate to the formal ceremonies.[87]

Although aware of the enormous problems facing both Jinnah and Pakistan, American newspapers and periodicals, as well as key American officials, agreed that Jinnah had proved himself a great statesman not only of Asia but also of the world.[88] As Edgar Snow noted, even if one only appraised Jinnah as a barrister, it would be to acknowledge that 'he had won the most monumental judgment in the history of the bar.'[89]

NOTES

1. Mary Louise Becker, 'Some Formative Influences on the Career of Quaid-i-Azam, M.A. Jinnah,' in Ahmad Hasan Dani, ed., *World Scholars on Quaid-i-Azam: Mohammad Ali Jinnah* (Islamabad, 1979), p. 83.

2. Christopher Thorne, *Allies of a Kind: The United States, Britain, and the War Against Japan,* 1941-1945 (Oxford, 1978), pp. 335-64; Gary Hess, *America Encounters India,* 1941-1947 (Baltimore, 1971), pp. 1-2.

3. Hess, *America Encounters India,* pp. 2-20.

4. M.D. Abul Khair, *United States Foreign Policy in the Indo-Pakistan Subcontinent, 1939-1947* (Dacca, 1968), p. 30.

5. Paul H. Alling, American ambassador to Pakistan, to George C. Marshall, secretary of state, 22 March 1948, 845F.00/3-2248, Decimal Files, Department of State, National Archives (hereafter cited as DSNA); Military Intelligence Division, report no. 4265, RG 226, Modern Military Records, National Archives (hereafter cited as MID Report, NA), Hess, *America Encounters India,* p. 21.

6. Becker, 'Some Formative Influences on the Career of Quaid-i-Azam,' p. 83.

7. *Statesman,* 13 September 1948; *Amrita Bazar Patrika,* 13 September 1948; *Hindustan Standard,* 13 September 1948; *Advance,* 12 September 1948; Lawrence Ziring, 'The Phases of Pakistan's Political History,' pp. 148-49; Fazlur Rahman, 'Iqbal, the Visionary; Jinnah, the Technician; and Pakistan, the Reality,' pp. 1-9, Barbara Metcalf, 'Iqbal: Ideology in Search of an Audience,' pp. 133-45 and Anwar H. Syed 'Iqbal and Jinnah on Issues of Nationhood and Nationalism,' pp. 77-107, all in C.M. Naim, ed., *Iqbal, Jinnah, and Pakistan: The Vision and the Reality* (Syracuse, 1979); Penderel Moon, ed., *Wavell: The Viceroy's Journal* (London, 1973), pp. 314-15, 368, 442, Beverly Nichols, *Verdict on India* (Bombay, 1944); Edgar Snow, 'The World's Queerest State,' *Saturday Evening Post* 221 (17 June 1948): 24-25, 120. As late as 1930 Muhammad Ali, Gandhi's friend and coworker, stated that Jinnah was one of the few who might be a future prime minister of India. Rias Ahmed Jafri Nadvi, ed., *Selections from Muhammad Ali's Comrade* (Lahore, 1965), p. 141. In 1940 another Congress leader, Subhas Chandra Bose envisaged the possibility that Jinnah might lead India. Sheila McDonough ed., *Mohammad Ali Jinnah: Maker of Modern Pakistan* (Lexington, MA, 1970), p. viii.

8. Sir Alfred Watson, 'The Man Who Made a Nation,' *Daily Telegraph,* 13 September 1948.

9. 'W. Norman Brown, *The United States and India and Pakistan* (Cambridge, MA 1963), is primarily an American introduction to that area of the world. A. Guy Hope, America and Swaraj (Washington, DC, 1968) is a cursory account. Khair, Indo-Pakistan Subcontinent is helpful. Hess, *America Encounters India* offers the fullest treatment.

10. Matiubul Hasan Saiyid, *Mohammad Ali Jinnah*, 2d ed. (Lahore, 1953) pp. 1-2, 37-40; Hector Bolitho, *Jinnah: Creator of Pakistan* (London, 1954), pp. 4, 9-11, 17-21, Abdul Qadir, 'The Quaid-i-Azam's Early Life' *Illustrated Weekly of Pakistan* (23 December 1951): 15; *Manchester Guardian*, 13 September 1948, Atique Zafar Sheikh 'Quaid-i-Azam's Family Environment,' in Dani, *World Scholars*, p. 55.

11. His Highness the Aga Khan, *The Memoirs of Aga Khan: World Enough and Time* (New York, 1954), pp. 124-25.

12. Aga Khan, *Memoirs*, pp. 124-25: 'Quaid-i-Azam, Mohammad Ali Jinnah' *The United Nations Biographical Record* 1 (July 1948): 1; Sir Stanley Reed, ed., *The Indian Yearbook: 1914* (Bombay, 1914), p. 476; Saiyid, Jinnah, pp. 37-40.

13. Bolitho, *Jinnah*, pp. 57-58; Reed, *Indian Yearbook: 1914*, p. 476; Saiyid, Jinnah, p.94.

14. Sir Stanley Reed, ed., *The Indian Yearbook: 1918* (Bombay, 1918), pp. 659-61; Brown, *United States and India and Pakistan*, p. 73.

15. Saiyid, *Jinnah*, p. 95; David Page, 'The Development of Mr Jinnah's Constitutional Ideas,' in Dani, *World Scholars*, pp. 272-73.

16. *Jawaharlal Nehru: An Autobiography* (London, 1936), pp. 67-68.

17. Sir Verney Lovett, *A History of the Indian Nationalist Movement*, 3d ed. (London, 1921), pp. 184, 276.

18. Wiffred Cantwell Smith, *Modern Islam in India and Pakistan*, 2d ed. (Lahore, 947), pp. 239-40, 244.

19. *Resolutions of the All India Muslim League*, May 1924–December 1936 (Delhi, nd), pp. 1-2.

20. Hope, *America and Swaraj*, pp. 6-7; Hess, *America Encounters India*, p. 10.

21. Saiyid, *Jinnah*, pp. 276-79; Bolitho, *Jinnah*, p. 95; Khair, *Indo-Pakistan Subcontinent*, p. 9; Josef Korbel, *Danger in Kashmir* (Princeton, 1954), p. 37; Khalid B. Sayeed, *Pakistan: The Formative Phase*, 1857-1948 (New York, 1968), pp. 72-75.

22. Ahmad Hamid, *Muslim Separation in India* (Lahore, 1971), pp. 181-82; McDonough, *Mohammed Ali Jinnah*, p. viii.

23. *New York Times*, 13 November 1930.

24. *Ibid.*, 15 November 1930.

25. *Ibid.*, 13 November 1930.

26. Barnby, 'Hindu or Moslem?—The Undying Problem,' *New York Times*, 28 December 1930. It should be noted that the issue of Hindu-Muslim conflict had been previously addressed not only in regular news items but also in feature articles. Indeed, editorials concerning Hindu-Muslim

differences had begun to appear as early as 1922. For example see *New York Times*, 1, 18 January 1922, 10 March 1922, 20 May 1923, 14 November 1923, 3 October 1924, 15 November 1930, and 28, 31 December 1930.

27. *New York Times*, 18 December 1930.

28. George Percival Spear, *India, Pakistan and the West*, 4th ed. (New York, 1967) pp. 132-33.

29. Claude Van Tyne, *India in Ferment* (New York, 1923), p. 217. A similar view was expressed by the noted political scientist Professor James W. Garner in 1935. Khair, *Indo-Pakistan Subcontient*, p. 29.

30. Muhammad Iqbal, 'Presidential Address Delivered at the Annual Session of the All-India Muslim League at Allahabad on the 29th December, 1930,' in Naim, *Iqbal, Jinnah, and Pakistan*, pp. 191-209; 'Shamloo,' ed., *Speeches and Statements of Iqbal* (Lahore, 1948), p. 8.

31. 'Shamloo,' *Speeches and Statements*, pp. 12-13.

32. Anwar H. Syed, 'Iqbal and Jinnah on Issues of Nationhood and Nationalism,' *The Indian Review I* (Autumn 1978): 23-42; Richard Symonds, *The Making of Pakistan*, 2d ed. (London, 1950), pp. 56-59; Larry Collins and Dominique La Pierre, *Freedom at Midnight* (New York, 1975), pp. 41, 115-16.

33. Aga Khan, *Memoirs*, pp. 242-43.

34. Bolitho, *Jinnah*, p. 100; Korbel, *Danger in Kashmir*, p. 37.

35. *New York Times*, 4 January 1932. Later in the spring of that year the *New York Times* again ran a feature article on Hindu versus Muslim differences that analyzed not only the religious but also the social and economic differences that had brought about the recent bloody riots in Bombay. *Ibid.*, 22 May 1932.

36. Saiyid, *Jinnah*, p. 304.

37. Bolitho, *Jinnah*, p. 109; *Manchester Guardian*, 13 September 1948.

38. Presidential address, Lucknow session, October 1937, *Presidential Addresses of Quaid-i-Azam* (Delhi, 1946), p. 5; *Nehru-Jinnah Correspondence: Including Gandhi Jinnah and Nehru-Nawab Ismail Correspondence* (Allahabad, nd), pp. 76-77.

39. *Nehru-Jinnah Correspondence*, p. 77.

40. *Letters of Iqbal to Jinnah* (Lahore, nd), pp. 17-18.

41. *Ibid.*, p. 19.

42. Becker, 'Some Formative Influences on the Career of Quaid-i-Azam,' p. 89, Sir Reginald Coupland, *India: A Restatement* (London, 1945), pp. 155-57, 171-76, app. 3; Philip Woodruff, *The Men Who Ruled India: The Guardians* (London, 1952), pp. 272-73.

43. Becker, 'Some Formative Influences on the Career of Quaid-i-Azam,' pp. 87-89; Manzooruddin Ahmed, 'Iqbal and Jinnah on the Two Nations Theory,' in Naim *Iqbal, Jinnah, and Pakistan*, pp. 41-77. See also Saleem M.N. Qureshi, 'Iqbal and Jinnah: Personalities, Perceptions and Politics,' in *ibid.*, pp. 11-41; and McDonough, *Jinnah*, pp. ix-x.

44. Abdul Hamid, *Muslim Separatism in India: A Brief Survey*, 1858-1947 (Lahore, 1967), p. 224; Hess, *America Encounters India*, pp. 17-18; Thorne, *Allies of a Kind*, p. 233; Mohammad Ayub Khuhro, 'Quaid-i-Azam Mohammad Ali Jinnah's Directive to Celebrate "Day of Deliverance"', in Dani, *World Scholars*, pp. 193-94. Jinnah's action was bitterly resented by Nehru and the Congress. See Syed Sharifuddin Pirzada, ed., *Quaid-e-Azam Jinnah's Correspondence*, 2d rev. ed. (Karachi, 1966), p. 147.

45. *New York Times*, 6 October 1939; 5, 6, 7, 8 November 1939, and 9, 14 December 1939.

46. John Gunther, *Inside Asia* (New York and London, 1939), p. 466.

47. *Time*, 4 December 1939, pp. 32-33.

48. *New York Times*, 8 January 1940 and 25 February 1940.

49. *New York Times*, 25 February 1940. For American stereotypes of the Indian Muslims as 'more aggressive' and 'able to fight' as compared with the Hindus, see Harold Isaacs, *Images of Asia: American Views of China and India* (New York, 1958), pp. 276-79.

50. Hess, *America Encounters India*, pp. 18-21; Jawaharlal Nehru, 'India's Demand and England's Answers,' *Atlantic Monthly* 165 (April 1940): 449-55; Khair, *Indo-Pakistan Subcontinent*, p. 30.

51. Hess, *America Encounters India*, p. 19.

52. K.A. Abbas, 'Jinnah the Enigma of India', *Asia* 40 (August 1940): 432-34; Humayun Kabir, 'Even the Muslims Disagree,' *Asia* 40 (August 1940): 435-38.

53. Khair, *Indo-Pakistan Subcontinent*, p. 30.

54. Hamid, *Musilm Separatism in India*, p. 215.

55. Jamil-ud-Din Ahmad, ed., *Some Recent Speeches and Writings of Mr Jinnah*, 2 vols. (Lahore, 1942-51), 1:149-51.

56. *New York Times*, 23 March 1940; Hess, *America Encounters India*, p. 21.

57. *New York Times*, 23, 24 March 1940.

58. Wilson to Cordell Hull, secretary of state, 5 April 1941, DF 845.00/1226, DSNA. For an illuminating and sympathetic article on Pakistan by the oldest daily newspaper published by Indians with strong Congress leanings, see 'A Plea for Pakistan,' *Amrita Bazar Patrika*, 5 March 1941.

59. Wilson to Hull, 8 May 1941, DF 845.00/1226, DSNA; *Amrita Bazar Patrika*, 6, 8 May 1941.

60. *Time* (10 November 1941): 30.

61. Sayeed, *Pakistan: The Formative Phase*, pp. 118-20; *Current Biography*, 1942 (New York, 1942), p. 418.

62. For example, see *New York Times*, 16 July 1942, 25, 26 April 1943, 2 July 1945, and passim; Milwaukee *Journal*, 29 March 1942; *Newsweek* (10 May 1942): 26, 29 (25 September 1944): 50, 52, (25 June 1945): 56, (23 July 1945): 54, and (3 June 1946): 43-44, *Time* (14 June 1943): 31, (9 July 1945): 34, (16 July 1945): 34-37, and (23 July 1945) 48; *Nation* (7 July 1945): 2, (14 July 1945): 51, and (28 July 1945): 79-81; *The New*

Republic (15 July 1945): 91-92; and *Life* (27 May 1946): 101-7. *Time* finally did a cover story on Jinnah in 1946 that pictured him as an aloof, arrogant, wealthy troublemaker. *Time* (22 April 1946): 28-31.

63. *New York Times*, 7, 9 September 1942, 4 October 1942, 7 February 1943, 25, 26 April 1943, and 7, 8 May 1943; Herbert L. Matthews, 'India: A Year's Visit Summed Up,' *Think* (September 1942): 40.

64. DF 845.00/2169, DSNA; MID Report no. 64265, RG 226, NA.

65. Churchill to Roosevelt, 4 March 1942, U.S., Department of State, *Foreign Relations of the United States*, 1942 1 (Washington, 1960): 612 (hereafter cited as FRUS, followed by appropriate year); *Roosevelt and Churchill: Their Secret Wartime Correspondence*, ed. Francis L. Lowenheim, Harold D. Langley, and Manfred Jonas (New York, 1975), pp. 183-84.

66. Harriman to Hull, 26 February 1942, *FRUS*, 1942, 1:608.

67. Memorandum by Wallace Murray, chief of the Near Eastern Division, 28 February 1942, DF 845.00/1299, DSNA.

68. MID Report, no. 25895, RG 226, NA.

69. MID Report, 22 August 1942, no. 549, RG 226, NA.

70. Johnson to Hull, 4 May 1942, *FRUS*, 1942, 1 648: *New York Sun*, 16 April 1942.

71. Hull to Johnson, 27 April 1942, and Roosevelt to Johnson, 8 May 1942, *FRUS*, 1942, 1:645, 650.

72. *New York Times*, 13 June 1942; 'Gandhi Chastises,' Newsweek 29 (11 May 1942): 46; Khair, *Indo-Pakistan Subcontinent*, p. 114. Hull later clarified the position of American forces in India in an effort to relieve tension. *The Memoirs of Cordell Hull*, 2 vols. (New York, 1948), 1:46.

73. Hess, *America Encounters India*, p. 35. The State Department was interested in investigating any points of view that might offer reconciliation between the Hindus and Muslims. Secretary Harry C. Herman to A.A. Berle, Jr., assistant secretary of state, 19 January 1942; Berle to Herman, 24 February 1942, DF 845.00/1294 and DF 845.00/1293 DSNA; Berle to Sumner Welles, undersecretary of state, 17 February 1942, *FRUS*, 1942, 1:602-4.

74. DF 845.00/1347, DSNA. Davies refers only very briefly to his encounters with Jinnah during his nine months' special assignment to the Indian subcontinent in *Dragon by the Tail: American, British, Japanese and Russian Encounters with China and One Another* (New York, 1972), pp. 237, 261.

75. John P. Davies, Jr., 'The Indian Problem Fall and Winter, 1942-1943.' Enclosure in William Phillips to Hull, 8 February 1943, DF 845.00/1821, DSNA. Lampton Berry American consul in New Delhi, who had a two-hour discussion with Jinnah later in the year corroborated many of Davies's observations. Berry to Hull, 15 September 1942, DF 845.00/1600, DSNA.

76. Alling, chief of Near Eastern Division, to Berle, Welles, and Hull, 2 July 1942, DF 845.00/1439, DSNA.

77. DF 845.00/10-1242, DSNA; Alling to Berle, Welles, and Hull, 2 July 1942, DF 845.00/1439, DSNA.

78. MID Report, New Delhi, 30 November 1942, no. 26270, RG 226 NA, Research and Analysis Report, Office of Strategic Services (OSS), 30 December 1942, no. 356, RG 226, NA (hereafter cited as R&A Report, NA).

79. Memorandum by Murray, 17 June 1942, DF 845.00/142, DSNA.

80. William Phillips, *Adventures in Diplomacy* (Boston, 1952), pp. 373-74; observations by Phillips, 10 June 1943, R & A Report, OSS, no. 923, RG 226, NA. Howard Donovan, American consul in Bombay, also paid high compliments to Jinnah's organizing ability, political astuteness, and incorruptibility. Donovan to Hull, 6 August 1943, and 25 January 1944, DF 845.00/2130 and DF 845.00/9744, DSNA.

81. Observations by Phillips, 10 June 1943, R & A Report, OSS, no. 923, RG 226, NA. For similar more favorable estimates of Jinnah, see G. Forbes, 'I Know These Indian Leaders,' *The Catholic World* 155 (July 1942): 413-14; *Newsweek* (10 May 1943): 26, 29; and *Time* (14 June 1943): 31.

82. Donovan, consul at New Delhi, to Marshall, 12 July 1947; MacDonald, consul at Bombay, to Marshall, 17 July 1947, DF 845.00/7-1247, DF 845.00/1747, DSNA; 'How Strong is Muslim Hostility to a Self-Governing India?,' 4 March 1942, R & A Report, OSS, no. 550 RG 226, NA; memorandum on nationalist groups in India, 26 March 1942, DF 845.00/1407, R & A Report, OSS, no. 700, RG 226, NA; memorandum, Division of Near Eastern Affairs, 22 June 1943, DF 845.00/2004, DSNA; Office of Intelligence Research Report, 1 August 1946, no. 4162.1, NA.

83. Lampton Berry, 'Political Situation in India,' 8 January 1946, DF 845.00/1-846 NA; MID Report, 10 January 1946, New Delhi, DF 845.00/1-1046, NA, office memorandum, 31 January 1946, DF 711.45/1-3146, all in DSNA. For the significance of the elections, see William J. Barnds, *India, Pakistan and the Great Powers* (New York 1972) pp. 26-30; Hugh Tinker, *India and Pakistan: Political Analysis* (New York 1966), p. 34 and *New York Times*, 9 September 1945. The elections also brought forth additional reviews of Jinnah's leadership and policies: George E. Jones, 'Jinnah—India's Political Question,' *New York Times Magazine* (5 May 1946): 13, 44-46, Margaret Bourke-White, 'India's Leaders,' *Life* (27 May 1946): 101-7; and *Newsweek* (3 June 1946): 43-44. *Time*, in an article entitled 'The Ham,' reported Jinnah's triumph in sarcastic and unflattering terms. *Time* (17 June 1946): 30 33.

84. George Merrell American commissioner at New Delhi, to James F. Byrnes secretary of state, 10 June 1946, DF 845.00/6-1046, NA; FRUS, 1946, 5:100-112; *FRUS* 1947, 3:143-46; Hess, *America Encounters India*, pp. 178-79, Merrell to Marshall 22 April 1947, 2 May 1947, and 20 May 1947, DF 845.00/41247, DF 845.00/5-247, and DF 845.00/5-2047, respectively; *Statesman*, 1 May 1947; Loy Henderson, director of Office of Near Eastern Affairs, to Dean Acheson, assistant secretary of state, DF FW 845.00/6-347, DSNA.

85. Samuel H. Day to Marshall, New Delhi, 9 June 1947, DF 845.00/6-947 and DF 845.00/6-347, DSNA; Marshall to President Harry S. Truman, 17 July 1947, DF 701.45F11/7-1747, DSNA, US, Department of State *Bulletin* (22 June 1947); 1249, *New York Times*, 10, 11, 25 June 1947 and 8 July 1947, *Christian Science Monitor*, 16 August 1947; *Time* (16 June 1947): 39-40; Newsweek (16 June 1947): 38, *Nation* (14 June 1947): 702; Phillips Talbot, 'Report from New Delhi,' *The New Republic* (6 June 1947): 7; *Christian Century* (23 July 1947): 892; Hess, *America Encounters India*, pp. l79-81.

86. Henderson to Marshall; 2 June 1947, DF 845.01/6-247, DSNA, Day to Marshall, 9 June 1947, DF 845.00/6-947, DSNA; Henry Grady, ambassador to India, to Marshall 2 July 1947, DF 845.00/7-247 and 11 July 1947, DF 845.00/7-1147, DSNA; Henderson to Marshall and Truman, 8 July 1947 DF 701.45F11/7-847, DSNA. See also DF 845.00/7-747 and DF 701.45F11/7-2147, DSNA.

87. Grady to Marshall, 8 August 1947, DF 701.45F11/8-847, DSNA; Marshall to Charles W. Lewis, charge d'affaires at Karachi, 9 August 1947, DF 701.45F11/8-847 DSNA; Lewis to Marshall, 10 August 1947, DF 701.45F11/8-947, 14 August 1947, DF 845F.01/8-1447, 16 August 1947, DF 845.00/9-1647, and 16 August 1947, DF 701.45F00/8-1647, all in DSNA.

88. For example, see Andrew Roth, 'Jinnah's New Republic,' *Nation* 165 (13 December 1947): 647-49; *Time* (22 December 1947): 37; Bourke-White, 'Pakistan's Struggle for Survival,' *Life* (5 January 1948): 16, 20, 23-26; *Scholastic* 53 (29 September 1948): 3; *Newsweek* (20 September 1948): 45-46; *Time* (20 September 1948): 36; *Christian Century* 65 (26 September 1948): 966; *United Nations Bulletin* 5 (I October 1948): 774 *New York Times*, 11 July 1947 and 12, 13 September 1948; and Christian Science Monitor, 16 August 1948. Donovan to Marshall, 12 July 1947, DF 845.00/7-1247, DSNA, MacDonald to Marshall, Bombay, 17 July 1947, DF 845.00/7-1747, DSNA; Marshall to Sir Mohammed Ali Zafrullah Khan, 12 September 1948, Truman to Alling, 12 September 1948, and Truman to Liaquat Ali Khan, prime minister of Pakistan, 12 September 1948, all in DF 845F.001/9-1248, DSNA.

89. Snow, 'The World's Queerest State,' *Saturday Evening Post* 221 (17 June 1948): 24-25, 120.

13

Indian Writers on Jinnah
Muhammad Reza Kazimi

Where do we place the cause of an historical event? And, if we subscribe to the great man theory, as everyone from adherent to adversary does in the case of Mohammad Ali Jinnah, do we place an event like the creation of Pakistan somewhere in the consciousness of its founder? If so, do we only mark the impress left by a personality on his followers, or do we also try and plot the reaction of those who viewed him as an enemy? For Muslims, Partition is a political issue; for Hindus, the unity of India is a religious concept. It is natural then that the leader who brought about the division of the country should be viewed as an enemy in India.

The representative Indian view about the Quaid-i-Azam is the one presented by Arun Shourie in his series of articles titled 'The Man Who Broke Up India'.[1] Is it in the foreground of this hostility that the portrait of Pakistan's founder can be penned? In the background of the Quaid-i-Azam's mission lie also the hopes and fears of the Hindus of India. The Partition could be the consequence of one cause; or the cause could be subdivided into a complex series of options. For the communal-minded Hindu, the explanation is simple. Jinnah with the deliberate help of the British, carved up India to frustrate its aspirations and derail its destiny. For the communal-minded Muslim, it is enough that Hindus and Muslims are separate nations. Whether the Hindus and the British were accommodative or not is irrelevant. India had to be divided.

Not all Hindus, nor all Muslims are communal-minded, therefore, they seek a closer analysis of the events preceding

Partition. All Hindus consider Partition a tragedy. It is in fixing the cause of the tragedy that they differ. Some sympathised with Jinnah while they decried Partition. To this group belongs Sachchidananda Sinha. Some reconcile to Partition but are critical of Jinnah's personality. To this group belongs Bhimrao Ramji Ambedkar. The representative of the majority of Indians are those who are critical of both his politics and his personality.

I

It is not surprising then that the first full length study of Jinnah by a Hindu should be critical on both counts. As far as I have been able to trace, the first such book is Kailash Chandra's *The Tragedy of Jinnah* (Lahore, Varma Publishing, 1941). A revised version was published in 1943. What is notable is that this book is not a trendsetter. Subsequent notices of Jinnah are not in this mould. In order to categorize it, we need to point out that *The Tragedy of Jinnah* typifies an attitude not an analysis, and as such helps us locate the milieu in which it was written. There are two markers to the book. Firstly, it is occasioned by the Lahore Resolution, which was found abhorrent by the author, and secondly, it is accompanied by the hope that Pakistan shall never come into existence. It is Kailash Chandra's hopes and fears which need to be made tangible, to be viewed in the background for any political portrait of Mohammad Ali Jinnah to be properly positioned.

About Kailash Chandra, we must place our inquiry on the following lines. Firstly, if he did not expect Pakistan to come into existence, why did he feel the need to write a full length study of Jinnah? Secondly, does he base his study on the proper premises, that is, how do they stand up to later events or later research? To answer the first question, let us see the reasons he addresses as to why Pakistan cannot come into being. The first reason is that no Muslim country has ever become a first rate power (p. 223). Secondly, he doubts whether Jinnah has the backing of Muslims (p. 230). Third, Mr Jinnah is old and infirm, 'He fainted while travelling to Madras' (p. 270).

As to why Pakistan should not come into being; i) Pakistan is not economically viable (p. 224), ii) Pakistan is close to the Russian border (p. 224) and iii) Muslim League demagogues say that Pakistan shall be an Islamic Theocratic State (p. 227). Kailash Chandra does not specify which demagogue, and does not venture to quote Jinnah on this point. Again, after decrying theocracy he decries Jinnah's fondness for ties by saying that ties are a reformed emblem of Christianity! (p. 227).

These observations do not stand up to later events: On p. 18, Kailash Chandra recounts the pan-Islamic (or Khilafat Movement) then says: 'It was under those circumstances that we got the Lucknow Pact of 1916'. Kailash Chandra forgets that the Lucknow Pact preceded the Khilafat Movement, and that Gandhi was in its favour while Jinnah was not. He gives Jinnah the credit for boycotting the Simon Commission but alters the sequence by saying that Jinnah began to fall foul of the Nehru Report. The Nehru Committee had been formed as a challenge to the Simon Commission. A question which Kailash Chandra ignores is, what was Mahatma Gandhi doing at the time of the Simon boycott? Another Indian writer, in time would answer this question.

Kailash Chandra says that a handful of Muslim Leaguers were elected in Hindu majority provinces, not because of their own party influence, but because of the influence of the Ulema (p. 135) whereas all the Ulema were on the side of the Congress, not the Muslim League. The Ulema of Deoband in particular, had ruled that it was possible to cooperate with the Congress but not with the Muslim League.

Again, where Kailash Chandra calls Muslim complaints of discrimination under 1937 to 1939 Congress ministries 'concoctions of damnable falsehood (p. 232), he forgets that people like N.B. Khare, a Mahasabhaite Chief Minister of CP, attested to discriminatory treatment awarded to Muslims.[2] Even Netaji said that the Congress had failed the Muslims. One of Kailash Chandra's misconceptions, which have been refuted by research, is his over estimation of Abul Kalam Azad's power and position in the Congress. He writes:

It is an open secret that in matter of Congress discipline he is rather harsh and autocratic and even leaders like Mahatma Gandhi dare not interfere with him. (p. 233).

Quite apart from the scene recounted by Sudhir Ghosh about Azad lying to Gandhi in the face of documentary evidence, we have Mahatma Gandhi's own letter to Pandit Nehru regarding Azad:

I do not understand him, nor does he understand me. We are drifting apart on the Hindu-Muslim question as well as on other questions. Therefore, I suggest that the Maulana should relinquish Presidentship.[3]

Kailash Chandra's arguments are indicative not only of rancour but also confusion. Contrary and disparate considerations colour the attitude of a party, this is a common phenomenon. But when such contradictions are reduced to cold print, we begin to wonder whether these contradictions are particularly apparent to those who find such arguments palatable. Perhaps Kailash Chandra's diatribe is an indication of why the Congress never evolved a long term policy to deal with the Muslim League, believing that it did not matter. How deep Kailash Chandra's presentation sank in, is of course, a matter of speculation, but it is quite noteworthy that Ms. Jethi T. Sipahimalini, Deputy Speaker, Sindh Assembly, does point out in the Foreword—which is traditionally only for commendation—that:

The author's criticism at certain places is rather strong and I wish he had rather left it out.(pv)

In fact, she has penned her Foreword in such vague terms that nowhere can she be accused of endorsing Kailash Chandra's views. Perhaps those who read them closely had begun to realize the magnitude, if not the gravity of what Jinnah represented to them. Kailash Chandra's arguments have internal contradictions but are typical of a prevailing attitude, being critical both of Jinnah's personality and his politics. Far more difficult to place is Bhim Rao Ramji Ambedkar, who endorsed Jinnah's policy but criticised his personality.

II

B.R. Ambedkar's concurrence with M.A. Jinnah's political demand is contained in *Thoughts on Pakistan* (Bombay, Thacker, 1941) and his denunciation is contained in *Ranade, Gandhi and Jinnah* (Bombay, Thacker, 1943) Justice Mahadev Govind Ranade (1842-1901) had favoured the idea of the Marhatta kingdom becoming the precursor of modern independent India. What attracted him to Ambedkar was Ranade's giving precedence to social reform over political reform. Ambedkar knew that without social emancipation, the Harijans or schedule castes would never benefit from political emancipating.

The key word in Ranade's thought was 'sanction' (p. 54) meaning the ability to fulfil a political will. Both Gandhi and Jinnah possessed 'sanction', paradoxically Ambedkar decried this trait in *Ranade, Gandhi and Jinnah*, calling them both egoists. How Ambedkar differentiated between the sanction of Gandhi and the sanction of Jinnah needs just a word of explanation. Ambedkar wrote that the absence of sanctions in Ranade's political philosophy need not detract much from its worth' (p. 55). Now, Ambedkar is confusing sanctions as a component of Ranade's thought, and sanctions as a means of enforcing Ranade's philosophy.

It is within the colonial hierarchy that Ranade's dictum was formulated. It is not often realized that the knot which binds the servient nation to the dominant nation is more necessary to the servient than the dominant nation' (p. 68). Only a leader of the scheduled caste could focus on the necessity of British colonialism. Gandhi was backed by a majority and Jinnah was backed by a minority, and it is this factor which created an ambience about Jinnah in Ambedkar's view. He expressed himself clearly in his *What Congress and Gandhi have done to the Untouchables* (Bombay, Thacker, 1945).

All that Jinnah had done was to hail the Gandhi–Ambedkar Pact whereby Ambedkar was forced to forgo Separate Electorates for Schedule Caste members. Jinnah himself did not accept a corresponding concession for the Muslims. Jinnah, as a champion for Muslim rights is to be admired, Jinnah, for being able to obtain a sanction for his people is to be envied. In *Thoughts on Pakistan*, Ambedkar had this to say about Jinnah's personality,

> An egoist without the mask and has perhaps a degree of arrogance which is not compensated by any extra-ordinary intellect or equipment. It may be on that account he is unable to reconcile himself to a second place.

Such remarks usually precede a finding that a leader is sincere but misled, but instead we find Ambedkar not sympathising or asking his readers to afford due consideration to M.A. Jinnah's demands, but rather identifying completely with Jinnah's solution to the communal problem. Ambedkar said in *Thoughts*:

> Integral India is incompatible with an independent India (p. 56). Even if India remained one integral whole it will never remain an organic whole (p. 57). The Muslims will be freed from the nightmare of Hindu Raj and Hindus will save themselves from the hazard of a Muslim Raj (p. 58). The mischief is caused not so much by the existence of mutual antagonism as by the existence of a common theatre for its display (p. 58).

III

Ambedkar was a contemporary politician, not a personal friend of M.A. Jinnah. Ambedkar's reaction is not that of an individual but a politician with a cause and that is what shapes his judgement. We now come to a small account by Sachchidanada Sinha, called *Jinnah—As I Know Him*. This small book proceeds from one of the oldest friends of Mohammad Ali Jinnah. He knew Jinnah when he was studying for the Bar. He personally witnessed Jinnah's role during the Lord Salisbury and Sir Dadabhai Naoroji election contest for the Finsbury constituency. Sinha tells us that Naoroji's victory was especially indebted to Jinnah. He speaks of Jinnah's part in the 1906 Calcutta session of the Congress. He recalls to readers the speech Jinnah made against separate electorates. Sachchidanada Sinha gives us a close look at the young Bombay barrister,

I and Jinnah became friends, and in Bombay we met in the chambers of Sir Feroz Shah Mehta. All of us, Jinnah included, conducted ourselves with the utmost politeness...This assembly was Plato's academy on a small scale.[6]

Sinha recounts that he expected Jinnah to preside over the 1911 Congress 'but fate had decreed otherwise'.

As to why Jinnah changed his stance, Sinha puts down to Jinnah's ambition and vanity. He differs with Jawaharlal Nehru's opinion that Jinnah left Congress because he did not relish the dust and grime of mass politics. Sinha makes a psychological distinction. He says Jinnah left Congress because he could never play second fiddle to Gandhi. For a close friend, he is most curiously ignorant about what went on behind the scenes in Nagpur during that fateful 1920 Session. Also, while imputing the emergence of Pakistan to Jinnah's vanity, he is intriguingly silent about the whole Cabinet Mission episode. Sinha returns to the view that had Jinnah not been insulted at Nagpur, Pakistan would never have come into existence.

IV

What really happened at Nagpur has been revealed by Kanji Dwarkadas, but before we come to his writings we must review V.N. Naik's *Mr. Jinnah: A Political Study* (Bombay Sadbhakti, 1947). This is perhaps the last book about the Quaid-i-Azam written in his life-time. His book is not a eulogy; it begins and ends with the hope that India and Pakistan shall reunite (p. 1 and 84). His general portrayal of Jinnah is that of a wrecker of Indian independence saying that he co-operated with Winston Churchill in checkmating Congress. He is critical of Gandhi as most of Jinnah's admirers are about Gandhi. He says that: 'The mystic and saint in India has spiritualized politics and landed Indians in a quandary' (p. 33); but when he discusses post-partition riots, he praises Gandhi and criticizes Jinnah (p. 84).

There is one scene recorded by V.N. Naik dating to 1922 or 1923 which he personally witnessed. Mohammad Ali Jinnah was presiding over a meeting in Bombay to promote the candidature of R.P. Paranjype. Jinnah dealt firmly and deftly with tough hecklers and their political patrons (pp. 38-41). This is a rare personal anecdote which belies the common notion that Jinnah was only a drawing room politician, unused to the rough and tumble of a political life.

On balance, but only on balance, Naik blames Congress and not Jinnah for the partition. Naik refers to the 1937 Congress refusal to accommodate the Muslim League in coalitions:

> Mr. Jinnah as a bitter Communalist is the creation of the Indian National Congress…It is events that make the fortune of slogans, not slogans that make the fortune of events (p. 18).

On two points Naik's interpretation is odd and unusual, that is on Jinnah's role during the Cabinet Mission Plan, and secondly, on the Quaid-i-Azam's speech of 11 August 1947. Throughout his book, he decries the division of India, but he disregards Jinnah's acceptance of the Cabinet Mission Plan, rather he says that Jinnah did not act as a statesman, but only in a manner that would shift the blame of the Plan's failure to the Congress. Naik says Jinnah played with Lord Wavell as a cat with a mouse. He does not know how Jinnah could manipulate the reactions of Gandhi and Nehru. This runs counter to most accounts, notably Azad's account that Congress was responsible for the Plan's failure, not Jinnah.

About the 11 August 1947 speech, Naik says that Jinnah spoke of the minorities with condescendation and generously because he was pleased with himself for having achieved Pakistan (p. 78). It is remarkable that having plotted the Congress' career of Jinnah so meticulously (pp. 30f). Naik fails to see in the Jinnah of 1947, the Jinnah of 1917. V.N. Naik has made the same mistake which many Pakistanis have since then consistently made, that is, reading Jinnah's 11 August speech in isolation. It should be read in conjunction with Jinnah's interview with H.V. Hodson.[7]

This book was a genuine attempt at reconciliation, but the author was unable to cope adequately with the horrendous events following Independence.

V

Straddling the earlier and later Indian writings on Jinnah are the works of Kanji Dwarkadas. He is not directly a biographer of Jinnah, only a biographer of Ruttie Jinnah. However, an Urdu translator, with the blessings of the author, culled a volume on Jinnah from the two books Dwarkadas had written on the Indian Freedom Movement. No study of Jinnah can be complete without reference to Kanji Dwarkadas' books because he was privy to the most intimate political secrets of Jinnah's career, as well as to the innermost recess of his heart. Dwarkadas revealed to Jawaharlal Nehru, that the reason behind Jinnah's opposition to Gandhi's non-cooperation resolution at Nagpur had been that Motilal Nehru had made this request to Jinnah (pp. 286-87).

This put Jinnah in a quandary, for though Jinnah was opposed to extreme measures like boycott of schools and courts, he was in favour of some forms of non-cooperation which would not rebound on the Indians. He protested in the Assembly when the British put his name on a list of politicians opposed to non-cooperation. What happened was that after he had primed Jinnah to oppose Gandhi, Motilal Nehru himself voted with Gandhi in the open session. I have never come across any account where Jinnah ever referred to the real reason he suffered oblogy for leaving Congress. Jinnah never replied, even when Motilal's own son advanced the reason that Jinnah left Congress because he could not stand up to mass participation. Had Kanji Dwarkadas not witnessed the Nagpur scene himself and mentioned it personally to Jawaharlal we would never know the truth. Dwarkadas spoke to Jawaharlal after Jinnah's death.

Kanji Dwarkadas also tells us how the inner counsels of Congress regarding Jinnah were shaped. He recounts his conversation with Sardar Patel while the Cabinet Delegation had gone to Simla, and remarks that once Congress came to terms with the British, there would be no need to settle with Jinnah or the Muslim League. This explains why Congress leaders tried to scuttle the Cabinet Mission Plan in 1946 and demanded that it be imposed as an award in 1947.

The account about Sardar Patel's observation reveals no secret, however, since Kanji Dwarkadas had known Ruttie Jinnah very closely, M.A. Jinnah called him the day following his wife's funeral. In his *Ruttie Jinnah*, Bombay, author, 1963:

> Never have I found a man so sad and so bitter. He screamed his heart out, speaking to me for over two hours, myself listening to him patiently and sympathetically, occasionally putting a word here and there. Something I saw had snapped in him (p. 58).

Hector Bolitho has mentioned how another friend had called on Jinnah to offer his condolence but held back when he saw a forbidding look in Jinnah's eye. No Muslim friend of Jinnah, not Liaquat, not Mahmudabad can be imagined recounting such a scene. Kanji Dwarkadas is the most indispensable writer on Jinnah.

VI

The two books written by Kanji Dwarkadas were published when a new crop of books on Jinnah were being published. The five books which together form the subject of this phase are:

1. S.K. Majumdar's *Jinnah and Gandhi: Their Role in India's Quest for Freedom* (Calcutta, L.K. Mukhopadhyay, 1966)
2. J.J. Pal's *Jinnah and the Creation of Pakistan* (Delhi, Sidhuram, 1983)
3. Sailesh Kumar Bandopadhaya's *Quaid-i-Azam Mohammad Ali Jinnah and the Creation of Pakistan* (New Delhi, Sterling 1991)
4. Ajeet Javed's *Secular and Nationalist Jinnah* (New Delhi, Kitab, 1998).
5. Prakash Almeida, *Jinnah: Man of Destiny* (Delhi, Kalpaz 2000).

We shall proceed again in a chronological order, beginning with S.K. Majumdar's book. Since this is the first book to be written after the ravages of Partition had abated, there is a natural curiosity about how a book praising Mohammad Ali Jinnah and critical of Mohandas Karamchand Gandhi came to be written in India by a non-Muslim author and that too, so soon after the 1965 war. Majumdar ends with a plea for peace and re-unification. He does not mention the Tashkent Declaration. Should we probe his motives negatively? After all, finding the substance of his argument impregnable, we can take recourse to questioning his bias. This will not be an isolated case. Let us concede then, at the outset that Majumdar is a Bengali nationalist. We have only to count the number of Bengali stalwarts Gandhi countered ideologically or politically; Raja Ram Mohan Roy whose modernist influence Gandhi sought to controvert by his medievalism, then among his contemporaries Rabindranath Tagore, Sir Asutosh Mukherji, Chitaranjan Das, and of course, Netaji Subhash Chandra Bose. When Bose was elected President of the Congress despite his opposition, Gandhi criticized the Congress bitterly and instructed dissidents to withdraw from the Congress.

> Congress is fast becoming a corrupt organization of bogus members … I must remind all Congressmen, that those who being Congress-minded remain outside it by design, represent it the most. (pp. 297-8).

This treatment of Subhash Bose in 1939 made Majumdar understand Jinnah's position in the 1920 Nagpur session of the Congress … Gandhi's convoluted thinking, his recoiling from the majority decision when it went against him, seems to have provided Majumdar the clue to Gandhi's mental process; also, it was the partition of Bengal which made him contemplate the partition of India ….

Whatever the bias, whatever his motive, we have to consider firstly whether Majumdar's reconstruction of the Freedom Movement is valid or not, whether his delineation of Gandhi's role and Jinnah's role is correct or not, going, as it does against the Indian estimate of Gandhi's role and the Pakistani appraisal of Jinnah's role; whether the publication of documents since 1966 has materially altered his findings or not, and whether a Pakistani could have produced such a study then, and finally, what position it occupies in the historiography of partition.

Another observation is in order here. In his introduction, S.K. Majumdar gathers all the main points of his submission, realizing fully that otherwise a novel and unpopular case would never be heard. There is more elaboration than substantiation in the text as the process of substantiation begins from the introduction itself. Again, it needs emphasis that Majumdar writes from a nationalist and not a communal standpoint. As mentioned above, he pleads for re-unification and repudiates the Two Nation Theory. How then does he come to admire Jinnah? This we can answer after having considered his analysis of Gandhi's role.

Majumdar first traces the ideological profile of Gandhi, spelling out his aims and objectives, and attempts to determine which of them he was able to achieve. Majumdar says that Gandhi's mission was to nullify the benefits of civilization and scientific progress. Majumdar calls it Gandhi's New World Order or New Civilization. Gandhi wanted to shun cities and go back to the villages, to nature. Gandhi held scientific development responsible for increasing the forces of violence. Gandhi stated that for him defence was the least important component of national reconstruction. Majumdar quotes from Gandhi's 1909 publication *Hind Swaraj*:

Medical Science is the concentrated essence of black magic. Quackery is infinitely preferable.(pp. v. vi).

Gandhi's inclination was looked upon with suspicion even among his compatriots. This is illustrated by the process with which he appropriated the Home Rule League. When Mrs Annie Besant, the founder president, was interned in 1916, Jinnah stepped in as President, and then publicly proposed Gandhi as his successor. The Home Rule League Secretary, M.R. Jayakar was skeptical. He wrote to Gandhi expressing his fears that Gandhi would attempt to change the aims and objectives of the Home Rule League and 'even try to secure in our creed a place for some of your pet theories which many of us may be inclined to regard as fantastic fads.[8]

Although Gandhi protested at his theories being called fads, he reassured Jayakar that apart from proposing a common language for India, 'you need have no apprehension that any other theories of mine, your League will be called upon to accept.' However, once he had secured the Presidentship of the Home Rule League, he announced his intention of utilizing the League for 'the advancement of causes in which I had specialized.' Gandhi changed not only the creed but the name of the League, calling it Swaraj Sabha, inviting even a life member to leave if he thought he could not remain a member of the Sabha under its altered constitution (p. 39). He thus drove out those very leaders who had brought him in. Jinnah seems to have been the only Muslim to resign. He was followed by M.R. Jayakar, Jamnadas Dwarkadas, Mangaldas Pakwasa, Nagindas Master and K.M. Munshi, among others.

How Gandhi took over the Home Rule League relates not only to his ideological aspect but psychological make-up. Majumdar recounts Gandhi's speech at the foundation ceremony of Benaras Hindu University. He insulted the western educated Congressmen, advised the princes to strip themselves of their jewels and protested against the security arrangements for the Viceroy, Lord Hardinge, advising him to risk being shot rather than have such elaborate precautions. There was pandemonium and every one left. This scene is attributed obliquely by Majumdar not only to Gandhi's political commitment but also to Gandhi's instinct for destruction. Majumdar quotes from C.F. Andrews[9] to bring out this trait in him:

> I remember having thrown into the sea a pair of beautiful field glasses because they were a constant bone of contention between a dear friend [Kallenbach] and myself ... I can remember having broken to bits, when a young man, the loved bangles of my dear wife because they were a matter of difference between us (p. 93).

Obviously any source of innocent pleasure was not acceptable to this saint and apostle of non-violence, all of whose efforts were directed at being able to exercise power. Caprice is a symptom of such desire, and Majumdar lists the inconsistencies in Gandhi's political career. This he achieves first by relaying Gandhi's definition of civil resistance. 'A civil resister never seeks to embarrass the government.' A poignant commentary on his boycott of the Prince of Wales visit, and the Quit India Movement. The episode relates to Gandhi's loyalist stand during the First World War. He attended the war conference called by Lord Chelmsford and distributed leaflets proclaiming:

> The easiest and straight way to win Swaraj is to participate in the defence of the Empire. If the Empire perishes, with it will perish our cherished aspiration.

This was the very argument which left him unmoved in 1942. In 1918, he went against the wishes of Rabindranath Tagore, C.F. Andrews and Surendranath Banerjee. Furthermore, when Bal Gangadhar Tilak sent a cheque with the proviso that 'he advocates making Indians eligible for Royal Commissions', Gandhi returned the cheque (p. 41). Tilak had also disapproved of Gandhi's involvement in the Khilafat Movement, deprecating the introduction of theology into politics (p. 90). Majumdar also mentions that the country did not take kindly to the ratification of the Gandhi–Irwin Pact as it coincided with the execution of Bhagat Singh and his compatriots. In all of this exposition, the fast until death undertaken by Gandhi to force the Government of India to remit Pakistan's share of her financial assets has an enigmatic aspect. Majumdar provides the framework for explaining even this action. In the backdrop of Gandhi's Salt Satyagraha, Motilal Nehru had said that were Gandhi to agitate against the Salt Act while he was prime minister, his government would take Gandhi to a place where even the British government dare not take him (p. 131). On the eve of Partition his son, Jawaharlal Nehru had frustrated and bypassed Gandhi by resisting the emergence of an independent and united Bengal by which step he intended to explode Jinnah's Two Nation Theory. He called Jawaharlal a 'King' in derision (p. 261) and took no part in the Independence ceremony, and twenty-four hours before he was assassinated, Gandhi had attempted to replace Congress with a Lok Sevak

Sangh, which was to consist of such bodies as the All India Spinners Association and the Gao-Seva Sangh etc.

Now how does Majumdar account for Jinnah's inconsistencies? How does he succeed in potraying Jinnah as a nationalist? Majumdar puts across convincing evidence derived from Jinnah's own words; yet he does not get off directly. In all the three episodes Majumdar cites above; Gandhi's loyalist role in the War Conference of 1918, his espousal of the Khilafat cause and his indifference to the fate of Bhagat Singh, Jinnah had played a positive role and in all the three episodes Majumdar ignores Jinnah's role in a study which is avowedly comparative. This can hardly have been intentional. Other writers were to point to this aspect.

This brings us to the documentation. Neither *Wavell: The Viceroy's Journal,* nor the *Transfer of Power Papers* were available to him. Leonard Mosely's *Last Days of the British Raj* he had consulted; H.V. Hodson's *The Great Divide* was yet to published. Kanji Dwarkadas' *India's Fight For Freedom* was published simultaneously with Majumdar's book, and *Ten years to Freedom* was two years away, so that Majumdar had no way of knowing that it had been Motilal Nehru who had pressed Jinnah to oppose Gandhi's Non-Cooperation resolution at the 1920 Nagpur Congress Session.

This conceded, we should examine the sayings of Jinnah from which Majumdar draws his conclusion that ideologically Jinnah had always remained a Congressman, and that it was Gandhi who forced him out. These are parts of Jinnah's speech as President of the Home Rule League:

> My message to the Mussalmans is to join hands with your Hindu brethren. My message to the Hindus is to lift your backward brother up (p. 37).

This was in 1919. In 1924, five years after he had resigned from Congress, Jinnah said:

> The League is not in any way going to adopt a policy or programme which will, in the least degree, as far as I can judge, be antagonistic to the Indian National Congress (p. 107).

In 1937, after Jinnah had rebutted Jawaharlal Nehru's assertion that there were only two parties in India, the British and the Congress, he still stated:

> The Hindus and Muslims must be organised separately, and once they are organised, they will understand each other better and then we will not have to wait for years for an understanding.

Although Majumdar does not so comment, it now seems rather obvious that here lay the clue to Jinnah's thinking. As a politician he disliked separate electorates, as a lawyer he had prudence. Almost upto the last, his ideal remained a free and united India; his method became separate organization. Majumdar almost closes in on this point when he quotes Jinnah exposition of the Lahore Resolution. Speaking on 22 February 1941, Jinnah had asserted:

> Mussalmans of India are proud to be Indians and believe in India for the Indians. It is in that spirit that the Lahore Resolution was adopted (p. 184).

Majumdar comments: 'It is clear that all Jinnah and the Muslim League wanted *at this time* was a constitution which guaranteed rights of self-determination for Muslims in the Muslim majority areas while retaining the fundamental unity of India' [emphasis added] (p. 84). Majumdar makes clear that whatever the cause of Jinnah's differences with Gandhi, it was not pride. Even after the humiliating scene at Nagpur in 1920, Jinnah was calling for swaraj (p. 107). He was with Gandhi at Ahmadabad on 18 December 1921 (p. 98) and even as late as 1929 Jinnah went to Sabarmati to see Gandhi. (p. 124). His differences with Gandhi were impersonal. Jinnah knew that the genie of communalism released by Gandhi during the Khilafat Movement would not be put back into the bottle. Also, as his resignations from the Home Rule League and the Congress show, he considered not the aim but the method of Gandhi to be wrong. Writing to Gandhi on 1 January 1940, Jinnah plainly stated that 'Ahimsa and spinning are not going to win India's freedom' (p. 185).

But again, how does Majumdar reconcile this formidable evidence of Jinnah's nationalistic sentiments with the actual fact that he presided over the partition of India? This is the point where reappraisal becomes necessary. How does Majumdar apportion the responsibility and how does he balance praise and censure? This is vital, because unless his study is balanced, it is not valid. Majumdar's praise of Gandhi is meaningless. He praises Gandhi for Indianising the freedom struggle (p. 69). This is exactly the trait he has been criticizing throughout his book. He owed it to us to explain how, with such a formidable opposition arrayed against him at Nagpur, Gandhi was still able to prevail. One of the other writers was to project this as an indication of Gandhi's stand. An explanation was due as it differed from Gandhi's appropriation of the Home Rule League.

Then again, he criticizes Gandhi's obsession with the spinning wheel, even to the extent of saying that Gandhi's boycott of foreign cloth was for the benefit of Ahmadabad millowners. Gandhi had actually supported a strike against Cotton millowners. Majumdar does not commend Gandhi's plan to induct school boys for spinning. Their combined production, as Majumdar admits, would meet the requirements of India. Gandhi could have combated British fabrics economically and not politically. It would not even be contingent on the boycott of schools.

As for Jinnah, Majumdar explains:

No other force was available to him except a communal force. The moment he achieved his aim to create a state where the writ of Gandhi and Gandhian Congress would not run, he threw off the mask of communalism he had been wearing for the time being....Every sensible man must repudiate the Two-Nation Theory as Jinnah himself did in his first speech to the Constituent Assembly (p. xiii).

This needs some clarification. Majumdar does not explain how Jinnah came to acquire a communal force. The entire Muslim cadre was with Gandhi during the Khilafat Movement. Even after its dissipation, Jinnah did not actively woo it. Even after Nagpur, he continued to co-operate with the Congress, against the Simon

226   M.A. JINNAH: VIEWS AND REVIEWS

Commission and against the National Agriculturist Party. Majumdar is one of the few authors to concede that the Congress had a tacit electoral understanding with the Muslim League in UP in 1937. Thus, Jinnah himself did not gather a communal force against Gandhi. This force gravitated towards Jinnah after it had been abandoned by Gandhi.

Majumdar explained Jinnah's actions uptil this point, thereafter, he criticized Jinnah's vote at the Simla Conference onwards:

> Jinnah's intransigence in Simla paid him high dividends; with all his pious wishes for an undivided India, Lord Wavell's infirmity of purpose lent strength to those who wanted to divide India (p. 215).

The Viceroy's decision, indeed, had this effect, but where do we place this fact against Jinnah's deeds being called a 'Historical Necessity' by Majumdar (p. xiv). Majumdar next criticizes Jinnah for his Direct Action and the subsequent Great Calcutta Killing. He disregards the report of the Chief Justice, Sir Patrick Spens, that there was Hindu incitement and a sudden, concerted and unprovoked attack on Muslims in North Calcutta.

Thus, we see that Majumdar's attempt at reconciliation leads him only half-way. Could one reasonably expect more? We have seen how Majumdar had mentioned, though admittedly without emphasis, Jinnah's trait that he considered separate organization an instrument for unity. Thus, he is justified in deducing that the Two Nation Theory was drafted for the equal emancipation of India and Pakistan. Beyond this, Jinnah's personal inclinations had a limited role in the Pakistan Movement. Jinnah deprecated Separate Electorates right up to 1937. It was only in 1942 that he shed his reservations about them to reject the Cripps offer which made partition contingent on Joint Electorates. Similarly, his personal inclination to preserve the unity of India, which peaked during the visit of the Cabinet Mission, was irrevocably shed when he made the call for Direct Action.

After all, Pakistan resented and rejected Jinnah's decision that Urdu be the sole official language of the State; it is still undermining Jinnah's pledge that Hindus and Muslims would be equal citizens of Pakistan. Jinnah's role was not guided but subsumed by what Majumdar calls Historical Necessity. In evaluating Majumdar's treatise we must fathom the equation between the real and the ideal in Jinnah's cognition. Jinnah had fought religious discrimination in India, he would not permit it in Pakistan. He went to the extent of telling Muslim migrants not to abuse the laws or hospitality when anti-Hindu riots broke out in Karachi.

Thus, the contradiction in Jinnah which we belabour was apparent and not inherent. What S.K. Majumdar has bequeathed is a landmark in the historiography of Partition and its neglect by scholars is unfair. His book cuts across most of Stanley Wolpert's *Jinnah of Pakistan* by depicting a Jinnah of India. His book very clearly foreshadows Ayesha Jalal's *The Sole Spokesman*, despite being impeded by lack of documentation. This is the first revisionist version of the Partition saga. This book, as we said at the outset, does not represent the majority view in India. Yet this book could have been written only in India.

VII

J.J. Pal's tone throughout his *Jinnah and the Creation of Pakistan* (Delhi, Sidhuram, 1983) is hostile. In his conclusion, however, he is unstinting in his praise of Jinnah's leadership, and in the same passage points to the fundamental differences between Hindus and Muslims; in effect an endorsement of the Two Nation Theory. On both counts, no Pakistani shall take issue with him. What blame he apportions to Jinnah and the Muslim League becomes irrelevant. It is unfair on Roger Long's part to characterize J.J. Pal's book as a diatribe.[10]

Yet we pause, because of all the Indian books on M.A. Jinnah, this alone is a Ph.D. thesis, and a Ph.D. thesis compared to a general book needs to be consistent and clear. Unlike most authors chosen for our study, Pal does not defend Jinnah on the score of the Cabinet Mission Plan. Citing the 5 June 1946 speech Jinnah made

before the All India Muslim League Council, Pal asserts that even
with the acceptance of the Plan, Jinnah's struggle for Pakistan
would not cease. It is not incumbent on him to demonstrate the
discrepancy between Jinnah's rhetoric and the Plan's mechanics.
Indeed, the question to be posed by an Indian scholar should be:
Why did the Congress not wait for the British to depart before
rejecting the Plan? The date for withdrawal had been set, the date
for the framing of a constitution had not.

As for clarity, where Pal quotes Gunnar Myrdal to the effect that
Jinnah's political transformation was caused by Gandhi, he needed
to make clear whether it was due to Gandhi's takeover of the Home
Rule League or because of his arousing the religious sentiments of
Muslims during the Khilafat Movement in the face of Jinnah's
express disapproval. One original interpretation does surface in
Pal's thesis and he is far more astute about the Bengal factor than
S.K. Majumdar.

> The Congress leaders welcomed annulment of the partition of Bengal
> and accepted the separation of Bihar and Orrisa to make Bengal into
> a Muslim majority province (p. 146).

Thus, J.J. Pal demonstrates how Bengali nationalism hurt Indian
nationalism and how the reunification of Bengal sundered the unity
of India. It is a pity that J.J. Pal did not develop this theme nor
did he reach again this depth of analysis from which three
nationalists stand to benefit; Indian, Pakistani and Bengali.

VIII

Sailesh Kumar Bandopadhaya's *Quaid-i-Azam Mohammad Ali
Jinnah and the Creation of Pakistan*, gives in its preface the
impression of being the author's inadvertent discovery of a secular
and nationalist Jinnah, but in reality it is an oblique refutation of
S.K. Majumdar's view. Since the evidence regarding Gandhi's
psychological make-up is incontrovertible, Bandopadhaya has
excluded Gandhi from his formal scheme of study and has
concentrated on Jinnah's psychology instead, which in his

estimation is the same as the estimation of Jawaharlal Nehru—success came to him late in life, he was a 'toff' and detested mass politics. Bandopadhaya contends that the achievement of Pakistan was a psychological necessity for Jinnah, as a widower with an enstranged daughter.

Time and again, S.K. Bandopadhaya imputes personal motives to Jinnah's political decisions, but intermittently; he makes concessions which modify or negate his arguments. For example, Bandopadhaya speculates that Jinnah opposed Non-cooperation in 1920 because he needed his lucrative law practice to keep his wife and daughter in the luxury they were accustomed to (pp. 43-4). He ignores the fact that Jinnah was opposed only to the medievalist brand of Non-cooperation otherwise he had stated that some form of Non-cooperation was necessary. This is what Mrs Jinnah had told Gandhi, that she (and her husband) considered Gandhi's scheme impracticable. She herself was a fire-brand revolutionary who had abandoned the luxury of her father's house and braved police brutality shoulder to shoulder with her husband. Their daughter, then a baby, would hardly protest. Unlike Majumdar, Bandopadhaya had access to Kanji Dwarkadas' *Ten Years to Freedom*, where it surfaces that Jinnah had taken the lead in opposing Gandhi's resolution at the instigation of Motilal Nehru. Bandopadhaya himself concedes that Jinnah had objected to his name being included in a government list of politicians opposed to Non-cooperation.

As for the other trait, conceit, Bandopadhaya recounts that Jinnah, along with Jayakar and Nataranjan wrote a letter to Gandhi on 2 February 1922, addressing him as 'Mahatmaji'. Two years later, in 1924, Jinnah participated in the Delhi All-Parties Conference presided over by Gandhi. As late as 30 November 1929, he went to see Gandhi in his Sabarmati Ashram. The other explanation advanced for Jinnah's conduct in the 1920 Nagpur session (ironically by Motilal's son) is that he abhorred mass politics. Jinnah told Durga Das the day after that 'I part company with mob hysteria. Politics is a gentleman's game.' Bandopadhaya interprets the word 'gentleman' in the class sense, but in view of

Motilal's conduct, it is more probable that Jinnah was using the word in the moral sense.

The second such episode was the controversy over the Motilal Nehru Report. Bandopadhaya attributes Motilal's *volte-face* over the Delhi Muslim Proposals to the rising tide of communalism. Shuddhi, Sanghatan, Tabligh and Tanzim movements had come up amidst the growing frequency of Hindu-Muslim riots. Bandopadhaya explains:

> The Congress representatives almost under a *duress* were *eager* to meet the demands of those obscure groups [Hindu Mahasabha and Sikh League] by the agreeing to curtail parts of the concessions agreed earlier to the Muslims (p. 63).

First juxtapose the words 'duress' and 'eager' and then note that Bandopadhaya does not mention what crucially happened between December when the Congress ratified the Delhi Muslim Proposals, and March, when it resiled from them. Far from an upsurge in communal tension having taken place, on 1 January 1928, M.A. Jinnah had welcomed to the stage of All India Muslim League Pandit Madan Mohan Malaviya and the Hindu Mahasabha saying that he valued their fellowship more than any concession made by the British (p. 57). Could there be any other reason for rejecting the Delhi Proposals than the rank communalism which Jinnah had bent over backwards to avoid?

In the third stage of estrangement relating to the 1937 elections, Bandopadhaya again invokes a personal motive?

> The socialist and democratic 'jargons' used by Jawaharlal were yet another point of discord. Jinnah was allergic to them not only because of his attachment to his personal properties to which a reference had been made earlier (p. 123).

But further on he concedes:

> There is also no edge in the plea that League leadership was specially pro-landlord interests; to be honest to facts, the class character of the bulk of the leaders was elitist, the difference being that of tweedledum

and tweedledee...Further, both parties rallied together to confront the Agriculturist Party (p. 131).

Far from being allergic to socialist and democratic jargon, Jinnah was not above using them himself, plainly telling a Calcutta audience that he was exerting himself for the poor, not for the capitalists.[11] Rather, Nehru's socialistic jargon was the cause of discord between him and Rajendra Prasad during that election year. The second half of Bandopadhaya's psychological argument is however valid,

> Jinnah had the privilege of participating in politics on equal terms with Motilal, and therefore was not in a position to entertain the snob and highbrow son of his one-time colleague (p. 127).

This is true as Jinnah told Frank Moraes when his differences with Jawaharlal Nehru were being discussed, 'I liked Motilal.'[12]

Commenting on Gandhi's role in the decision of Congress ministries to resign at the outbreak of the Second World War, Bandopadhaya expostulates:

> Getting active support of Gandhi in War efforts with his commitment to non-violence was a matter of conjecture (p. 154).

This remark marks the extent of divergence between Majumdar and Bandopadhaya. Majumdar had clearly shown that his creed of non-violence had not prevented Gandhi from becoming a recruiting sergeant in the First World War, much to the direct discomfiture of both Tilak and Jinnah.

Again Bandopadhaya asserts that 'Jinnah with his ego' was after power, but that Gandhi's case was different as Gandhi's role was the 'spiritualization of politics' (p. 161). Evidently, Bandopadhaya takes Gandhi's resignation from Congress at face value. It was Gandhi who forced Congress, over the opposition of Nehru, to launch the Quit India Movement, going to the extent even of asking the Congress President, Azad, to resign.

To drive home his point that Jinnah was driven by ambition, Bandopadhaya contends, 'he occupied the post of Governor-General with undue haste even though at an earlier stage he had conceded the proposal of Mountbatten becoming common Governor-General (p. 162)'. This is, of course, completely without foundation, underpinning the fact that Bandopadhaya has only a nodding acquaintance with *The Transfer of Power Papers.*

Whether Jinnah was driven by ambition is best determined by his part in the Cabinet Mission deliberations, and from this phase in the freedom struggle, Bandopadhaya has not spared attention. Rather, he devotes maximum space to the AIML's role in it, characterizing its 12 May 1946 proposals in the following words:

> The propositions of a central government and central legislature were clearly envisaged. The difference between League and Congress was only quantitative and not qualitative (p. 259).

Normally after this admission, all Bandopadhaya's intervening analysis of Jinnah's conceit and ambition would have been nullified, but Bandopadhaya intrudes a number of qualifications here as well. To begin with, Bandopadhaya surmises that Jinnah must have been under some pressure from some quarter in the Muslim League. Where this pressure group was during the Simla Conference, he does not say. Furthermore, he contradicts his own assessment above by conceding that Jinnah was prepared to forego a sovereign Pakistan in exchange for zonal autonomy. Further on, he characterises Jinnah's acceptance of the Cabinet Mission Plan as dishonest, and to this end he quotes from Jinnah's speech: 'Acceptance of Mission's proposals was not the end of their struggle for Pakistan' (p. 289).

Bandopadhaya ties in this observation of Jinnah with the advice he received from Jamiluddin Ahmad: work the plan to the group stage and then 'create a situation to force the hands of the Hindus and British to concede Pakistan of our conception' (p. 273 n. 21). Jamiluddin Ahmad also provided a blueprint on how the Muslim League could sabotage the Indian Constituent Assembly after entering it. As far as this evidence goes, Bandopadhaya has justification on his side. We cannot in fairness press upon him to accept Woodrow Wyatt's disclosure that he had suggested to Jinnah that he could make acceptance of the Cabinet Mission Plan palatable for the Muslims by terming it a means to achieve Pakistan.[13]

However, Bandopadhaya was not aware there was evidence of another nature. On 21 May 1946, Liaquat Ali Khan had sent to Jinnah detailed objections to the Cabinet Mission Plan which made plain that since all the coercive apparatus of the state would vest with the Hindu majority, the Cabinet Mission Plan, far from serving as a stepping stone to Pakistan, would not secure even the stated safeguards. What is more, Bandopadhaya does not mark the subtle difference between accepting a statement on 16 May and forwarding a set of proposals on the 12th in which a clear concession of sovereignty was made. In other words, Bandopadhaya vaccilates between his assessment and his modification, mainly because (i) he does not discriminate between reliable and unreliable sources, and (ii) he stresses the psychological factor too strongly. Where Bandopadhaya itemizes the communal behaviour of Jinnah, he does not probe deeply enough. For example, he blames Jinnah for the Sindh Muslim League Resolution of 1938 which called for two Federations in India, not knowing that Jinnah had actually watered it down.[14] Similarly, he accepts unquestioningly Wali Khan's assertion that Sir Zafrullah Khan had drafted the Lahore Resolution at the behest of the British. Ashique Hussain Batalvi's well documented refutation based on the Zetland–Linlithgow Correspondence has not reached him.[15]

Nevertheless, Bandopadhaya has this in his favour that he is not a Bengal Nationalist. Unlike Majumdar, Bandopadhaya does not bemoan the bifurcation of his province:

> If once the principle of transfer of power to a certain province was conceded, that may open the flood gates of several others provinces making similar claims. Particularly some of the rulers of native states had already voiced such demands (p. 323).

Similarly, he deduces from circumstantial evidence that Jinnah had no clear conception of Direct Action. This is the point where he changes places with Majumdar, who, while being laudatory of Jinnah generally, is highly critical of Jinnah's call for Direct Action. Unlike Majumdar, Bandopadhaya also accepts that the Congress statement of 6 January 1947 accepting HMG's statement of 6 December 1946 was contradictory.

Bandopadhaya's conclusions are confounded because of his efforts to adjust the merits of Jinnah with the merits of Gandhi. This stems from the motives he assigns to both of them. S.K. Bandopadhaya's essential estimate of Jinnah is:

> Such occasional sparks of nationalism in the background of communal overtones will be evident in the life of Jinnah even hereafter [19 January 1937] (p. 75).

He does not seem to think that to establish such a trait of inconsistency, examples were needed. He begins by admitting that on the personal side there were many instances in which Jinnah, at a cost to himself, (considering his fondness, as Bandopadhaya stresses, of personal wealth) provided succour to Hindu individuals (p. 6) but he labels these incidental, although the burden of his strictures against Jinnah are not only personal, they are also psychological. Here he takes his cue from Stanley Wolpert: Jinnah was obsessed by Gandhi, Nehru goaded Jinnah into mass agitation, bringing home the fact that Wolpert's biography of Jinnah is not as laudatory as is generally assumed. By treating the nationalist trait of Jinnah in isolation, Bandopadhaya admits to the shortsightedness of the Congress but insists that every lapse on its part should have been overlooked. That the change in Jinnah could have been a justifiable reaction to Hindu communalism does not cross his mind. Thus, at the end of Bandopadhaya's study we do not know whether his quest to reconcile the 'unbelievable and yet true fact of history' that Jinnah the nationalist created the state of Pakistan failed or was abandoned.

IX

Ajeet Javed reverts basically to the position of S.K. Majumdar. She refers to his book but not to S.K. Bandopadhaya's intervening work. Is her work redundant for being a re-statement of Majumdar's position? Hardly, because she adds significantly both to our knowledge and understanding. Unlike Majumdar, she concentrates on the religious rather than the psychological aspect of Gandhi's mission. Again, as opposed to Majumdar, she is sympathetic to Jinnah's role between 1940 to 1947 and interprets his moves in tactical terms. She provides pieces missed by both Majumdar and Bandopadhaya. While her documentary sources are not very comprehensive, she mentions works containing contemporary estimates of Jinnah, such as V.N. Naik's *Mr. Jinnah—A Political Study* covered above and M.S.M. Sharma's, *Peeps into Pakistan* (Patna, 1954) which have rarely, if ever, been considered by later scholars. This rebounds greatly to her credit.

The core of her *Secular and Nationalist Jinnah*, is, like Majumdar's tract a comparative study of Gandhi and Jinnah, and it is from her that we learn what M.K. Gandhi was doing in the shadows when M.A. Jinnah was in the limelight. Ajeet Javed begins by putting the basic utterances of Gandhi and Jinnah side by side. 'I am a Hindu first and therefore a true Indian'—Gandhi, 'I am an Indian first and a Muslim afterwards'—Jinnah (p. 187). Her narrative begins with 1916, the year following Gandhi's return to India. In the 1916 Lucknow Session, Gandhi could not be elected to the Congress' Subjects Committee, and had to be nominated by the President. Ambica Charan Majumdar, (p. 194). Consequently, Gandhi's view of the Self-Government Resolution was not enthusiastic: 'It may be good, it may be bad, but I do not have any high opinion of it' (p. 195).

Jinnah had refused to join the peace celebrations because of the Jallianwala Bagh tragedy, but Gandhi chose to participate (p. 47). Ajeet Javed also stresses that Jinnah adopted a nationalist stance during the First World War as against the loyalist stance of Gandhi. She also recounts that Gandhi refused to participate in the Jinnah-led demonstration against the Bombay governor, Lord Willingdon, on the ground that he belonged to Ahmadabad and not Bombay! (p. 198). Thus, as against Stanley Wolpert, Ajeet Javed demonstrates that it was Gandhi who was obsessed by Jinnah and not the other way round. She tells us how it had been Jinnah who had proposed the name of Gandhi to be President of the Home Rule League, and how once elected by sixty-seven members present out of six-hundred in Bombay and six thousand in India—he ousted Jinnah and the other founder-members (p. 208).

Jinnah criticised the Montagu-Chelmsford Reforms 1919, whereas Gandhi not only welcomed them but threatened to traverse the length and breadth of India in their support, claiming that it was against 'Indian Culture' to refuse the British hand of friendship (p. 207). Gandhi refused to offer any comments on the Delhi Muslim Proposals to Mrs Sarojini Naidu, while Jinnah explained them to her at length and in detail. During the Round Table Conference, Gandhi signed a requisition enabling Ramsay MacDonald to announce the Communal Award while Jinnah had refused (p. 279).

The most dramatic contrast between Gandhi and Jinnah was over the trial of Bhagat Singh. Uptil now it had been only conceded that Gandhi adopted a luke warm attitude towards Bhagat Singh because he wanted to save his pact with Lord Irwin. Here we find Gandhi displaying open hostility. Gandhi said: 'Hunger strikes have positively become a plague. On the *slightest pretext*, some people want to resort to hunger strike [emphasis added] (pp. 226-7) while Jinnah had stated: 'Well you know perfectly well that these men are determined to die. It is not a joke. I ask the Hon'ble Law Member to realise that it is not everybody who can go on starving himself to death. Try it for a little while and you will see....The man who goes on hunger strike has a soul. He is moved by the soul and he believes in the justice of his cause'.[16]

Ajeet Javed also recounts the most ironic *volte-face* by Gandhi, not without adding a comment. Gandhi asked Muslims to give up their rigid view of religion as the Muslims in Turkey had done: 'He forgot the role he played in arousing Muslims for the Khilafat, despite stiff opposition from Jinnah' (p. 219). This reveals how Gandhi's views had come to tally with that of the Hindu Mahasabha and Ajeet Javed actually supplies the details. Gandhi had expressed his admiration for the Rashtriya Swayamsevak Sangh (RSS) when he inspected its Wardha camp. This was long before they actually had Gandhi assassinated. Gandhi supported the RSS on the ground that: 'Every community is entitled, indeed bound to organise itself if it is to live as a *separate entity*[17] [emphasis added] (p. 218).

Jinnah had exhorted the Muslims to organize so as to co-operate better, Gandhi asked the Hindus to organise for separation. How close they were and how far. If Hindus were a separate entity, it automatically follows that he considered the Muslims a separate entity. Assassination loomed in the background of Jinnah's contact with the Mahasabha also. Baba Savarkar had tried to bribe Yashpal with fifty thousand rupees and a revolver to kill Jinnah. When his brother, Veer Savarkar made a secret appointment with Jinnah, Rafiq Sabir chose that day to make his assassination attempt.

In depicting Jinnah directly she emphasises, quite naturally, his secular and nationalist trait. As if to contradict Nehru's assertion that Jinnah left the Congress because he did not relish mass participation, Ajeet Javed points out that Jinnah had undertaken to establish the Home Rule League because the British had started referring to the Congress as an elitist body. (p. 38). While negotiating the Lucknow Pact, Jinnah had said that Muslims should not display only self-interest; for the rest seventy million were enough (p. 91).

Even after Jinnah had left the Congress, he had not abandoned Non-cooperation. 'There is no other course open to the People, except to inaugurate the policy of Non-co-operation, though not necessarily the programme of Mr Gandhi' (p. 49). In 1925, Jinnah publicly disclaimed having called the Congress a Hindu institution (p. 156). 'I do not see eye to eye with the present policy and programme of the Congress', Jinnah stated on the floor of the Indian Legislative Assembly. 'Nevertheless I have profound reverence for those men who are working in that organization.' This raises the question that if Jinnah still retained such sympathy for the Congress, why did he not attempt to join it again; for example when the Khilafat Movement had dissipated itself, or when Gandhi had formally dissociated from the Congress. Jinnah was tempted but Ajeet Javed shows that Jinnah's sense of propriety had prevented him. Referring to Madan Mohan Malaviya having lately been called a descendant of Ravan, Jinnah said that if he rejoined the Congress and differed even mildly on any issue, he would be dubbed a descendant of Yazid (p. 231).

Five years after having told seventy million Muslims that being confident of their numbers they should co-operate with the Hindus, he told them that seventy million Muslims should learn not to lean on the British or the Hindus. 'Organise yourselves in this country, and you will be a power' (p. 225). 'Organise yourself' the method remained the same, the purpose changed. Initially, Jinnah was against referring the minority issue to the League of Nations, considering it to be a domestic matter. Ajeet Javed gives us a comprehensive and rounded figure of Jinnah both politically and biographically, Ayesha Jalal would have secured a much more tangible basis for her revisionist theory had she also covered the earlier phase of Jinnah's career.

Unlike both Majumdar and Bandopadhaya, Ajeet Javed does not take exception to Jinnah's espousal of the Muslim cause. She cites a number of authors to the effect that the change in Jinnah resulted from Congress high-handedness. V.N. Naik calls the communal Jinnah a creation of the Congress (p. 262), as the political ire of Jinnah was aroused. This implies that once his ire was aroused, he steadfastly worked for Pakistan. This also implies that his ire overcame his scruples. Brian Lapping wrote that the creation of Pakistan must be attributed not to Jinnah, but to the Congress leaders[18] (p. 277). This is an opinion which is contempraneous to Ayesha Jalal's findings. Shiva Rao[19] asserts that Congress leaders realized too late the price they would have to pay 'for their failure to be accommodating when Jinnah was prepared to be reasonable' (p. 264). M.N. Roy,[20] the famous Marxist leader, held that Jinnah 'out of spitefulness because of being ignored went on to create Pakistan' (p. 264).

Thus far, Pakistani readers, though they may deprecate such petty sentiments as ire and spitefulness being held responsible for the creation of their state, will not dissent from the basic contention that Jinnah had attempted accommodation before opting for

Pakistan. There is a threshold they will not cross, and this is signified by M.N. Roy's observation that Jinnah was not serious in his partition demand. 'Jinnah was driven to the bitter end of gaining a victory he himself dreaded and which he did not survive' (p. 281). Falling in the same category is the report of H.K. Ramani,[21] who quoted Jinnah to the effect that he had not wanted Pakistan, but it was forced on him by Sardar Patel and he did not want to accept defeat (p. 281).

Clearly we are confronted with conflicting statements being issued by the same leader. We need, therefore, to establish a criterion to sift such statements. Mahatma Gandhi had said in 1941 that 'if Indian Muslims become determined to separate, no power can prevent them from doing so' (p. 226). In 1944, Gandhi had said that there would be a 'fight to the knife' if Muslims insisted on complete separation. Clearly then, if Gandhi had been insincere in 1941, calling, so to say, the bluff of Muslim separatists, Jinnah could also be deemed to be calling the bluff of the Congress by the Lahore Resolution, or by his call to Direct Action, even though, Ajeet Javed has adduced, on the basis of character, that if Jinnah was sincere in 1916, he was sincere in 1946.

Ajeet Javed has effectively challenged the Great Man Theory. As against the common contention that Pakistan could never have come about without Jinnah, she claims that Pakistan came into being despite him. Jinnah's tactical move had dragged him into a situation from where he was unable to cry halt to partition. In this connection, she relays M.S.M. Sharma's story[22] that after having given his assent to the 3rd June Plan, Jinnah went back to Lord Mountbatten to say that he did not want Pakistan but only an honourable settlement based on a united India. (p. 279).

This is not just gilding the lily but dragging the revisionist theory into ridicule. Not only does it go against archival evidence, it goes against human possibility. In the first place, as Viceroy, Lord Mountbatten would never have refused. Later, as a raconteur, he would recount with relish this scene to Collins and Lapierre, rather than complain of Jinnah's obstinacy. Ajeet Javed has gone through a wealth of printed matter; she has gone deep into the Legislative

Assembly records, but she has not consulted the *Transfer of Power Papers*.

Whether Jinnah was finally resolved to attain Pakistan after his July 1946 call for Direct Action or not, can be determined by tracing the course of his negotiations with the leaders of the Sikh community.

X

Prakash Almeida's *Jinnah: Man of Destiny* is a model of political obcurantism. Normally such a work would not merit academic attention. The Indian attitude to Jinnah is of such a nature that even such a strand of opinion needs representation. Apart from a deep seated veneration for Subhash Chandra Bose, there is no perceptible thread which connects Almeida's treatise to the earlier mentioned works. Firstly, the book lacks method, it is not thought out, and the bibliography is superficial. He refers once to volume X of the *Transfer of Power Papers*, but it is clear that his acquaintance with it is most cursory. He opines that Jinnah emancipated womenfolk like Begum Shahnawaz (p. 121), showing that he has never read her *Father and Daughter*. Then his thought process is somewhat novel. Before we come to his estimates of Jinnah or Gandhi, we need to cite his main demand:

> I have every reason, as a student of history to condemn Lord Mountbatten, this culprit Briton who had much to answer for the lacs of Indians killed in the streets and fields of India in the partition violence ... he merely facilitated the passage it all with mighty disasters. I herewith demand a clear apology from the British Parliament for the betrayal of His Ex. Mountbatten for his calculated failure to avert the holocaust in India — It is absolutely clear that Mountbatten created the Kashmir problem so subtly as a provision against the future (pp. 181-2).

Lord Mountbatten may not have foreseen that an Indian writer would accuse him of creating the Kashmir problem, but he was prudent enough not to destroy, as Krishna Menon had pleaded, his letter of 14 June 1947, to the effect that there would be dire consequences for Anglo-Indian relations were the State of Jammu and Kashmir allowed to go to Pakistan. In fact, it was the other Menon (V.P.) who, even before the arrival of Lord Mountbatten asked for Gurdaspur to be separated from Pakistan, vide his most secret Letter No. R 205/46 dated 23 January 1946. On 17 June 1947, Jawaharlal Nehru followed up Krishna Menon's communication with a note to Mountbatten:

> The normal and obvious course appears for Kashmir to join the Constituent Assembly of India. This will satisfy both the popular demand and the Maharaja's wishes. It is absurd to think that Pakistan would create trouble if this happens.[23]

Thus, the direction of Prakash Almeida's accusation is opposite to the records. Lord Mountbatten did not create the Kashmir dispute, he only succumbed to the pressure of Nehru and the Menons. One would think that Almeida's indictment of Mountbatten was to set the stage to shower praise on Jinnah, but this is not so, for among the five books chosen for study, this is the one in which Jinnah comes in for the harshest criticism. Almeida's strictures are based on i) Jinnah's demand for dominion status rather than outright independence ii) his assessment that the Round Table Conference was Jinnah's dream and that his political existence depended on its success, and iii) Jinnah's psychological need to counter Gandhi.

i) Then why did Jinnah consider 'complete independence' as anathema for his country? It becomes absolutely clear that Jinnah the nationalist was definitely against complete independence as the national goal and unlike (*sic*) preserving the status of imperialist connection. Here may be the real root cause of Jinnah's conflicts. It is indeed strange and very distressing that a person like Jinnah should fail to understand the Congress demand for complete independence, that was more than justified, as voiced by the young blood in Congress.

Gandhi, too, was earlier not for 'complete independence'—why then did Jinnah fail to join hands with the Mahatma? Maybe the root cause of Jinnah's tragedy lies in his failure to realise the indispensability of the national goal of complete independence. Could one imagine a scenario where Jinnah replaced the young blood's Bapu and lead Subhash Bose and Jawaharlal towards the goal of complete independence?

'Thus, Jinnah betrayed his country by making himself available for the British policy of divide and rule to knock down the Congress demand of complete independence. No wonder Jinnah was never arrested and sentenced by the British' (pp. 95-96).

Unfortunately, we have to go into the substance of these accusations before we typify their nature. The proper place for Almeida to have posed these questions was when his narrative had come down to the Third June Plan. There it would have been manifest that the young blood, i.e., Jawaharlal was forced by Vallabhbhai Patel and not Mohammad Ali Jinnah to accept dominion status rather than complete independence. If Jinnah had been pressing for dominion status by stressing complete independence as an alternative, he was only demanding the first instalment of independence. Dominion status meant full democratic government. Defence was the consideration which prompted Jinnah to accept not only dominion status but also the Cabinet Mission Plan.

ii) As to why Jinnah did not follow Gandhi during the phase Gandhi was rejecting complete independence (as a resolution tabled by Hasrat Mohani), the earlier three authors have repeatedly stressed it was Gandhi who, with his loyalist stance in the first War Conference onwards, had continuously frustrated the revolutionary stance of Jinnah and Tilak. The psychological effect this had on Jinnah was to make him suspicious of Gandhi.

iii) As for imagining Jinnah leading Bose and Nehru towards freedom, in the case of Bose, imagination is not necessary. One has only to recall the scene of Bose listening to Jinnah with rapt attention when Jinnah addressed the Cambridge Majlis in the fateful year 1920. Even with Jawaharlal such a scene is imaginable, given the personal friendship that existed between Jinnah and Motilal Nehru. The latter's secretary (and renowned Urdu poet) Firaq Gorakhpuri has revealed that Gandhi offered to get Nehru a college lectureship the year his father had delayed depositing the customary one hundred thousand rupees to his bank account. Nehru detested Jinnah because Jinnah was a personal friend of his real father, Motilal; but averse to his political father, Gandhi. We only need to recall how Gandhi treated Subhash Chandra Bose in 1939, and how Nehru treated Gandhi in 1947 to concede that the scene of Jinnah leading Congress to freedom is not fantastic; unless of course, a Muslim was unacceptable to their rank and file. After all, Almeida has not refrained from calling Abul Kalam Azad a liar (pp. 232-33) when Gandhi repeatedly asked for Jinnah to be named Prime Minister of India, a constitutional impropriety—was he not hinting that he be made the first Governor-General? V.P. Menon noted that since Jinnah had already declined, it was unfair to raise this issue again and again. Stanley Wolpert, who considers Gandhi the greatest Indian after Buddha, has, in his very recent book, expressed the opinion that Gandhi wanted to be the first Governor-General of India.[24] As for why Jinnah did not follow Gandhi in Gandhi's loyalist phase, the more pertinent question is why Gandhi did not join Jinnah when Jinnah risked arrest by protesting against Lord Willingdon.

Prakash Almeida actually turns the psychological premises on its head when he states: 'Motilal understandably detested Jinnah for having wrecked his Nehru Report and the Dominion Plan' (p. 98). In the first place, Motilal did not 'detest' Jinnah, he only opposed him, in the second, 'understandably' is the last word to be used here. Almeida is breaking the sequence of events at the wrong turn. It was actually Motilal Nehru who wrecked the Delhi Muslim Proposals, which were not only accepted but also ratified by the Congress—as repeatedly stressed by the other three authors. Jinnah was hurt but did not detest Motilal for this, that is, for making him cut a sorry figure before Lord Birkenhead (the Secretary of State) and making the Muslim League a laughing stock.

Therefore, to state that Jinnah's political existence was at stake in the RTC's or that the RTCs were a realization of his dream, is not only an exaggeration but an aberration. After all, as Ajeet Javed has shown, it was Gandhi who gave Ramsay MacDonald the discretion to announce his Communal Award, while Jinnah had refused. Jinnah was not even the leader of the Muslim delegation to the RTC, Sir Aga Khan and Sir Fazl-i-Husain (behind the scene) were the leaders. Jinnah had gone along with Sir Mohammad Shafi in concluding an agreement with Gandhi. Even though Gandhi went back on his agreement; Jinnah still praised Gandhi's agreement with B.R. Ambedkar, and publicly wished for a similar agreement between Gandhi and the Muslims (p. 101).

Jinnah's equation with Gandhi finds expression in the following observation of Almeida: 'Did he [Jinnah] derive some conclusion from Gandhi's refusal to save Bhagat Singh? Then surely he must come to see the potential of the Gandhian method of mass movements, but could not reconcile himself to it.' (p. 68). Gandhi's refusal to save Bhagat Singh does not show the potential of mass movement but its helplessness. The other implication is that Gandhi had the potential to save Bhagat Singh, but deliberately refrained from such a step; hardly an action calling for reconciliation. How could Jinnah, who had protested against the treatment meted out to Bhagat Singh, reconcile himself to the 'Gandhian method of mass protest' at the hour of its failure?

Now let us put into sequence the following observations of Prakash Almeida: i) 'Jinnah as a person cannot be understood unless viewed in the light of Gandhi' (p. 48). I believe that Jinnah failed to be the father of India and hence opted to become the father of the new nation Pakistan' (p. 10). 'One even has to accept the fact that the arrival of Gandhi misfocussed the politics' (p. 55) 'Gandhi's tragedy lies in his blunders and mistakes which resulted out of the conflict between the saint Mahatma Gandhi and the politician Mr. Gandhi' (p. 118). 'Till the word 'Pakistan' was pronounced by Jinnah, he was essentially secular and nationalist. He did not remain nationalist but one must accept the historical fact that even after the creation of Pakistan, he remained secular to the core, and he amply proved that. He clutched to Pakistan as only a thing that came handy as a bargaining pressurised tool' (p. 110).

Where shall we place the praise and where shall we place the denunciation? Shall we let these conflicting and confusing statements speak for themselves or add a few incidental instances? Almeida asserts that Jawaharlal Nehru was guilty of betraying India because he met with Clement Atlee and Cripps to discuss the means by which the next Labour government would transfer power to India:

> Significantly this secret Plan for transfer of power was discussed with conclusions even before the World War II actually exploded on the world horizons (p. 119).

One may dismiss as crass ignorance Prakash Almeida's invoking Jinnah's close association with the Raja of Mahmudabad as proof of Jinnah's love for private property (p. 112), but what is the significance that he attaches to Nehru's meeting with Atlee and Cripps. Was Nehru's demand for independence a closely guarded secret? Or were the three of them conspiring to spark off the Second World War?

There is little that we can add about the thought process of this author. How are we to view it?

XI

Mohammad Ali Jinnah was a campaigner for India's freedom. Mohammad Ali Jinnah was an instrument for India's partition. Both claims are valid. Whether this represented an advance or a derailment depends on the meaning of the word 'freedom'. The Hindus had not gained freedom on the fall of the Muslims. The Muslims would not gain freedom on the withdrawal of the British. Speaking before the All-Parties Conference in 1928, M.A. Jinnah said:

Every country struggling for freedom and desirous of establishing a democratic system of government has had to face the problem of minorities ... minorities cannot give anything to the majority and the majority alone can give.

Addressing the Constituent Assembly of Pakistan twenty years later, Jinnah said:

You may belong to any religion, caste or creed, that has nothing to do with the business of the state. We are starting with this fundamental principle that we are all citizens and equal citizens of one state.

Is this inconsistency, or is it the upholding of a life long principle? India was divided because one community subjected another to religious discrimination. Jinnah was resolved that there would be no discrimination in Pakistan. Now was the inconsistency in Jinnah's stand, the espousal of the Two Nation Theory in India and its rejection in Pakistan based on external or internal factors. The internal factor would encompass ambition, vanity and spite. The external factor would embrace anxiety for equitable human rights and survival. If both phases of Jinnah's political career are intrinsically consistent then a study of his earlier stance becomes as vital as the study of his later stand. This is the service performed by these Indian writers:

The Indian re-appraisal of Jinnah is not concordant. It has two distinct strands, but almost all the authors covered here represent some degree of divergence from the official Indian stand. When Govind Swaroop, the Cultural Affairs Secretary of Maharashtra, called Jinnah 'a great freedom fighter who contributed to the freedom of India' he was accused by his Chief Minister, Murli Manohar Joshi, of 'dereliction of the highest order' and promptly punished (August 1997).

The line of thought represented by S.K. Majumdar and Ajeet Javed is the farthest from the official stand, but in one curious respect it resembles the stand of the RSS and its latter day successors. This was the organization which accepted responsibility for Gandhi's assassination and its current leaders have no compunction about referring to Gandhi's 'gopis'. This is too bizarre a note for any serious author to adopt, nevertheless sometimes even S.K. Majumdar and Ajeet Javed overstep the limit of political criticism.

They are critical of Gandhi and the Congress mainly on the basis of their inconsistency, their loyalist phase and their induction of religion in politics. Their basic premise is that Jinnah was a sincere nationalist only wishing for his community to partake equally of the freedom to be gained from the British. They refer specifically to the Cabinet Mission Plan to emphasise that by rejecting the grouping of provinces, the Congress left only one alternative: partition. But while they absolve Jinnah of the charge of communalism or vanity in bringing about partition, they do not regard partition as a fair solution. Their objection to partition does not seem to be chauvinistic. Nowhere do they express a feeling that a section of Indian Muslims escaped the domination of caste Hindus. Their desire for a united India is sentimental, a sentiment only indirectly nurtured by religion. They stop short of conceding that since Jinnah was a genuine nationalist, his espousal of the partition plan demonstrates that it was an unavoidable outcome of the freedom struggle.

The attitude of Sailesh Kumar Bandopadhaya and Prakash Almeida seems to be that no matter how unreasonable the attitude of Congress, no matter how vulnerable the position of the Muslims had become, Jinnah should have ultimately sacrificed the survival of the Muslims at the altar of Indian unity. They realise that the officially sponsored view of Jinnah's role is one sided and misleading. They are willing to praise Jinnah but not to criticise Gandhi and the Congress leadership. They desire a Jinnah who would bow before Nehru; they do not favour a Jinnah who would stand up to Mountbatten.

The change in Jinnah's attitude can be attributed to external factors. The abjuration of the Lucknow Pact, the Delhi Muslim Proposals, the electoral understanding of 1937, and finally, the Grouping clause. This helps us draw a line between territorial loyalty and communal survival. Was Partition a mistake? Jinnah solemnly and publicly deliberated over this question, four days before the establishment of Pakistan. There were only two types of regions, Hindu majority and Muslim majority. A Muslim majority region is Kashmir, where for the last decade, armed repression on an unprecedented scale has taken place. A Hindu majority area is Mumbai, where thousands of Muslims protesting over the demolition of the Babri mosque were decimated within a day. The Congress chose non-violence to counter the British, but resorted to violence against the Muslims, which has only vindicated their decision to divide India. However, Indian interest in the life and work of Jinnah has the potential to rise above academics and engage the attention of the public at large. This can become a source of understanding and confidence building between the two countries who share—willingly or unwillingly—the political legacy of Mohammed Ali Jinnah.

NOTES

1. Arun Shourie, 'The Man Who Broke Up India' in *The Illustrated Weekly of India*, Bombay 20 and 28 October, and 3 November 1985.
2. K.K. Aziz, *Muslims Under Congress Rule*, Islamabad, NIHCR, 1979 vol. 1, pp. 734-35.
3. Stanley Wolpert, *Gandhi's Passion*, New York, Oxford University Press, 2001, p. 203.
4. B.R. Ambedkar *Thoughts on Pakistan*, Bombay, Thacker's, 1941. Reprinted in Mushirul Hasan (ed.) *Inventing Boundaries*, New Delhi, Oxford University Press, 2000.
5. Mushirul Hasan, *Ibid.*, pp. 56-58.
6. Reprinted in Urdu translation by Ahmad Yusuf as *Woh Jinnah Jinhein Mein Janta Tha*, Patna, Khuda Bukhsh Oriental Public Library, 1996, pp. 287-310.
7. Waheed Ahmad, (ed.) *The Nation's Voice*, Vol. IV Karachi, Quaid-i-Azam Academy, 2000, pp. 831-43.
8. M.R. Jaykar, *The Story of My Life*, Bombay, Asia Publishing House, 1958, vol. I, p. 318.
9. C.F. Andrews, *Mahatma Gandhi's Ideas*, London, George Allen and Unwin, 1949, pp. 271-74.
10. Roger D. Long, *The Founding of Pakistan*, Lanham, Scarecrow Press, 1998, p. 228.

11. Hector Bolitho, *Jinnah; Creator of Pakistan*, London, John Murray, 1954, p. 158.
12. Frank Moraes, *Witness to an Era*, New Delhi, Vikas, 1973.
13. Woodrow Wyatt, *Confessions of an Optimist*, London, Collins, 1985, p. 156.
14. Saad R. Khairi, *Jinnah Reinterpretted*, Karachi, Oxford University Press, 1994, p. 354.
15. Daily *Jang* (Urdu) (ed.) Mir Khalilur Rahman, Karachi, 25 August 1985, p. 3.
16. A.G. Noorani, *The Trial of Bhagat Singh*, Karachi, Oxford University Press, 2001, p. 273.
17. Vide *Young India*, 6 January 1929.
18. Vide Brian Lapping, *End of Empire*, Delhi, Granada Publications, 1985, p. 66.
19. Shiva Rao, *India's Freedom Movement*, New Delhi, Orient Longman 1972, p. 13.
20. M.N. Roy, *Men I Met*, New Delhi, Lalwani Publications, 1968, p. 33.
21. Hashoo Kewal Romani, *Pakistan X Rayed*, Delhi, New Age, 1951. p. 111.
22. M.S.M. Sharma, *Peeps into Pakistan*, Patna, Pustak Bhandar, 1954, p. 147.
23. N. Mansergh and E.W.R. Lumby (eds.) *The Transfer of Power*, London, Her Majesty's Stationary Office, 1981, Vol. xi, pp. 442-48.
24. Stanley Wolpert, *op. cit.*, p. 246.

List of Contributors

David Page. Producer and Editor, BBC. He has lectured on South Asian affairs at the University of Oxford and the University of London. He is the author of *Prelude to Pakistan*, Karachi, Oxford University Press, 1987.

Andrew Roberts. Writes and reviews books for the *Sunday Telegraph*, London. Author of *Eminent Churchillians*, London, Weidenfeld and Nicholson, 1994 and many other publications.

Stanley Wolpert. Professor Emeritus of History, University of California, Los Angeles. Author of *Jinnah of Pakistan*, New York, Oxford University Press, 1984 and *Gandhi's Passion*, New York, Oxford University Press, 2001, and many other publications.

R.J. Moore. Professor Emeritus of History, Flinders University, Author of *Churchill, Cripps and India*, Oxford, Clarendon, 1979, *Escape From Empire*, Oxford, and Clarendon, 1979.

Ian A. Talbot. Director, Centre for South Asian Studies, Coventry University, England. Author of *Provincial Politics and the Pakistan Movement*, Karachi, Oxford University Press, 1996 and *Pakistan A Modern History*, New Delhi, Oxford University Press, 2002.

Francis Robinson. Professor of South Asian History and Vice-Principal, Royal Holloway College, University of London. Author of *Separatism Among Indian Muslims*, Cambridge University Press, 1974.

Alan Whaites. Professor of Politics, School of Asian and African Studies, University of London and Director, International Policy and Advocacy World Vision International.

Ayesha Jalal. Professor of Tufts University, Massachusetts. Author of *The Sole Spokesman*, Cambridge, CUP, 1985 and *Pakistan: The State of Martial Rule*, Cambridge, CUP, 1990 and many other publications.

Roger Long. Professor of History, East Michigan University. Editor *Foundations of Pakistan*, London, The Scarecrow Press, 1998 and *Dear Mr Jinnah: Selected Correspondence and Speeches of Liaquat Ali Khan*, Karachi, Oxford University Press, 2004.

Sharif Al Mujahid. Founder Director, Quaid-i-Azam Academy. Author of *Jinnah: Studies in Interpretation*, Karachi, Quaid-i-Azam Academy, 1981.

Syed Jaffar Ahmed. Director, Pakistan Study Centre, University of Karachi. Author of *Federalism In Pakistan*, Karachi, PSC, 1990.

Betty Miller Unterberger. Regents Professor, Texas A and M University. Author of *The United States, Revolutionary Russia and the Rise of Czechoslovakia*, University of North Carolina Press, 1989.

Muhammad Reza Kazimi. Associate Professor of Islamic History and Pakistan Studies, National College, Karachi. Author of *Liaquat Ali Khan: His Life and Work*, Karachi, Oxford University Press, 2003 and *Pakistan Studies*, Karachi, Oxford University Press, 2005.

Index